CHRISTMAS CRAFTS
& ENTERTAINING

CREATIVE
PUBLISHING
international

MINNETONKA, MINNESOTA

CONTENTS

Introduction 4

First Impressions 7
Snowflake Wreath 9
Classical Gold Wreath 13
Birch-bark Sconce 17
Light Sphere 19
Topiary of Lights 23
Bird Feeders 25

Around the House 29
Star Tree Topper 30
Beaded Ornaments 33
Victorian Ornaments 36
Shell Ornaments 38
Patchwork Santa Tree Skirt 42
Boot Stockings 50
Mantel Cloth 54
Advent Wreath 59
Advent Calendar 63
Patchwork Santa Wall Quilt 66
Shaped & Tasseled Pillows 71
Pillow Changers 76
Santa's Pillow Collection 80
Shell-trimmed Christmas Tree 84
Mr. & Mrs. Frost 87

Share the Joy 93
Paper Art Cards 94
Hostess Gifts: Bottles & Jars 99
Mitten Gift Bags 103
Painted Santa Gift Boxes & Bags 105

Holiday Table Linens 109
Table Linen Basics 111
Metallic Appliqué Linens 118
Paper-pieced Placemats 123
Silk Ribbon Embroidered Linens 127
Holiday Bells Table Topper 133
Placemat with Sheer Insert 137
Texturized Table Linens 141
Easy Painted Placemats 144
Placemat Table Runner 147

Centerpieces & Candlelight 151
Cascading Fruits & Roses 153
Fresh Advent Wreath 157
Molded Beeswax Candles 163
Beeswax Ornaments & Garlands ... 166
Embellishing Purchased Candles ... 168
Painted Glass Candleholders 171

Entertaining Accessories 175
Woodburning Designs 176
Hooked Rug Trivet 182
Tree Trivet 189
Napkin Rings 192
Scented Coasters 198
Paper-pieced Coasters 203

Breakfast & Brunch 205
Egg Dishes 207
Breads 209
Beverages 214

Appetizers 217
Finger Food 218
Dips & Spreads 224
Cheese 230

Main Dishes 235
Poultry 237
Game Birds 243
Pork 248

Side Dishes 253
Vegetables 254
Potatoes & Dressings 262
Accompaniments 266

Desserts 269
Fruit Desserts 270
Puddings & Creams 277
Cakes 281

Candies & Cookies 285
Candies 286
Bars & Cookies 295

Patterns 304
Index 316

CHRISTMAS CRAFTS & ENTERTAINING

There's no Christmas like a handmade Christmas. Whether you enjoy making ornaments for your tree or decorating your home with fresh wreaths and garlands, the personal touch is what makes the season merry. Christmas cards, hostess gifts, and stocking stuffers made by hand truly come from the heart. And the rich treasures that come from the Christmas kitchen speak volumes about the spirit and caring of the Christmas cook.

Christmas Crafts & Entertaining is brimming with projects, ideas, and recipes for decorating your home and hosting holiday gatherings. Beginning with your front yard and entrance, you'll find unique lighting projects, wreaths, and containers for feeding winter birds. Spread cheer throughout your home with ornaments, wall hangings, tree skirts, and pillows. Hang handmade stockings and Advent calendars in anticipation of Christmas Day. Make the giving season special with painted gift boxes or handmade paper art cards. Prepare fancy jars and bottles filled with hostess gifts from the kitchen.

Because much of your entertaining centers around the holiday table, you'll find lots of ideas for making holiday table linens, including tablecloths, placemats, napkins, and table runners. Dress up your table with centerpieces, and add the warm glow of hand-poured beeswax candles. Add a personal touch with coasters and trivets in Christmas motifs. Or, decorate trays and chargers with woodburned and colored designs.

Christmas Crafts & Entertaining will tease your taste buds as you browse through more than one hundred recipes for holiday entertaining. You'll find ideas to make every meal special, from a simple family breakfast to a multicourse Christmas feast. Appetizers, snacks, and beverages help you entertain holiday drop-in guests or host gala open-house gatherings. Mouthwatering cookies, candies, and desserts tempt you to try them all.

FIRST IMPRESSIONS

SNOWFLAKE WREATH

Create this unique evergreen snowflake wreath, naturally embellished with pinecones, to greet holiday visitors. Select from a wide variety of natural pine branches for a needle style that appeals to you. Use short needles for a full wreath or long, feathery needles for a more open wreath. Also consider how needle density will affect the wreath's crystalline design.

Gather or purchase a few pinecones to cluster at the center. Choose cones matching in size and shape, or search for a variety of cones to add interest. Add holly or other greens with a contrasting color and texture to the center.

Spray green needles with an aerosol colorant, such as a white enamel paint or a flocking medium, or add a festive touch using an iridescent or glitter spray.

Wear work gloves to protect your hands from sharp needles.

MATERIALS

* Six natural pine spray branches, with or without pinecones; 18" (46 cm) long for 32" (81.5 cm) wreath.
* Green floral wire, 24-gauge; wire cutter; work gloves.
* Pinecones as desired; hot glue gun, optional.
* Fresh, dried, or artificial greens for center embellishment.
* Aerosol colorant, optional.

HOW TO MAKE A SNOWFLAKE WREATH

1 Trim foliage from lower 7" (18 cm) of two branches; save trimmings. Lap bare lengths so branch tips are 32" (81.5 cm) apart; bind branches together at each end, using floral wire. Repeat twice to prepare three sets. Arrange sets so branches form small triangle at wreath center; bind branches at each intersection, using wire.

(Continued)

9

2 Select six or more small branches for center; use trimmings from step 1. Arrange branches so they meet at center and just cover bare branches; point all needles away from center. Secure at triangle, using wire.

3 Wrap 9" (23 cm) wire around bottom layers of larger pinecones; twist to secure. Insert wires near wreath center; twist wires on back to secure. Trim excess wire. Layer small cones on larger, using hot glue. Embellish center of wreath with other greens.

4 Secure twisted wire loop at center back of upper branch, for hanging. Apply colorant to wreath, if desired; spray from top to cover upper and extended edges, or spray the entire wreath.

MORE IDEAS FOR SNOWFLAKE WREATHS

Add battery-operated lights; secure hidden battery pack on back. Replace pinecones with elements that reflect other holiday decorations, such as shell ornaments (page 38), silver bells, or other dried pods; avoid using embellishments that may be damaged by nature.

Purchase seven artificial sprays for a wreath that will last many years; cut seventh spray for small branches. Bend wire core to secure at center. Arrange clustered cones in a star formation.

CLASSICAL GOLD WREATH

Transform an artificial evergreen wreath into an elegant display of classic golden nature with textured fruits, gilded nuts, and dried artichokes.

Give inexpensive artificial fruits a rich, dramatic surface, using a texturizing medium such as DecoArt™ Decorating Paste™. Then paint them with an antique crackled finish, touched with gold.

HOW TO MAKE A CLASSICAL GOLD WREATH

MATERIALS

* Artificial evergreen wreath.
* Artificial fruit stems.
* Texturizing medium; craft stick.
* Crackle medium; small sponge applicator.
* Off-white acrylic craft paint.
* Antiquing medium and soft cloth.
* Gold wax-base paint.
* Dried artichokes; gold aerosol paint.
* Pinecones; glossy aerosol wood tone, optional.
* Assorted nuts; hot glue gun.
* Green floral wire, 24-gauge; wire cutter.
* Dried floral material.

1 Apply rough coat of texturizing paste to fruits, using craft stick. Dollop and spread paste in some areas; leave some areas bare. Allow to dry thoroughly. Brush crackle medium on fruits; allow to set.

2 Brush off-white paint on fruit, leaving some original fruit color showing; paint will crackle almost immediately. Allow to dry. Apply stain, using cloth; wipe off excess.

(Continued)

3 Lightly rub gold paint on areas of fruits and nuts. Paint artichokes gold. Spray pinecones with glossy wood tone, if desired.

4 Secure fruit stem ends at center top of wreath; wrap wreath branches around stems. Weave fruit stems partially around wreath, leaving bottom of wreath bare; secure with wreath branches.

5 Wrap wires around bottom layers of pinecones; twist to secure, leaving long tails. Insert wires at center top of wreath so pinecones hang into opening; twist wires at back.

6 Wrap wires around artichokes, as in step 5; secure in arc over pinecones. Secure dried floral stems, evenly spaced, around wreath, using wreath branches. Secure nuts, using hot glue.

MORE IDEAS FOR CLASSICAL GOLD ARRANGEMENTS

Plant a small tree in a classic urn; weave a decorative ribbon and small lights through its branches, and embellish it with assorted textured fruits and golden artichokes. Arrange larger fruits at the bottom and smaller fruits near the top.

Hang a garland so it cascades down the sides of the door or across balcony and porch railings. Scatter fruits, artichokes, nuts, and ferns throughout its length. Weave ribbon in and out of garland.

BIRCH-BARK SCONCE

Hung on the door or beneath a porch light, this birch-bark sconce arrangement is a rustic celebration of the season.

Dramatic color variations occur naturally in birch bark; the papery white surface peels to reveal a peach core, and dark, rough blemishes are common. Lichen and mushrooms grow in wonderful clusters, adding more colors and textures. Birch bark may be gathered from fallen trees or purchased at floral shops.

The tefe rose is an exploded seed pod attached to stem wire; it resembles a blossoming flower and is available at floral shops.

Assorted evergreens, such as fir, spruce, cedar, boxwood, and juniper, are appropriately used alone or mixed.

HOW TO MAKE A BIRCH-BARK SCONCE ARRANGEMENT

MATERIALS

* Birch-bark piece, at least 14" × 6" (35.5 × 15 cm); six to eight screws, depending on bark size; utility knife, optional.
* Leather lacing, length depending on bark size; leather needle; clip.
* Floral foam; serrated knife.

* Three tefe roses.
* Assorted evergreen sprigs; seeded eucalyptus.
* Floral stem wire; floral tape; wire cutters.
* Bell reed stems.
* Three brass jingle bells.

1 Tear or cut birch bark to desired size. Soak bark in very hot water until pliable, at least one hour. Roll cone, taking advantage of unique characteristics of bark; leave opening at bottom and clamp upper edge with clip. Twist screws through lapped ends to make four to six holes. Twist two screws through bark, near top of back.

2 Cut 9" (23 cm) from lacing; secure at back, for hanger. Knot end of remaining lacing; insert other end at inside bottom of cone, using leather needle, if desired. Weave lacing through holes; remove screws as needed. Knot lacing on inside; turn lacing over upper edge, to outside. Cut foam to fit sconce, using serrated knife; place in sconce.

(Continued)

HOW TO MAKE A BIRCH-BARK SCONCE
ARRANGEMENT (CONTINUED)

3 Insert longest rose at back; insert other roses at front sides. Bend front roses slightly forward. Insert evergreens and eucalyptus, distributing variations throughout arrangement; lengthen stems, using wire and floral tape, if necessary.

4 Cut assorted lengths from bell reed stems; scatter reeds throughout arrangement. Attach jingle bells and evergreen sprigs to lacing tail as desired.

MORE IDEAS FOR SCONCE FILLERS

Depict a Christmas carol *by using holly and ivy stems. Secure the sconce using narrow ribbon or cord; replace the bells with a bow.*

Repeat the natural colors *of the bark, using giant lotus pods, green or brown eucalyptus, and sage or salal. Dangle pinecones.*

LIGHT SPHERE

This glorious sphere of small lights will brighten your outdoor decorating in a unique way. It blends into the natural setting of your yard during the day and explodes into color or bright white at night.

Purchase a package of clear plastic party glasses and simply melt them together to create the sphere. Choose multicolored lights or a string of single-color or white lights. Suspend the spheres from tree branches, and enjoy!

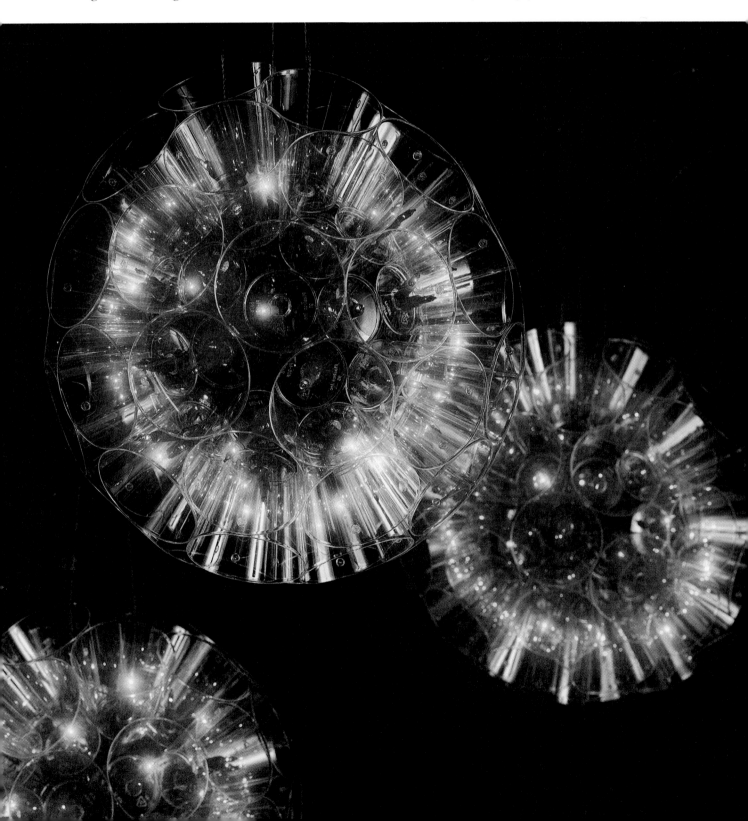

HOW TO MAKE A LIGHT SPHERE

MATERIALS

* Fifty clear, flexible plastic old-fashioned glasses with slanted sides.
* Hot glue gun.

* Weatherproof string of 50 or 100 miniature lights.
* Weather-resistant cord, for hanger.
* Outdoor-rated extension cord; brown duct tape.

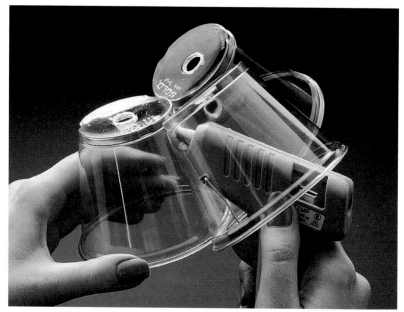

1 Make hole in bottom of each glass, using hot glue gun tip; rotate gun to make hole large enough to fit one or two lights.

2 Hold two glasses together so top and bottom edges meet. Fuse glasses together as near bottom as possible; press glue gun tip to inside of one glass until hole begins to form, then quickly press tip at same point in other glass, melting glasses together. Allow plastic to cool. Fuse third glass to both of joined glasses. Test joints for stability.

3 Continue adding glasses, fusing adjacent glasses, to form sphere; leave opening to fit hand. Place light string inside sphere; allow plug and cord to hang outside. Insert one or two lights into bottom hole of each glass, using all lights.

4 Thread cord through fusing holes in opening row; pull up three evenly spaced loops, and knot together. Suspend sphere as desired.

5 Secure plug end of extension cord to tree trunk, using duct tape; position cord so light strand will reach it without stretching. Plug cord into outdoor-rated circuit receptacle. Plug lights into outlet; wrap light strand around nearby twig or branch to prevent unneccessary stress on lights.

MORE IDEAS FOR LIGHT SPHERES

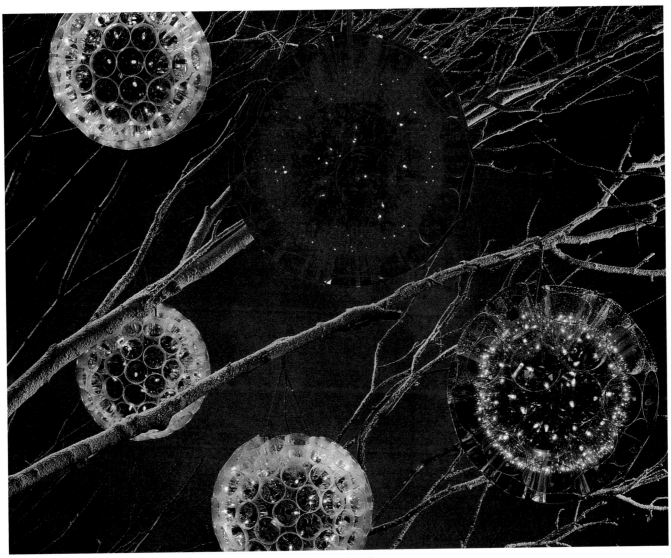

Substitute colored or faceted glasses. Create smaller spheres, using plastic shot glasses.

TOPIARY OF LIGHTS

$\mathcal{C}$reate this small, shaped tree of miniature lights for a delightful way to mark your entry and to brighten steps during dark winter nights.

Wrap a tomato cage with garland and small lights; use two light strings to maximize points of light within safety regulations. Place it on top of an empty urn for a classic topiary, or on a large overturned terra-cotta saucer for a tiny country tree.

HOW TO MAKE A TOPIARY OF LIGHTS

MATERIALS

* Tomato cage, 30" (76 cm) high.
* Galvanized steel wire, 12-gauge; wire cutter.
* Electrical tape.

* 16 yd. (14.72 m) metallic garland.
* Two weatherproof, end-to-end strings of 100 miniature lights.
* Outdoor-rated extension cord.

1 Turn cage upside down. Cut three wire pieces 1" (2.5 cm) longer than existing supports. Bend back 1" (2.5 cm) around bottom hoop. Secure wires to hoops halfway between supports, using electrical wire. Tape all wires together at top. Secure one light string at top; drop male plug so it rests easily on ground.

2 Secure end of garland to top of cage. Wrap garland around cage toward bottom, holding lights out of way. Join garland lengths as necessary to cover cage. Wrap light string around cage; turn bulbs out as string winds toward bottom. Join light strings as necessary, hiding plug ends in garland. Plug lights into cord; plug cord into outdoor-rated circuit receptacle. Fluff garland to partially cover strings. Place tree on urn or at side of steps.

BIRD FEEDERS

Sharing the joy of the season with feathered friends is a tradition in many parts of the world, especially where winter snows make food hard to find.

Birds gather at grain sources; they like regular and bearded wheat, oats, barley, millet, sorghum, and foxtail. Miniature corn and dried sunflowers are other favorites, and many birds love raw peanuts. Seeds may be pressed into a layer of peanut butter spread over cones. Breads and popcorn should be avoided; they are filling and don't provide sufficient energy. Suet is a favorite attraction because it provides long-lasting, warming energy. Plain suet is available at groceries; garden centers and specialty bird-feed stores offer suet blended with nuts and grains.

Assorted berries, such as cranberries, holly, bittersweet, rose hips, and red pepperberries, provide colorful embellishments as well as food; avoid using dyed naturals or imitations. Small fresh fruits, such as crabapples and kumquats, are sweet treats. Dried fruit slices may be purchased or dried at home in a dehydrator or oven. Use well-colored, unblemished fruits, such as apples, oranges, and pomegranates; choose firm citrus with thick rinds and minimal juice. Small cones, colorful peppers, and a variety of pods, such as lotus and poppy, may be added for interest.

Bird feeders also attract squirrels, which easily jump to feeders from overhanging branches or roofs. Metal hardware cloth discourages their visits to suet feeders; a convenient bowl of shelled corn will delight them.

HOW TO OVEN-DRY FRESH FRUIT FOR EMBELLISHMENTS

Soak apple slices in 1 qt. (0.9 L) water with 2 tbsp. (25 mL) lemon juice, to prevent discoloration. Pat dry, using paper towel. Arrange 1/4" (6 mm) slices of assorted fruits on baking sheet; separate slightly. Place in slow oven set at 200°F (95°C); use exhaust fan to remove humidity as fruit dries. Bake about two hours; timing varies with fleshiness and quantity of fruit. Remove when fruit is leathery.

HOW TO BUILD A SUET HOUSE

MATERIALS

* ⅔ yd. (0.63 m) rough-sawn 1 × 8 cedar or redwood; saw.

* Drill; drill bits in assorted sizes.

* Four galvanized screws, 1½" (3.8 cm) long.

* ½" (1.3 cm) hardware cloth, cut into two 6" × 4½" (15 × 11.5 cm) pieces; staple gun.

* 1 yd. (0.95 m) heavy leather lacing or polyurethane cord; two screw eyes.

* Embellishments as desired; string or raffia.

* Suet block, about 4½" × 4½" × 1½" (11.5 × 11.5 × 3.8 cm).

CUTTING DIRECTIONS

Cut one 8" (20.5 cm) length of wood, for the base. Cut one 8" × 5" (20.5 × 12.5 cm) piece, for the roof. Cut two 1¾" × 5" (4.5 × 12.5 cm) pieces, for the uprights. Include knots, if desired; avoid placing any knots near the center of the short sides on the base and roof, and near the ends of the uprights.

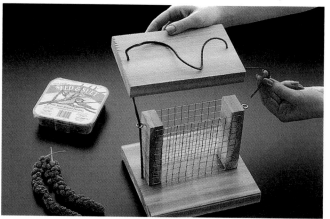

1 Drill hole ½" (1.3 cm) from edge, at center of each short side of base, using drill bit in same diameter as lacing. Repeat on roof. Drill two ⅛" (3 mm) holes on each short side of base, drilling each hole ½" (1.3 cm) from center and 1⅛" (2.8 cm) from edge. Drill two ⅛" (3 mm) holes on centerline of one upright end, 1" (2.5 cm) apart; repeat on other upright. Secure uprights to base, inserting screws through small holes from underside of base.

2 Secure hardware cloth to upright sides, using staples. Drill hole on outside of each upright, ⅜" (1 cm) from top; insert screw eyes. Knot lacing end. Slip lacing from base bottom through screw eye, roof holes, and opposite screw eye; return to base bottom. Knot loose end. Tie knot near lacing center to form 3" (7.5 cm) loop, for hanger. Insert suet into holder; tie other edibles to screw eyes, using string or raffia.

HOW TO MAKE A GRAIN STAND

MATERIALS

* Container, such as wooden tote, window box, terra-cotta pot, or urn.

* Sand to fill container; paper.

* Grain stalks; string.

* Birdseed as desired.

* Embellishments as desired.

1 Measure container depth. Trim grain stalks so total length is no more than five times container depth; tie bundles near the center, using string.

2 Line container with paper to prevent sand spills; partially fill container with sand. Push bundles to container bottom; add additional sand, and top with birdseed to container rim. Embellish container with greens, berries, or grain garlands as desired.

MORE IDEAS FOR
BIRD FEEDERS

Purchase bell-shaped suet or seed; *secure embellishments to edible hanger.*

Fill pomegranate or citrus shell *with suet or seed. Cut fruit in half; scoop sections and seeds out. Punch three evenly spaced holes around shell, 3/8" (1 cm) from rim. Slip cord through each hole and knot ends, to hang; allow shell to air-dry several days before filling. Secure edible embellishments to cord, if desired.*

Fill a birch-bark sconce *with wheat stalks. Secure the stalks, using a suet plug, and add orange slices for colorful nourishment. Insert evergreen sprigs along the upper edge, for perch.*

27

STAR TREE TOPPER

Create this lightweight, beautiful star for a glorious tree topper. Form a raised design on a papier mâché star using hot glue. Apply spray paint, small sheets of imitation metal leaf, and an antiquing medium to give it a special glow.

Purchase a papier mâché star; several styles are available in craft stores, including tree-topper cones. Play with various letters of the alphabet to make a design that complements your star; simply connect elongated S and C curves for intricate scroll designs, and join mirror images of the connected letters with a V to fill a star's point.

Paint the star before applying metal leaf for an interesting secondary color; the leaf will split slightly and reveal the color around the raised design. Select gold, silver, or copper leaf to complement your other ornaments. Age bright metallic finishes with an antiquing medium, if desired.

Secure the star to your treetop using elastic cord. Use decorative gold or silver cords to match the star's finish, or choose white or black cords so they will disappear among flocked or natural needles.

HOW TO MAKE A STAR TREE TOPPER

MATERIALS

* Papier mâché star in desired style.
* Hot glue gun.
* Acrylic paint: dark red, black, or green.
* Metal-leaf adhesive; brush.
* Imitation metal leaf in desired color; soft brush, optional.
* Antiquing medium in desired color; soft brush; soft cloth.
* Aerosol clear acrylic sealer.
* ⅓ yd. (0.32 m) elastic cord; curved upholstery needle, optional.

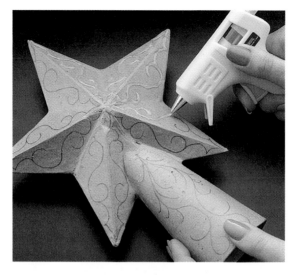

1 Draw lines for raised design on star, using pencil. Apply hot glue to design lines, holding glue gun at 45° angle while gently squeezing. Keep tip slightly above star surface until line ends; touch tip to line end, and lift straight up. Allow to harden and cool. Repeat on back, if desired.

2 Paint star, using acrylic paint. Allow to dry. Apply leaf adhesive to star; allow to set, following manufacturer's directions.

3 Cut metal leaf into manageable pieces. Apply metal leaf to surface, following manufacturer's directions. Apply clear acrylic sealer; allow to dry.

4 Apply antiquing medium, following manufacturer's directions, if desired. Wipe off excess, using soft cloth; allow some to remain in crevices around design. Apply clear acrylic sealer; allow to dry.

For stars without tree-topper cone, cut elastic cord in half. Insert one end through curved upholstery needle; push needle through star back so it pierces star each side of center. Pull cord half-way through star; knot ends loosely. Pull second cord through star back, 2" to 3" (5 to 7.5 cm) below first one; knot ends. Slip cords over vertical branch at treetop. Adjust knots to tighten loops, if necessary; rotate knots to star surface.

Beaded fruit in a bowl (above) offers holiday sparkle for the buffet or coffee table.

Three-dimensional pearl cage (left) showcases a glimmering trinket.

Shimmering crystal bead icicles (opposite) drip from the tree.

32

BEADED ORNAMENTS

Create a beautiful collection of beaded ornaments for your tree and home. Add elegant crystal icicles to your tree, or hang them in a window for rainbows of light. Hang three-dimensional cages to enjoy their pattern of beads; use them to emphasize a special ornament or suspend a sprig of mistletoe. Colorful fruits and balls make trees special; gather them in a bowl for unique centerpieces.

Select beads in a variety of colors, shapes, and sizes for added interest. Consider crystal and pearl beads for an elegant look, or use wooden beads for a casual country home; use metallic beads with any style.

Purchase unique beads individually or buy bulk packages to arrange a variety of bead patterns. Beads of uniform size and color also come in prestrung hanks of 10 or 12 strings; although many colors are available, you may choose to string your own beads for the fruit and ball ornaments.

HOW TO MAKE AN ICICLE

MATERIALS

* Crystal or metallic beads in assorted sizes and colors.

* 24-gauge wire; wire cutter; needlenose pliers.

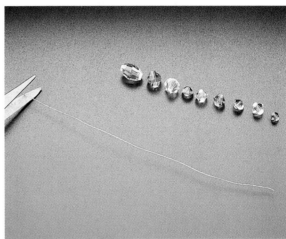

1 Arrange beads in a line according to size, alternating colors and shapes as desired. Measure approximate length; cut wire about 2" (5 cm) longer.

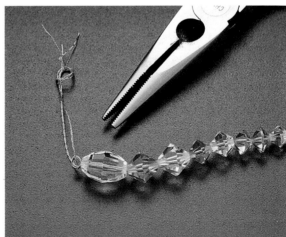

2 Form small loop in wire end, using pliers. Slide smallest bead onto other end; continue, working from smallest to largest bead, stacking beads snug. Trim excess wire ¾" (2 cm) from largest bead; form wire loop for attaching hanger.

33

HOW TO MAKE A THREE-DIMENSIONAL CAGE

MATERIALS

❋ 24-gauge wire; wire cutter; permanent marker; pliers.

❋ Beads in desired sizes.

❋ Small decorative ornament, if desired.

❋ ½ yd. (0.5 m) ribbon, ⅛" (3 mm) wide, for bow.

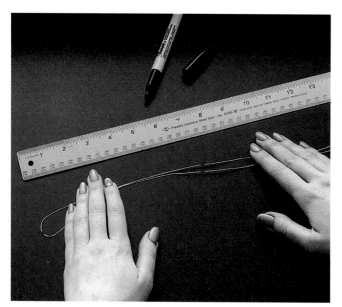

1 Form wire loop to determine desired ornament size; consider size of suspended ornament, if one will be used. Cut wire with length equal to three times the determined measurement plus 3" (7.5 cm). Mark wire center, using marker. Measure half the original wire loop length to each side of center; mark.

2 Slide beads onto wire, forming symmetrical arrangement on each side of center. Snug beads to fill space between outer marks; twist wire at marks, forming loop. Mark the original wire loop length to each side of twist; mark halfway points.

3 Slide beads onto wire to fill space from twist to first mark; follow original arrangement, if desired. Wrap wire at mark between beads at wire's center. Slide beads onto wire to fill space to next mark, using same arrangement, if desired; wrap wire around first twist to complete circle.

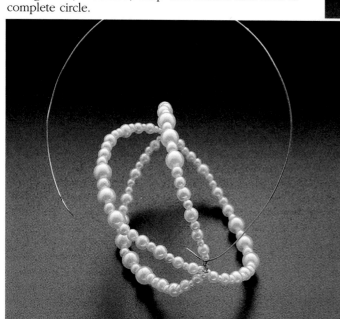

4 Repeat step 3 with remaining wire. Suspend inner ornament, if desired, using fine cord or wire; secure at top twist. Use one wire to form loop for attaching hanger; trim excess wire. Attach ribbon or cord to loop for hanging.

HOW TO MAKE BEADED FRUITS & BALLS

MATERIALS

❋ Styrofoam® or lightweight wood forms as desired; use six balls for grape cluster.

❋ Ribbon or cord, for hanging.

❋ Toothpicks; craft glue.

❋ Drill and small drill bit, optional.

❋ Prestrung seed or rochaille beads; 3½" (9 cm) forms and clusters of six 1" (2.5 cm) grapes use about one hank of 12 strings. Or bulk beads; beading needle; thread.

❋ Embellishments as desired; green floral wire and silk ivy leaves, for grape cluster.

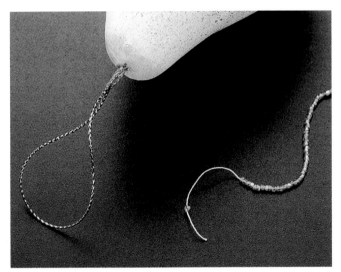

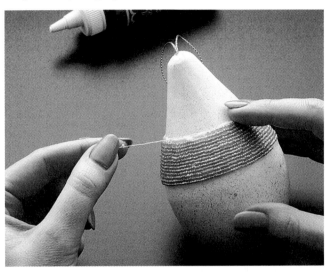

1 Create small hole at form top, using toothpick or small drill bit. Cut desired ribbon or cord length for hanger. Apply small amount of glue to ends; insert ends into hole, forming hanger. Allow to dry. Separate bead hank strings; tie knot to secure end beads.

2 Apply small glue band at form center; allow glue to set two or three minutes until tacky. Wrap bead string over glue, spiraling upward around form; apply more glue, and place strings end to end as necessary to cover upper half. Repeat to cover lower half. Allow to dry; trim excess bead strings. Embellish as desired.

For striped balls, alternate bead colors; start and finish each string at back of ball.

For grape cluster, wrap green floral wire around nail for tendril; twist around hanger base or glue to form as desired. Create five more grapes; cluster so each grape touches three or four others; glue. Add silk leaves as desired.

VICTORIAN ORNAMENTS

Visit the romance of the Victorian era with these two ornaments. Cover Styrofoam® forms with delicate netting or narrow ribbon. Adorn them with metal or resin Victorian charms, beads, and decorative trims, such as cording, ribbon, and gimp. Secure embellishments with craft glue or with escutcheon or dressmaker pins, for quick and easy finishing.

HOW TO MAKE A VICTORIAN CHARM ORNAMENT

MATERIALS

* Styrofoam form, 3½" to 4" (9 to 10 cm) tall.
* Acrylic paint, in desired colors.
* ¾ yd. (0.7 m) cording, lace, or ribbon.

* ½ yd. (0.5 m) tulle or sparkle illusion.
* Victorian charms as desired; hot glue gun.
* Beads and sequins as desired; straight or escutcheon pins.

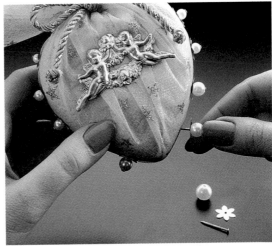

1 Paint form as desired; allow to dry. Tie small knots at trim ends to prevent raveling, if necessary. Tie square knot to form 3" (7.5 cm) loop at trim center. Set form on 15" (38 cm) tulle square. Gather tulle firmly at top. Place trim knot at back; tie bow in front to secure tulle.

2 Paint resin charms, if desired. Apply charms to front and back as desired, using hot glue. Apply beads as desired, using brass pins.

HOW TO MAKE A RIBBON BALL ORNAMENT

MATERIALS

* 10 yd. (9.15 m) ribbon, ¼" to ⅜" (6 mm to 1 cm) wide.
* 3" (7.5 cm) Styrofoam ball.
* Craft glue.

* Two or more beads as desired.
* Straight or escutcheon pins as desired.
* Embellishments as desired.

1 Secure end of ribbon to ball, using glue. Wrap ribbon very taut around ball, overlapping ribbon slightly, until ball is covered. Pull end of ribbon tight; secure at top of ball, using glue. Hold firmly until dry.

2 Leave 6" (15 cm) ribbon tail, for loop; glue end to top, forming loop. Pin bead, using straight or escutcheon pin, at top and bottom to prevent ribbon layers from slipping. Secure additional trims or beads as desired.

SHELL ORNAMENTS

Many areas of the world do not experience drifts of holiday snow; some people prefer warm days on the beach. These lovely ornaments are made of assorted seashells; they bring some of nature's beauty indoors, and they unite traditions of warm and cold climates.

Conical shells may be professionally cut; slices reveal the delicate patterns of the body cavity, and lily cuts resemble the furled petals of a flower. Umbonium shells are naturally compressed, with a buttonlike look.

Natural variations in bivalve shells can be used in the design of angel ornaments; some shells have "shoulders" at the hinge. Surface textures and color patterns may suggest gown folds, ruffles, and more.

Purchase sliced and lily-cut shells at nature shops or coastal tourist shops. Buy whole shells and miniature embellishments, or gather interesting pieces at the beach for added memories.

Consider how shells will relate in size and shape to others chosen for the same ornament; play with various pieces until they are pleasing to the eye. Look for a shallow halo shell if the body shell is deep; select a deep halo to cup the head if the body is nearly flat.

Use small sea life to embellish the angel. Choose a simple sea star heart, a broken shard trumpet, or tiny barnacle eyes. Discover tiny doves inside a sand dollar to imitate rays of halo light.

HOW TO MAKE A SEASHELL SNOWFLAKE ORNAMENT

MATERIALS

* 5" (12.5 cm) ribbon, ¼" (6 mm) wide, in desired color.
* 1" (2.5 cm) diameter plastic, wood, or tagboard disc.
* Six center-cut slices of equal length from chula or strawberry strombus seashells, for outer layer.
* Six lily-cut shells of equal length from chula or strawberry strombus seashells, for inner layer.
* One umbonium or snail shell, ¼" to ½" (6 mm to 1.3 cm) diameter, for center.
* Craft glue.

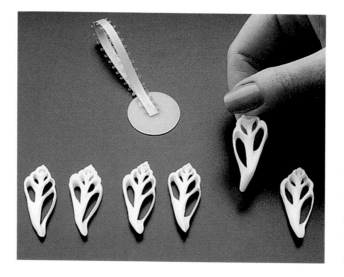

1 Lap ribbon ends to form loop; glue to disc, and allow to dry. Arrange chula slices side by side. Note curves and spaces; turn slices over as necessary so all longest spaces are on the same side.

38

2 Place ⅛" (3 mm) glue dot on underside of chula slice, at narrow tip. Lap about ½" (1.3 cm) of slice onto disc. Repeat quickly with remaining slices. Adjust lap amount so slices are evenly spaced on an imaginary circle. Allow to dry several hours.

3 Place ⅛" (3 mm) glue dot on lily-cut shell back, ¼" (6 mm) from narrow tip. Place tip over disc center so shell back rests between two slices and curled lip is on the top. Repeat quickly with remaining lily-cut shells; adjust so cut tops are evenly spaced on an imaginary circle. Glue umbonium shell at center to hide tips. Allow to dry overnight.

HOW TO MAKE A SEASHELL ANGEL ORNAMENT

MATERIALS

* 3/8" to 5/8" (1 to 1.5 cm) wood bead, for head; acrylic paints and fine-tip brush.
* 10" (25.5 cm) 8-lb. (3.5 kg) monofilament fishing line, for hanger.

* Craft glue; mat knife.
* Miniature shells, for hair.
* Round seashell, larger than head, for halo.
* Large attractive shell, for gown.

* Ribbon, felt, suede, or Ultrasuede® strip, 1/4" to 1/2" (6 mm to 1.3 cm) wide, for wings; scissors.
* Embellishments as desired.

1 Paint eyes and mouth on head. Knot ends of hanger to form loop; secure to bead hole or back of head, using glue. Glue miniature shells to top and sides of head, for hair, bringing hair close to face to prevent appearance of baldness; leave back of head bare.

2 Apply glue to halo hinge. Place gown hinge over halo, lapping shells about 1/8" (3 mm). Secure head to halo bowl and snug against body, using glue. Allow to dry thoroughly; check shells occasionally to make sure they remain snug.

4 Apply glue along upper edge and hinge of gown; secure wings. Trim ends diagonally, pointing away from gown. Embellish as desired. Trim any visible glue from ornament with mat knife.

3 Cut wing strip equal in length to four times body height. Place glue drop at strip center; turn strip onto glue at slight diagonal to form loop that is slightly more than half the body width. Repeat to form second loop.

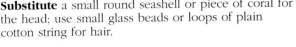

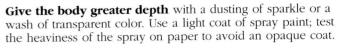

Substitute a small round seashell or piece of coral for the head; use small glass beads or loops of plain cotton string for hair.

Give the body greater depth with a dusting of sparkle or a wash of transparent color. Use a light coat of spray paint; test the heaviness of the spray on paper to avoid an opaque coat.

Collect broken or sand-washed shells, and consider design possibilities of the found treasures. Holes in small shells may be located perfectly for eyes or mouth; conical shells work well for the gown. Protruding nodules may imitate feet beneath a gown.

Use various shells for wings. Select pieces similar in size, shape, and color; they do not need to match. Arrange the wings behind the assembled angel, noting the contact points. Secure quickly, using hot glue; reinforce the bond, using craft glue.

PATCHWORK SANTA TREE SKIRT

Five jolly Santa faces are the focus of this three-dimensional tree skirt. A button mouth and painted eyes show his delight, wire spectacles rest on his big round nose, and a jingle bell dangles from the tip of his hat. Quotable panels join the faces in traditional holiday colors.

Select white faux fur for Santa's beard and hat trim. Choose from small cotton prints or solid reds for suitable hat and lettering fabrics; select a contrasting green fabric for the rest of the skirt and skirt lining.

Use a rotary cutter and cutting surface, and a wide see-through straightedge with 45° angle markings for fast and easy cutting of the various pieces. Or develop paper patterns, using the measurements given in the cutting directions. Fold or stack most fabrics to speed cutting; cut faux fur one layer at a time to ensure accuracy.

All seam allowances are ¼" (6 mm). To maximize the beauty of the faux fur, turn its pile away from the cut edges when stitching and press seams lightly to avoid crushing the pile.

Use a nail polish or acrylic paint bottle, or some other small sturdy cylinder with a similar diameter, to shape Santa's glasses.

MATERIALS

* ¼ yd. (0.25 m) fabric, for face and nose.

* ½ yd. (0.5 m) white faux fur, for beard and hat trim.

* ⅜ yd. (0.35 m) red fabric, for hat, border, and letters.

* 1¾ yd. (1.6 m) green fabric, for skirt panel.

* 2 yd. (1.85 m) fabric, for skirt lining.

* Rotary cutter, cutting surface, straightedge, optional.

* Tracing paper.

* Blush; black fabric paint or permanent fabric marker or embroidery floss.

* Polyester fiberfill.

* Five ⅝" (1.5 cm) red buttons, for mouths.

* Five brass jingle bells, ½" to ⅝" (1.3 to 1.5 cm).

* 60" (152.5 cm) 24-gauge brass wire, for glasses; small cylinder; invisible thread.

* Paper-backed fusible web; iron.

* Polyester quilt batting, 1½ yd. (1.4 m) square.

CUTTING DIRECTIONS

Cut two 1½" (3.8 cm) strips from the face fabric, using a straightedge and a rotary cutter; stack the strips. Cut five quadrilaterals for the faces, as shown below, with sides that measure 12½" (31.8 cm) and 9½" (24.3 cm).

Draw a 3" (7.5 cm) diameter circle on paper; use it as a pattern to cut five noses.

Cut 2" (5 cm) faux fur strips into five quadrilaterals, as shown below, with sides that measure 10½" (26.8 cm) and 6½" (16.3 cm); repeat four times to cut five hat trim pieces.

Cut three 9" (23 cm) squares from faux fur; cut them in half diagonally for the beards. Discard one beard. Or, if fur has a nap, make a pattern first. Cut five beards with nap running toward point.

Cut three 5½" (14 cm) squares from the red fabric; stack the squares. Cut them in half diagonally for six hats; discard one hat.

Cut five 4" (10 cm) strips from green fabric; stack three strips. Cut quadrilaterals, as shown below, with sides that measure 16" (40.5 cm) and 8¼" (21.2 cm). Cut a total of ten border pieces.

Trace the pattern on page 310 for the hat tip, and cut five from the red fabric.

Enlarge the skirt panel pattern (page 309). Cut five panels; cut one panel in half from the tip to the mark.

Cut an 18" (46 cm) length of fabric across one end of the skirt lining.

HOW TO CUT QUADRILATERAL PIECES

1 Align 45° angle mark of straight-edge along one side of stacked strips; trim end of strips, holding straightedge firmly.

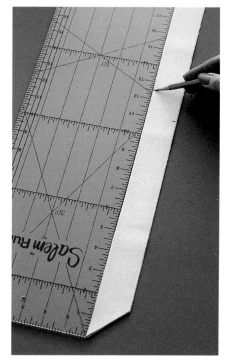

2 Mark long outer side and short inner side as required in cutting directions, using pencil; for example, measure 12½" (31.8 cm) from pointed end and 9½" (24.3 cm) from inner end, for face strips.

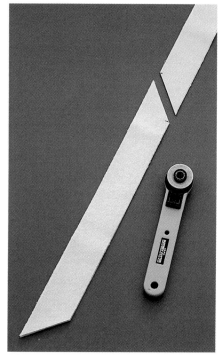

3 Reposition straightedge on marks; 45° angle mark will align with side of strip. Cut.

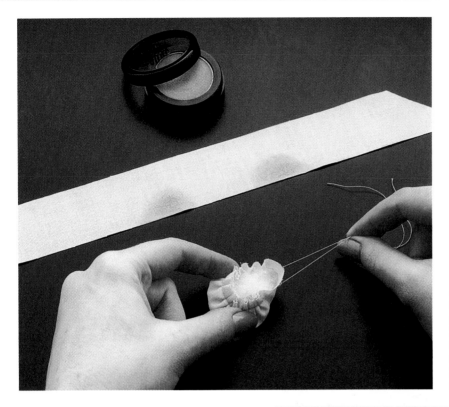

1 Apply two half circles of blush lightly to lower edge of face, for cheeks. Apply 1" (2.5 cm) circle of blush to center of nose circle. Machine-baste ¼" (6 mm) from cut edge of nose circle. Pull thread tails on right side of fabric tight, enclosing ball of fiberfill; knot, and trim tails.

2 Stitch long side of hat to short side of hat trim, right sides together. Stitch long sides of face and beard, right sides together. Stitch remaining sides of hat trim and face, right sides together. Press seams lightly toward hat and face.

3 Hand-stitch nose to center of face. Sew button on beard, for mouth; position directly beneath nose, about 1" (2.5 cm) from face seam.

(Continued)

4 Fold hat tip, right sides together, as indicated on pattern. Stitch from point B to point C; backstitch to secure each end. Turn right side out, aligning raw edges; press. Stitch jingle bell to point.

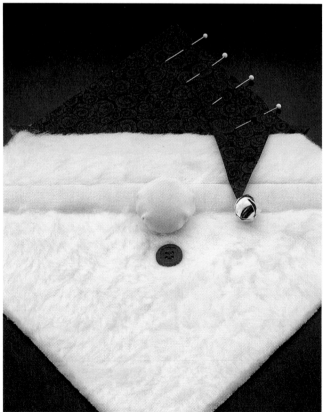

5 Pin hat tip to right side of hat, aligning raw edges along upper right side of hat, as shown.

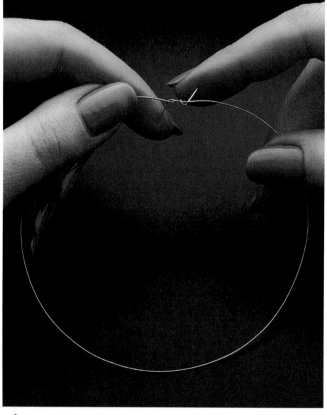

6 Cut 12" (30.5 cm) length of wire. Lap ends, leaving ¾" (2 cm) tails; wrap tails around wire to form circle.

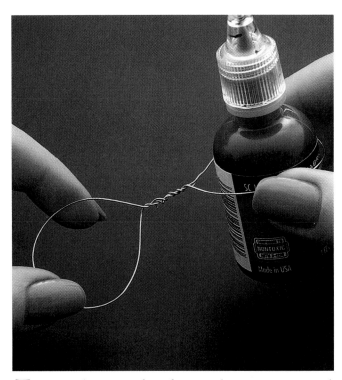

7 Twist circle once to form figure eight; position wrapped tails at center. Place one loop around cylinder, and twist center until loop is tight; remove cylinder. Repeat for opposite loop.

8 Bend twisted part slightly to form spectacles' bridge. Secure to face with a few stitches across bridge, using invisible thread. Draw eyes on face, using fabric paint or marker, or hand-stitch eyes, using floss.

HOW TO MAKE A SANTA TREE SKIRT

1 Make five Santa blocks, as on pages 45 and 46, steps 1 to 5. Mark wrong side of Santa blocks, panels, and borders where ¼" (6 mm) seams will intersect; place one mark at each corner.

2 Enlarge HO! pattern (page 309); trace on paper side of fusible web four times. Apply web to red fabric scraps, following manufacturer's directions; cut letters out and remove paper backing. Fuse one letter set on one skirt panel, as shown, following manufacturer's directions; repeat with three remaining sets and three whole panels.

(Continued)

3 Arrange blocks and panels as shown. Stitch adjoining block and panel sides, right sides together, backstitching at corner marks; keep jingle bell tip free.

4 Stitch adjoining short panel sides, backstitching ¼" (6 mm) from each end, as in step 3; leave long sides of two half panels open. Press the seam allowances toward panels.

5 Align short side of border piece to Santa beard; stitch as in step 3. Repeat with nine remaining border pieces. Stitch border end seams from corners to cut edges; press seam allowances toward borders.

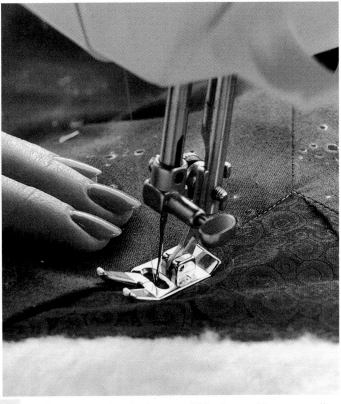

6 Mark selvage center of larger lining piece; mark cut edge center of smaller lining piece. Align pieces, right sides together, matching marks. Stitch; press seam allowance to one side.

7 Place batting on work surface so it is smooth, but not stretched. Place lining over batting, right side up, and pieced top over lining, right side down. Pin layers together along all raw edges. Trim excess batting and lining, using pieced top as pattern.

8 Stitch around tree skirt; pivot at each seam, and leave 6" (15 cm) opening on one long panel side. Trim seam allowances at all outer corners; clip to stitching at all inner corners. Turn skirt right side out; press seams lightly.

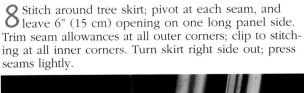

9 Stitch in the ditch around blocks, and between all border and panel pieces. Stitch close to edges of all fused letters. Complete Santa block as on pages 46 and 47, steps 6 to 8. Slipstitch opening closed.

BOOT STOCKINGS

These fun stockings reflect two of the most recognized holiday traditions, Santa and the Nutcracker. Santa's boot is buckled and strapped and has feather trim lapping his pants leg. The Nutcracker's boot is decorated with festive trims and buttoned laces.

Create stockings to mirror your holiday decor. Choose velveteens, bejeweled buckles and buttons, and rayon or metallic frogs, for rich elegance. Select denims, corduroys, or wool flannels, with buckles left uncovered, for a laid-back Santa. Use similar fabrics with plain wood or metal buttons, for an American Nutcracker; twisted weltings, narrow braids, and leather lacings work well for ties.

Choose bright white, tan, or an unexpected color for Santa's trim; marabou feather boas are available in a variety of colors at fabric and costume supply stores. Select from a wide variety of elegant or casual trims, such as laces, medallions, beads, and buttons, for the Nutcracker's boot; stitch narrow trims side by side, or layer them on top of wider trims, if desired.

To avoid crushing the pile when sewing on velveteen or corduroy, use a walking foot, if you have one, and press the seams lightly. Stitch the feather trim to Santa's boot by hand, using a whipstitch, or by machine, using a piping foot and a long straight stitch.

MATERIALS

* ¾ yd. (0.7 m) fabric, for lining.
* ¾ yd. (0.7 m) low-loft batting.

For Santa's boot:

* ½ yd. (0.5 m) fabric, for boot and boot strap.
* ½ yd. (0.5 m) fabric, for pants leg and hanger.
* ½ yd. (0.5 m) marabou feather boa, for trim.
* Topstitching thread.
* 1½" (3.8 cm) buckle.

For Nutcracker's boot:

* ¾ yd. (0.7 m) fabric.
* ⅝ yd. (0.6 m) trim; glue stick, optional.
* Six ¾" to 1" (2 to 2.5 cm) buttons and ¾ yd. (0.7 m) narrow trim or lacing, or three frogs.
* Embellishments as desired.

CUTTING DIRECTIONS

For the Santa boot stocking, cut two Santa boots, using the pattern on page 306; clip at the marks. Cut a 3½" × 4½" (9 × 11.5 cm) rectangle, for the boot strap. Cut two pants legs, using the pattern on page 307.

For the Nutcracker stocking, cut two stockings, using the pattern on page 306.

For either style, cut two stockings from the lining and two from the batting, using the pattern on page 306; clip the lining at the marks. Cut one 2" × 6" (5 × 15 cm) rectangle, for the hanger.

HOW TO MAKE A SANTA'S BOOT

1 Stitch boot to pants leg, right sides together, using ½" (1.3 cm) seam allowance, for front. Press seam open. On right side, zigzag over topstitching thread ⅜" (1 cm) from pants-leg sides. Avoid piercing thread with needle; leave thread tails. Stitch boa over seam; trim boa at cut edge. Repeat, for back.

(Continued)

2 Fold boot strap in half lengthwise, right sides together. Stitch across short end and along side, using ¼" (6 mm) seam allowance. Trim corner; turn and press flat. Pin open end to edge of one boot, between clip marks; baste a scant ½" (1.3 cm) from cut edges.

3 Fold hanger in half lengthwise, right sides together. Stitch long side, using ¼" (6 mm) seam allowance; turn and press. Pin folded hanger to right side of back pants leg so ends align to upper edge, 1" (2.5 cm) from back side.

4 Pin front stocking to batting along boot edges and ½" (1.3 cm) from top; secure upper thread tails to top pins. Pull lower tails, gathering pants-leg sides to fit batting. Baste a scant ½" (1.3 cm) around stocking. Repeat, for back.

HOW TO MAKE A NUTCRACKER'S BOOT

1 Position trims as desired on stocking front; cut trims even with stocking edges. Secure trims on stocking, using pins or glue stick; stitch along sides or through trim center as desired. Repeat on stocking back. Make and secure hanger to back as in step 3, above.

2 Pin stocking front to batting, right side up; baste a scant ½" (1.3 cm) around stocking. Repeat, for back. Follow steps 5 and 6, opposite, to line stocking. Position lining in stocking. Stitch buttons 1½" (3.8 cm) from seam, or stitch frogs across seam; avoid catching more than one layer of lining.

5 Stitch lining to stocking at upper edge, right sides together; use ½" (1.3 cm) seam allowance. Trim batting from seam allowance; press seam allowance toward lining. Edgestitch close to seam, securing lining to seam allowance.

6 Pin front to back, right sides together; pin boot to boot and lining to lining. Stitch around stocking, using ½" (1.3 cm) seam allowance; leave opening in lining, between marks. Trim batting from seam allowance; clip curves, and turn right side out. Slipstitch opening closed.

7 Position lining in stocking. Stitch buckle at desired location; avoid catching more than one layer of lining. Slip boot strap through buckle.

For chained buttons, cut three 6½" (16.3 cm) pieces of narrow trim or lacing. Tape ends of each piece together, forming three loops. Place loops around button sets; bend tape around back buttons.

For laced buttons, tie knot at each end of trim. Place trim center at seam between lower button set; wrap trim around buttons on alternating sides, wrapping to top set. Tie bow above top buttons.

MANTEL CLOTH

Create a beautiful mantel cloth to make your fireplace more festive. Outline the cloth with a twisted welting, suspend special ornaments at the front, and quilt holiday motifs or gentle swirls on the panels.

Develop the pattern pieces before purchasing fabric; you will want to railroad the fabric if the mantel length is longer than the fabric width to avoid seams in the mantel cloth. Measure patterns to determine yardage for cording or piping.

Select mediumweight fabrics and trims that coordinate with the rest of your holiday decorating. Calicos or textured linens, casual cotton welting, and wood or tin ornaments provide a casual or country feeling. Velvets, taffetas, or damasks, rayon welting, and crystal or polished metal ornaments are very elegant.

Choose a quilting motif that repeats or complements the ornaments; trace around cookie cutters or paper patterns. Use a walking foot to ease feeding of multiple fabric layers, if available. Or drop the feed dogs and stipple-

quilt the panels; use an all-over, free-form design or fill in a motif's background.

Use at least four drapery weights to keep the top panel against the wall; you may choose to use more if your mantel is more than 45" (115 cm) long, if you design drops longer than the mantel depth, or to counter-balance heavy ornaments.

MATERIALS

* Paper, to make pattern; flexible curve, optional.
* Decorative fabric.
* Batting.
* Lining fabric.
* Ribbon, ⅛" to ¼" (3 to 6 mm) wide.
* Decorative twisted
welting; transparent tape.
* Safety pins.
* Drapery weights, four or more.
* Ornaments; one for each upper point.
* ½" (1.3 cm) buttons; one for each ornament.

CUTTING DIRECTIONS

Cut three mantel fronts, using the pattern developed in steps 1 and 2; cut one each from fabric, batting, and lining. Cut six mantel sides, using the pattern developed in step 3; cut two each from fabric, batting, and lining. Cut three rectangles for the mantel top, with the length equal to the mantel length plus ½" (1.3 cm) of ease for every yard (meter) of length, and the width equal to the mantel depth; cut one each from fabric, batting, and lining.

Measure around the pattern pieces to determine the welting yardage; purchase an amount equal to the circumference of the front and side panels plus 6" (15 cm).

Determine the desired drop of the ornaments; cut one ribbon for each ornament equal to two times the drop plus 2" (5 cm).

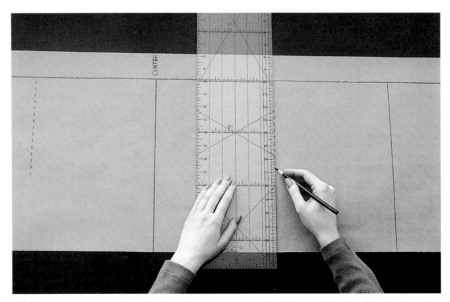

1 Measure mantel length; draw line on paper to this length plus ½" (1.3 cm) per yard (meter). Determine spacing of front points; divide length by desired number of points. Use perpendicular lines to mark location of each front point. Draw short dotted lines midway between perpendicular lines as shown.

(Continued)

55

2 Measure mantel height to determine minimum drop; mark this distance along dotted lines. Determine desired mantel drop at long points; mark this distance along solid lines. Draw front drop edge, using flexible curve, if desired. Add ½" (1.3 cm) seam allowances to all edges.

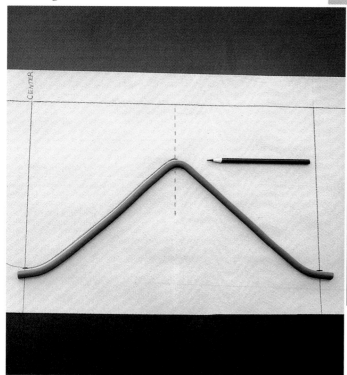

3 For side, draw rectangle with width equal to mantel depth and length equal to desired side drop. Shape drop as desired. Add ½" (1.3 cm) seam allowances to all edges. Cut out pattern pieces; tape to mantel to check size, proportion, and shape.

4 Mark quilting design on right side of front, using fabric pencil. Place front panel over front batting, right side up. Align all edges; pin. Machine-baste around panel. Repeat with side panels and top.

5 Identify right side of decorative welting; inner edge of tape is not visible on right side. Align welting to sides and front edge of top panel, right sides up, with cord along seamline; baste scant 1/2" (1.3 cm) from edges, using zipper foot. Clip tape to ease welting at corners and curves. Wrap transparent tape around ends to prevent raveling. Repeat with front and side panels, aligning welting to side and lower edges.

6 Place front over front lining, right sides together; pin all edges. Stitch sides and lower edge, using 1/2" (1.3 cm) seam allowances; use zipper foot, crowding welting. Trim batting from seam allowances; trim corners, and clip curves. Repeat for side panels.

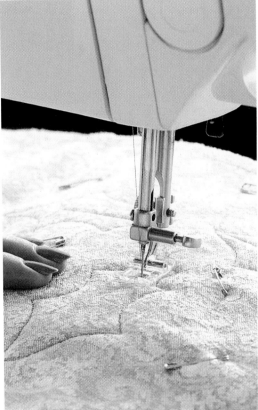

7 Turn pieces right side out; press lightly. Pin-baste around marked designs or at 3" (7.5 cm) intervals as desired. Stitch quilting designs as desired.

8 Pin side panels to top, right sides together, so side welting is 1/2" (1.3 cm) from long cut edges of top. Stitch, using zipper foot; crowd welting. Repeat, stitching front panel along front edge of top; welting of front and side panels should meet at corners.

(Continued)

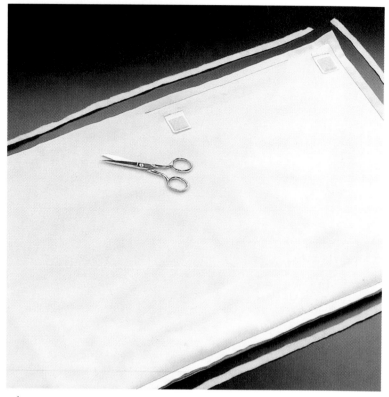

9 Attach drapery weights to wrong side of top lining, ⅝" to ¾" (1.5 to 2 cm) from one long edge. Secure one near each corner and two near center; secure more, if desired.

10 Place top lining on top, right sides together, so weights are at back; pin raw edges, carefully enclosing front and side panels. Stitch around top, using ½" (1.3 cm) seam allowances. Use zipper foot, crowding welting. Avoid catching panels in seams. Leave 6" (15 cm) opening on back edge. Trim batting from seam allowances; trim ½" (1.3 cm) at opening. Trim corners. Turn right side out and press lightly. Slipstitch opening closed. Stitch quilting design, if desired.

11 Stitch button to front panel lining and batting at each upper point, just above welting. Avoid catching front panel in stitches. Slip ribbon through ornament. Tie knot a distance from ornament equal to desired drop; tie second knot ⅝" (1.5 cm) from first knot. Repeat with each ornament. Attach ornaments at buttons, slipping button between knots.

ADVENT WREATH

This Advent wreath provides a unique way to share the joy of expectation all season long. Decorate a natural or artificial wreath to recall special memories, and open one small gift each day as you count down to Christmas.

Suspend a group of favorite mementos from the top of the wreath, and add embellishments that develop a favorite holiday theme. Cluster small embellishments on the top and sides to create an attractive flow for the eye; small bells or sturdy floral stems, such as mountain ash berries, work well and are available in several natural colors.

Purchase small, plain envelopes in stationery stores, or make your own envelopes using decorative or holiday wrapping papers. Number an envelope for each day; use a decorative pen, or select letter transfer sheets from assorted styles available at art and stationery stores.

Into the daily envelopes, slip coupons that may be exchanged immediately or throughout the coming year. Consider a small treat, a special privilege, or a day off from a specific chore; design them to please your family. Or purchase small, flat gifts, such as foil-wrapped candy coins or charms.

HOW TO MAKE AN ADVENT WREATH

MATERIALS

* Wreath, 36" (91.5 cm) in diameter.
* Clusters of small embellishments or berry stems.
* Paddle floral wire; wire cutter.
* One to three large ornaments.
* Small embellishments, such as berries.
* 1 yd. (0.95 m) ribbon, 3" (7.5 cm) wide.
* 7¾ yds. (7.1 m) ribbon, ¼" to ½" (6 mm to 1.3 cm) wide.
* Twenty-five envelopes, 2" (5 cm) square, or decorative papers to make envelopes.
* Decorative pen or transfer letters, ½" (1.3 cm) tall, and stylus or craft stick.
* Glue stick; paper punch.
* Twenty-five small gifts.

1 Secure clustered embellishments to wreath frame at center top, using floral wire; bend stems or secure more clusters to follow upper curve of wreath. Allow an unadorned arc to remain bare at bottom; arrange needles to partially cover floral stems, if used.

2 Suspend large ornaments at center top, using narrow ribbon. Secure small embellishments as desired.

3 Tie bow in wide ribbon. Secure bow to wreath, just above ornaments, using wire; arrange and trim tails as desired. Cut narrow ribbon into twenty-five 11" (28 cm) lengths. Secure ribbons randomly over wreath surface, using wire; allow at least 2" (5 cm) between ribbons. If using purchased envelopes, omit step 4.

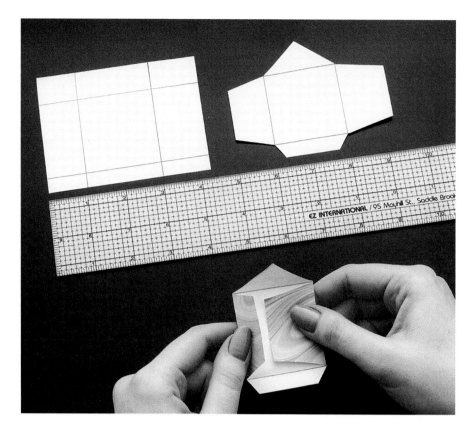

4 Cut 4¼" × 3¼" (10.8 × 8.2 cm) rectangle from decorative paper. Mark foldlines on wrong side of paper, 1" (2.5 cm) from one short side and 1¼" (3.2 cm) from other short side, ⅞" (2.2 cm) from top and ⅜" (1 cm) from bottom. Score foldlines, using table knife, if paper is heavy. Cut out four corners; shape flaps slightly, as shown. Fold envelope; secure narrow side over wide side and bottom flap over sides, using glue stick. Repeat to make twenty-five envelopes.

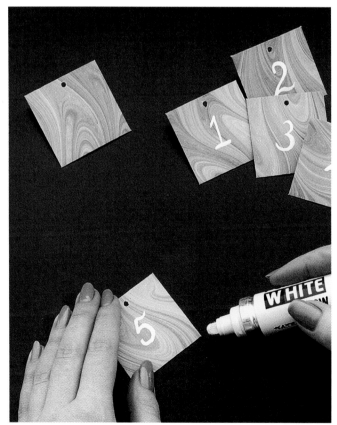

5 Label envelopes with numbers 1 through 25, using decorative pen. Or, position transfer sheet over each envelope, placing number near envelope center; rub number, using stylus or craft stick. Gently lift transfer sheet to ensure complete transfer.

6 Punch hole at tops of envelopes, using paper punch. Insert coupon or small flat gift in each envelope. Tie envelopes to wreath, using ribbons; arrange numbers randomly to avoid lopsided arrangement as envelopes are removed. Hang wreath, using wire loop on back.

ADVENT CALENDAR

This unique Advent calendar provides a visual reminder of your family's favorite holiday cookies. Create twenty-five polymer clay cookies, and count down to Christmas by hanging them on a beribboned baking sheet. Beginning December first, add one cookie each day until all are hanging on Christmas Day. Store the waiting cookies in a small cookie jar or mixing bowl.

Warm polymer clay to make it pliable; roll it between your palms, fold, and reroll until it is soft. Roll soft clay into a ball to eliminate bubbles before forming cookie shapes. Flatten balls slightly to make the simplest designs, like thumbprint cookies or a peanut butter kiss. Discover easy ways to duplicate other cookies in the tips, below. Refer to cookbooks for inspiration, or purchase holiday candy molds. Use disposable towelettes to clean your hands before working with another clay color.

Choose from a wide variety of traditional cookie decorations, including colored sugars, sprinkles, dots, and metallic balls; use baker's decorations that will not melt. Bake decorated shapes on a baking sheet, following the clay manufacturer's directions. Paint the cooled clay, if desired.

MATERIALS

* Polymer clay, assorted colors.
* Small Christmas cookie cutters; large dowel; Mylar® sheet.
* Candy molds; baby powder; small soft paintbrush; acrylic paints, optional.
* Decorative baker's toppings.
* Disposable towelettes; mat knife; toothpick; small dowel.
* Baking sheet, for baking clay.
* Acrylic spray sealer.
* Magnetic strip, ½" or 1" (1.3 or 2.5 cm) wide; scissors; all-purpose glue.
* Steel baking sheet, at least 17" × 11" (43 × 28 cm), with hole at one end; avoid the nonstick variety or the lower bow may not adhere well.
* Masking tape; permanent marker in desired color.
* ⅜ yd. (0.35 m) satin ribbon, ¼" (6 mm) wide.
* 4 yd. (3.7 m) reversible wired ribbon; 24- or 26-gauge wire.
* Hot glue gun.

TIPS FOR MAKING CLAY COOKIES

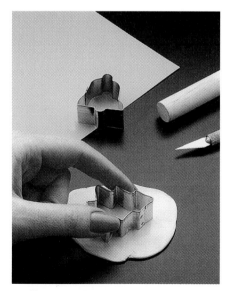

Roll slightly flattened clay ball on clean, smooth surface to about ³⁄₁₆" (4.5 mm), using Mylar sheet between clay and dowel. Use cookie cutters or knife to cut designs. Lift clay shapes using knife, if necessary.

Form rods by rolling ball on surface with fingers; avoid thick and thin areas by moving hands over full length. Place thick rods side by side, and twist gently for candy canes; place medium rods side by side, and spiral length around one end for pinwheels.

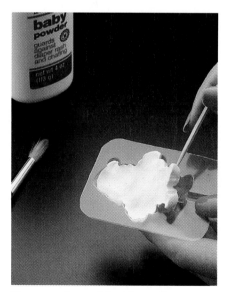

Dust candy mold with small amount of baby powder, using brush. Warm clay to fill mold about halfway; press ball into general shape, and push into mold. Insert toothpick gently at edge where design shows a dent or inner angle; gently pry clay from mold.

(Continued)

Decorate cookies as desired. Cut or pinch layered details from thin sheets. Arrange and gently press thin rods on cookie to imitate frosting. Shape small clay balls into chocolate kisses, cinnamon bits, or other candies as desired. Roll tiny clay balls or use decorative baker's toppings for additional color and detail; press small parts gently into clay to secure.

Use toothpick or small dowel to smooth edges and improve bond between colors. Use sharp tips or flat ends to add surface details or natural texture.

Paint details on cured and cooled cookies, if desired. Glue small decorations in place, if necessary. Spray cookies with acrylic sealer; allow to dry thoroughly.

Cut magnet strip as long as possible, so the weight of the cookie will not cause it to slip; trim width, if necessary, so strip is not visible from front. Glue to back of cookie, using an all-purpose glue; allow glue to cure as manufacturer directs.

HOW TO MAKE AN ADVENT CALENDAR

1 Plan placement of numbers on sheet, using tape; alternate four rows of four and three rows of three, as shown below. Write numbers 1 through 25 on baking sheet, using permanent marker; begin with 25 in the upper left corner.

2 Fold satin ribbon in half; pass fold through hole in end of baking sheet, and slip ends through loop, drawing tight. Knot ribbon about 2½" (6.5 cm) from sheet; tie bow over knot.

3 Cut 1½ yd. (1.4 m) length from wired ribbon. Wrap ribbon over thumb for center loop; form loop on each side. Form slightly larger loop on each side. Insert wire through center loop. Bend wire around ribbon; twist wire tightly, gathering ribbon. Secure wire to baking sheet at hole; trim excess wire. Shape ribbon loops; trim tails, if desired.

4 Make bow with tails, using remaining wired ribbon. Form three loops on each side of center loop, and secure loops with wire, as in step 3. Trim tails as desired. Glue bow to center bottom of baking sheet, using hot glue.

This three-dimensional Santa wall quilt has a button mouth, wire spectacles, a big round nose, and a jingle bell dangling from the tip of his hat, just like the patchwork Santa tree skirt (page 42). Piece three jolly Santa faces, following the general directions for the skirt, and join them with a merry Ho! Ho! Ho!

Quilt the layered top minimally by stitching around the lettering and along the outer block, sashing, and border seamlines. Or quilt the top more fully by stitching within areas; stitch small snowflakes in the air behind Santa, quilt Christmas designs in the borders, or stitch around printed designs in the fabric.

HOW TO SEW A SANTA WALL QUILT

MATERIALS

* ⅛ yd. (0.15 m) fabric, for face and nose.

* ¼ yd. (0.25 m) white faux fur, for beard and hat trim.

* ⅓ yd. (0.32 m) red fabric, for hat, corners, and letters.

* ¼ yd. (0.25 m) light or off-white fabric, for corners.

* 1 yd. (0.95 m) green fabric, for background, sashing, and borders.

* ¾ yd. (0.7 m) coordinating fabric, for quilt back.

* 27" × 45" (68.5 × 115 cm) quilt batting.

* Three ⅝" (1.5 cm) red buttons, for mouths.

* Three brass jingle bells, ½" (1.3 cm) or 15 mm.

* 1 yd. (0.95 m) 24-gauge brass wire, for glasses.

* Polyester fiberfill.

* Blush; black fabric paint or permanent marker or embroidery floss.

* Masking tape; safety pins; quilter's pencil, optional.

* 1⅔ yd. (1.58 m) ribbon, ¼" (6 mm) wide, for hanger loops and bows.

* One 24" (61 cm) cafe curtain rod, brass finish.

* ¾ yd. (0.7 m) decorative cord, for hanger.

* One decorative wall hanger, brass finish.

CUTTING DIRECTIONS

Cut one 1½" (3.8 cm) strip from the face fabric, using a straight-edge and rotary cutter. Cut quadrilaterals, as shown on page 44, so the sides measure 12½" (31.8 cm) and 9½" (24.3 cm); repeat twice to cut three faces.

Draw a 3" (7.5 cm) diameter circle on paper; use it as a pattern to cut three noses.

Cut one 2" (5 cm) strip of faux fur. Cut a quadrilateral, as shown on page 44, so the sides measure 10½" (26.8 cm) and 6½" (16.3 cm); repeat twice to cut three hat brims.

Cut two 9" (23 cm) squares from faux fur. Cut them in half diagonally for three beards; discard one. Or, if the fur has a nap, make a pattern first. Cut the beards so the fur brushes toward the lower point.

Cut two 5½" (14 cm) squares from the red fabric; stack the squares. Cut them in half

diagonally for three hats; discard one.

Trace the pattern (page 310) for the hat tip, and cut three from the red fabric.

Cut three 6½" (16.3 cm) squares from the red fabric; stack and cut them diagonally, for six corner pieces.

Cut three 6½" (16.3 cm) squares from the light or off-white fabric; stack them and cut diagonally, for six corner pieces.

Cut three 11¾" × 8" (30 × 20.5 cm) rectangles from the green fabric. Also cut four 2¾" × 19¼" (7 × 48.1 cm) strips, for the sashing and borders. Cut two 2¾" × 43¼" (7 × 110 cm) strips, for the side borders. Cut four 2½" (6.5 cm) strips across the width of the fabric, for the binding.

Cut the ribbon into five 3" (7.5 cm) lengths and five 9" (23 cm) lengths.

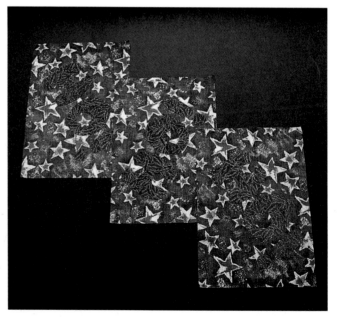

1 Make three Santa blocks, as on pages 45 and 46, steps 1 to 5. Stitch light background corners to upper sides of blocks and red background corners to lower sides of blocks, right sides together, keeping jingle bell tip free. Press seam allowances toward corners.

2 Enlarge, trace, cut, and apply one set of HO! letters to each green rectangle, as on page 47, step 2; arrange letters as shown.

(Continued)

3 Align rectangle that reads on an upward diagonal to left side of Santa block, right sides together; stitch. Repeat, aligning two downward diagonals to right side of remaining blocks. Press seam allowances toward rectangles. Arrange sashing and short border strips above and below Santa rectangles; stitch, right sides together, to make top as shown.

4 Stitch side borders to pieced top, right sides together. Press seam allowances toward sashing and borders. Mark additional quilting design, if desired, using quilting pencil lightly.

5 Tape backing to work surface, wrong side up, so it is taut, but not stretched. Smooth batting over backing. Center quilt top over batting, right side up; smooth.

6 Baste layers together using safety pins, working from center of quilt to sides; avoid pinning along seams. Remove tape from backing. Fold edges of backing over edges of quilt top; pin-baste.

7 Stitch in the ditch around Santa blocks and along all corner, sashing, and border seams; stitch from center to edges. Stitch close to edges of all fused letters. Stitch additional quilting designs, if desired. Remove pins.

8 Measure quilt top across middle; trim binding strip to this measurement. Press binding strip in half lengthwise, wrong sides together. Pin strip to upper edge of quilt top, matching raw edges; ease fullness as necessary. Stitch binding strip to quilt, using scant ¼" (6 mm) seam allowance. Trim excess batting and backing to a scant ½" (1.3 cm) from the stitching. Repeat at the lower edge.

9 Wrap binding strip snugly around edge of quilt, covering stitching line on back; pin in the ditch of the seam. Stitch in the ditch on right side of quilt, catching binding on back.

10 Repeat steps 8 and 9 for quilt sides, measuring quilt top down center and trimming strips to measurement plus 1" (2.5 cm), for ½" (1.3 cm) extensions at top and bottom. Fold extensions over finished edges before final pinning.

11 Complete Santa blocks, as on pages 46 and 47, steps 6 to 8. Fold 3" (7.5 cm) ribbon to form loop, and stitch ends securely to upper corner of quilt. Form small bow, using 9" (23 cm) ribbon; hand-stitch over loop, hiding ends. Repeat at opposite corner; space three more loops and bows evenly across upper edge. Insert cafe rod through loops. Attach cord to rod ends; hang on decorative wall hook.

SHAPED &
TASSELED
PILLOWS

Tuck these fun holiday-shaped pillows in surprising places to add a festive touch throughout the house, or add them to an existing pillow collection.

Select fabrics that reflect the shapes themselves, according to your own style. Add tassels to the corners of the tree pillow, and outline the star with a decorative cord. Use novelty or jeweled buttons and beads for more ornaments and added starlight, if desired.

MATERIALS

* Paper, for pattern; straightedge; fabric pencil.
* Polyester fiberfill.
* Fusible interfacing to back lightweight fabrics.
* ⅓ yd. (0.32 m) fabric, for tree center.
* ¼ yd. (0.25 m) contrasting fabric, for tree border.
* 4½" × 2" (11.5 × 5 cm) fabric piece, for tree trunk.
* Three tassels, for tree.
* ½ yd. (0.5 m) fabric, for star.
* 1½ yd. (1.4 m) decorative cord, ¼" (6 mm) wide, for star; liquid fray preventer.
* Buttons and beads, optional.

HOW TO MAKE A TREE PILLOW

1 Draw 12" (30.5 cm) line on paper; mark center. Draw 11" (28 cm) perpendicular line, starting at center; draw lines from each end of first line to top of second line, forming triangle, for pattern.

2 Cut two fabric triangles, using pattern. Cut six 2¼" × 20" (6 × 51 cm) strips for border; cut two strips in half, crosswise. Cut two 2¼" × 2" (6 × 5 cm) pieces for trunk. Fuse interfacing to wrong side of lightweight fabrics. Mark each point on wrong side of triangles where ¼" (6 mm) seams meet.

3 Stitch short strips to short sides of trunk piece, right sides together; finger-press seams toward trunk. Repeat for second trunk strip.

4 Center short triangle side on trunk strip, right sides together, and pin; strip will extend beyond triangle ends. Stitch ¼" (6 mm) seam between marked points, backstitching at each point. Stitch plain strips to adjacent sides, keeping strips free from new seams. Repeat, for back.

5 Fold triangle in half through one point, right sides together, aligning strip edges. Position straightedge along fold, as shown; mark line on strip, using fabric pencil. Stitch on line, backstitching at seam intersection. Repeat at remaining corners. Trim excess fabric. Repeat, for back. Carefully press seam allowances to one side; avoid distorting triangles.

7 Stuff pillow with fiberfill. Slipstitch opening closed. Add embellishments as desired.

6 Pin tassels at corners of back; part of cord will extend beyond cut edges. Pin pillow front to back, right sides together; stitch, using ½" (1.3 cm) seam allowances. Leave 5" (12.5 cm) opening on bottom. Trim corners, and press seam allowances open; turn right side out.

HOW TO MAKE A STAR PILLOW

1 Draw an 18" (46 cm) diameter circle on paper, using string tied to a pencil. Divide circle into five parts; marks should be about 11⅜" (29 cm) apart.

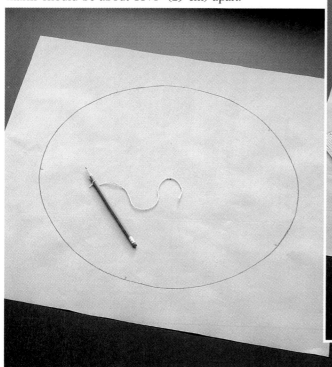

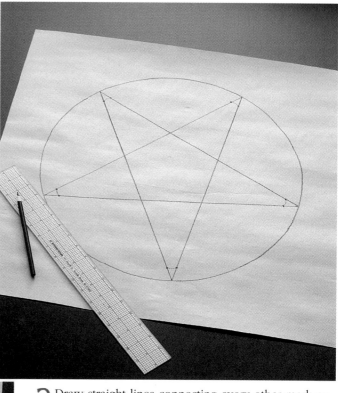

2 Draw straight lines connecting every other mark on circle. Round off star points 1" (2.5 cm) from ends.

3 Cut two stars from fabric, using pattern. Fuse interfacing to wrong side of lightweight fabrics. Pin stars right sides together, aligning edges. Stitch, using ¼" (6 mm) seam allowance; take short stitch across each point. Leave 3" (7.5 cm) opening on one side. Clip into each corner; trim points. Press seam allowances open; turn.

4 Stuff pillow with fiberfill; use pencil to pack fiberfill into
points. Slipstitch opening closed.

5 Seal cord end with liquid fray preventer;
allow to dry. Trim end clean. Whipstitch
cord over seam, starting at inner corner.
Seal cord where it meets end; trim
clean when dry, and secure
with hand stitches.

PILLOW CHANGERS

Dress up your everyday knife-edge pillows with these holiday ideas. Select fabrics that complement the pillows you wish to cover and that blend well with your home's decor.

Design pillow toppers to cover one-third to two-thirds of the pillow, shaping the lower edge as you desire. Embellish them with beads, bells, buttons, and more.

Reverse colors for toppers and overlays on contrasting pillows, if desired.

Select from a variety of colors in fabrics such as organza and ninon to make a sheer, flanged overlay for your pillow; choose a similar tone for a subtle change, or use a contrasting color for greater interest.

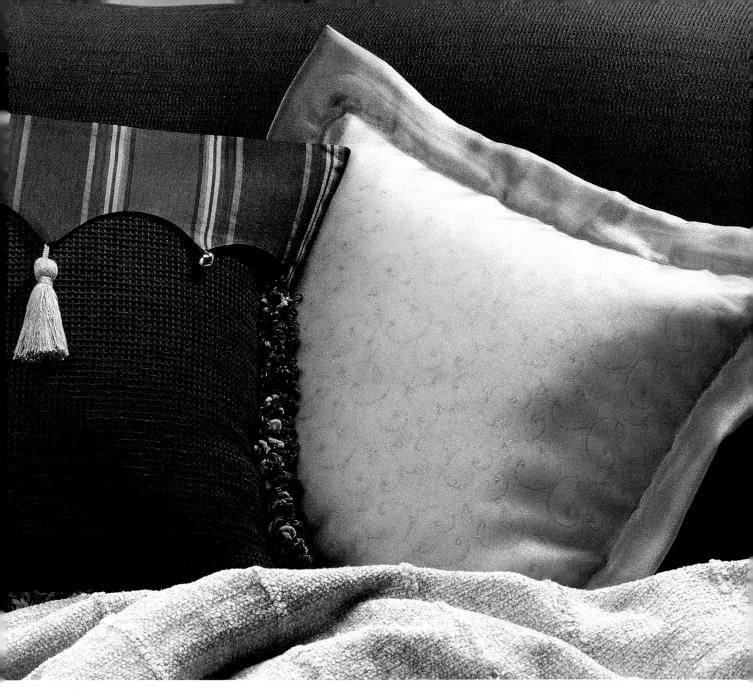

MATERIALS

* Paper, to draw pattern for topper.

* Fabric, for topper; ½ yd. (0.5 m) for toppers covering the upper third of pillows up to 20" (51 cm) square; ¾ yd. (0.7 m) for longer toppers.

* Sheer fabric, for overlay; pillows up to 14" (35.5 cm) square require only ⅝ yd. (0.6 m).

* Embellishments as desired.

CUTTING DIRECTIONS

For a topper, cut four pieces, using the pattern as drawn in steps 1 and 2.

For an overlay, cut one rectangle with the length equal to the pillow height plus 5" (12.5 cm) and the width equal to two times the pillow width plus 14" (35.5 cm).

HOW TO MAKE A PILLOW TOPPER

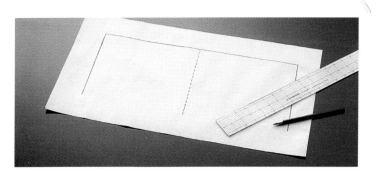

1 Measure pillow width, including trim; draw line on paper equal to this length plus ½" (1.3 cm). Draw perpendicular lines at each end that are at least one-third the pillow height; draw dotted line at center.

(Continued)

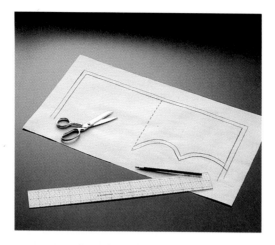

2 Draw desired hem shape; draw from one side to dotted line for symmetrical hem. Add ½" (1.3 cm) seam allowance to all sides. If symmetrical, fold on dotted line; cut on outer lines.

3 Align sides and upper edge of two pieces, right sides together, and stitch, using ½" (1.3 cm) seam allowance; leave hem open. Trim corners; press seam allowances open.

4 Repeat step 3 with remaining two pieces, for lining, using ½" (1.3 cm) seam allowance on sides and ⅝" (1.5 cm) seam allowance along upper edge; leave 5" (12.5 cm) opening along upper edge.

HOW TO MAKE A SHEER FLANGED OVERLAY

1 Press under ¾" (2 cm) double hem on each short end; stitch close to inner fold. Mark long sides at center and points 1½" (3.8 cm) from ends, using pins. Fold end marks to center mark, wrong sides together, so hems overlap 3" (7.5 cm); pin.

5 Add tassels at hem edge, as on page 148, step 2, if desired. Align seams and hem edges of topper and lining, right sides together; pin. Stitch, using ½" (1.3 cm) seam allowance. Trim points; clip curves. Turn right side out through opening; press.

6 Slipstitch opening closed. Hand-stitch any bells, beads, or decorative buttons. Place topper over upper edge of pillow.

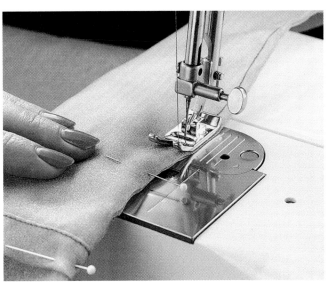

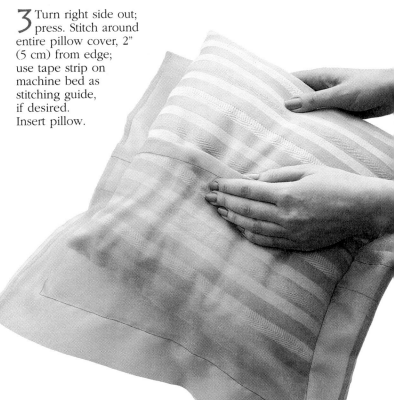

3 Turn right side out; press. Stitch around entire pillow cover, 2" (5 cm) from edge; use tape strip on machine bed as stitching guide, if desired. Insert pillow.

2 Stitch seams, using short stitches and ¼" (6 mm) seam allowances. Trim seams, using pinking shears, if possible. Turn wrong side out; press seam edges. Stitch again ¼" (6 mm) from edges.

SANTA'S PILLOW COLLECTION

Piece a merry Santa face, convert an everyday pillow into his hefty sack, and wrap an ordinary pillow to look like a gift. Set the three pillows together as a reminder of holiday folklore, or use the ideas separately for a simple decorative touch.

Choose fabrics used elsewhere in your home or select all new for a coordinated set. Use fabrics that reflect your personal style; make them elegant in velvet and satin, or casual in a coarsely textured linen, hopsacking, or calico. Select a non-directional print for the sack. Tie the sack simply with a knotted cord, or make matching ribbon bows for both the sack and gift.

MATERIALS

* Fabrics for Santa's face, nose, beard, and hat; ½ yd. (0.5 m) fabric for border and pillow back; 14" (35.5 cm) pillow form.

* Fabric for sack and gift; yardage will vary with pillow size.

* ½ to ¾ yd. (0.5 to 0.7 m) decorative cord, for knotted sack.

* 1 yd. (0.95 m) ribbon, for sack with bow.

* 1 to 3 yd. (0.95 to 2.75 m) ribbon, for gifts with bows, depending on pillow size.

CUTTING DIRECTIONS

For a Santa pillow, cut one face, nose, hat brim, beard, hat, and hat tip, following the general cutting directions on page 44. Cut two 3½" × 8½" (9 × 21.8 cm) strips and two 3½" × 15" (9 × 38 cm) strips from the border fabric. Cut one 15" (38 cm) square for the pillow back.

For Santa's sack, measure the pillow. For the sack, cut a rectangle with the height equal to three-and-one-half times the pillow height and the width equal to the pillow width plus 2" (5 cm). Cut a rectangle for the lining with the height equal to the pillow height plus 2" (5 cm) and the width equal to twice the pillow width plus 3" (7.5 cm).

To wrap a pillow, cut a rectangle with the height equal to two times the pillow height plus 9" (23 cm) and the width equal to the pillow width plus 9" (23 cm).

HOW TO MAKE A SANTA PILLOW

1 Make one Santa block, as on pages 45 and 46, steps 1 to 5. Align short border strips to opposite sides of block, right sides together; stitch, using ¼" (6 mm) seam allowances. Stitch long border strips to remaining opposite sides of block, right sides together; press seam allowances toward borders. Complete pillow as on page 73, steps 6 and 7; use pillow form and omit reference to tassels. Complete Santa block as on page 46, steps 6 to 8.

HOW TO GIFT WRAP A PILLOW

1 Press under ⅜" (1 cm) on each side of fabric. Unfold corner; fold diagonally so pressed folds match. Press the diagonal fold; trim corner as shown. Repeat at each corner.

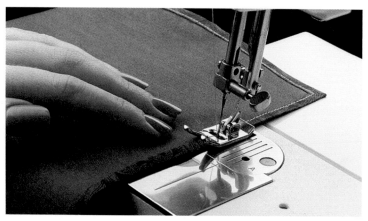

2 Fold under raw edges to pressed folds; press double-fold hems in place. Stitch around rectangle close to inner fold.

3 Place pillow on wrong side of fabric; wrap as you would a gift, securing flaps with safety pins. Wrap ribbon around pillow as desired, hiding pins; adjust pin location, if necessary.

HOW TO MAKE SANTA'S SACK

1 Fold sack fabric in half, crosswise; pin sides. Stitch, using 1/2" (1.3 cm) seam allowance. Trim corners. Pin short ends of lining together; stitch to form circle. Press seams open. Finish lower edge of lining, if desired.

2 Place lining in sack, right sides together, matching lining seam to side seam; pin upper edges. Stitch, using 1/2" (1.3 cm) seam allowance; press seam allowance open.

3 Turn lining down over wrong side of sack. Tack lining to sack at seam allowances. Topstitch upper edge, if desired.

4 Turn sack right side out; insert pillow. Tie sack closed above pillow, using decorative cord or ribbon.

SHELL-TRIMMED CHRISTMAS TREE

Collecting colorful shells and bits of sea life entrances children of all ages, and this miniature Christmas tree displays the smallest treasures beautifully.

Find small trees in gift and Christmas shops. Discover shells and colorful bits of coral while exploring the ocean beach or in nature shops.

Make a glue paste to ease shell positioning without sliding and to shorten setting times; it's very child friendly! Just pour white craft glue into a small container, and stir occasionally until thick.

MATERIALS

* Miniature trees.
* Wire cutter; white acrylic paint; fine glitter, optional.
* Paste of condensed craft glue; craft stick.
* Tiny seashells and sea life bits.
* Baby oil or mineral oil, optional.

HOW TO MAKE A SHELL-TRIMMED CHRISTMAS TREE

1 Separate connected tree branches, if necessary, using wire cutter. Paint tree base and branches; sprinkle fine glitter on wet paint, if desired. Examine all sides of shells and sea life bits. Select the most colorful pieces, planning at least one piece for each branch; separate by size and color strength.

2 Plan location of shells and bits on tree, spacing most colorful pieces evenly around tree; gradually increase size from top to bottom. Place small paste dollop on tip of branch; gently press colorful shell or bit on paste. Repeat with all colorful pieces; fill in with less colorful shells. Layer pieces as desired.

84

3 Position pointed shells so narrow ends point to tree trunk. Attach sea star at treetop with one leg pointing straight up.

4 Allow glue to dry thoroughly. Brush on light coat of baby oil or mineral oil, to restore color and sheen to well-worn or aged shells.

MR. & MRS. FROST

Mr. and Mrs. Frost are happy to be in from the cold. Set them by the fire or on a buffet table, or let them greet your guests near the front door. Mr. Frost stands about 14" (35.5 cm) tall; she's a little shorter.

Sew the bodies using snow-white cotton velour, terry cloth, or polar fleece. Create a carrot nose from a simple felt triangle. Use beads for their coal eyes and mouths; choose multifaceted beads to add a little twinkle. Dress them in country casual clothes; recycle an old pair of jeans to make his overalls, and select a small gingham check or tiny holiday print for his scarf and her apron.

Consider how you can use the jeans' features to add interest and imitate factory detailing. Use a tiny change pocket or the manufacturer's label for the bib's pocket, or stitch it to the back of the pants. Secure a size label at the pocket's side, if desired. Select topstitching thread in a color to match the original topstitching, if possible. Save rivets; glue them to overalls as embellishment, if desired.

Purchase small buckets or baskets for Mr. and Mrs. Frost to carry; fill them with silk holly clusters, poinsettias, or red berries, available in floral and craft shops. Use additional small florals to embellish the apron and hats. Or make a tiny firewood tote from a scrap of fabric.

MATERIALS

* ½ yd. (0.5 m) fabric, for bodies and arms; safety pins.
* Polyester fiberfill.
* White pearl cotton, size 3.
* Four ¾" (2 cm) buttons, to secure arms; 5" (12.5 cm) doll needle.
* Orange felt scrap; orange or gold topstitching thread.
* Four ⅜" (1 cm) black beads, for eyes.
* Ten small black beads, for mouth.
* Cosmetic blush; craft glue.
* ⅜ yd. (0.35 m) fabric for scarf and apron.

For Mr. Frost:

* One pair worn jeans.
* Topstitching thread.
* Four ⅜" to ½" (1 to 1.3 cm) buttons, for overalls.
* Hat, about 6" (15 cm) in diameter.
* Embellishments as desired.

For Mrs. Frost:

* ⅝ yd. (0.6 m) eyelet trim, ¾" (2 cm) wide.
* Two ⅜" to ½" (1 to 1.3 cm) buttons, for apron.
* Hat, diameter will vary with style.
* Embellishments as desired.

CUTTING DIRECTIONS

Cut a felt rectangle 1½" × 3" (3.8 × 7.5 cm); cut it in half diagonally to make two noses.

For Mr Frost:

Cut two body pieces, using the pattern on pages 304 and 305; follow outer line. Mark the neck and waist with safety pins. Cut four arms, using the pattern on page 305.

Cut one 5¼" × 4" (13.2 × 10 cm) rectangle from the bottom of a jeans leg, for the front bib; include the hem on the long side. Cut one 2¾" × 2¼" (7 × 6 cm) rectangle, for a pocket, if desired. Cut two 1¼" × 9" (3.2 × 23 cm) strips, for the straps. Cut one 8" × 9½" (20.5 × 24.3 cm) rectangle, for the pants; center it over the jeans seam.

Cut a 10" (25.5) square of scarf fabric, then cut it in half diagonally, for the bandanna; discard one triangle. Or cut a 1¼" × 22" (3.2 × 56 cm) strip, for a muffler.

For Mrs. Frost:

Cut two body pieces, using the pattern on pages 304 and 305; follow inner line. Mark the neck and waist with safety pins. Cut four arms, using the pattern on page 305.

Cut a 12" × 3¼" (30.5 × 8.2 cm) rectangle, rounding the bottom corners, for the apron skirt. Cut a 2½" × 5" (6.5 × 12.5 cm) rectangle, for the bib. Cut a 1½" × 24" (3.8 × 61 cm) strip for the waist tie. Cut a 1½" × 9" (3.8 × 23 cm) strip, for the neck strap.

HOW TO MAKE A SNOWMAN

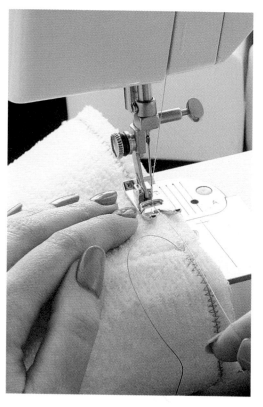

1 Align body pieces, right sides together; pin. Stitch, using ¼" (6 mm) seam allowance; leave bottom open. Zigzag over topstitching thread ⅜" (1 cm) from opening, right side up; avoid piercing thread with needle. Leave topstitching thread tails.

2 Stuff body to neck safety pin, using fiberfill; remove pin. Wrap neck tight, using pearl cotton. Push more fiberfill into head area, using eraser end of pencil, to make firm round head about 4½" (11.5 cm) wide.

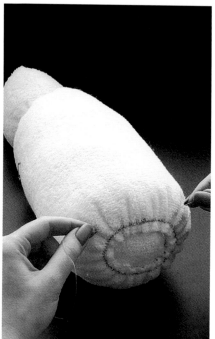

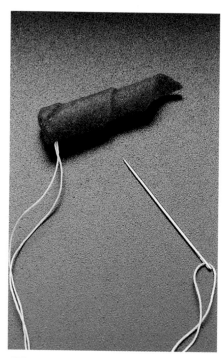

3 Stuff remaining body; place fabric scrap over fiberfill. Gather bottom, pulling thread tails; leave small opening. Wrap pearl cotton around body at waist pin, pulling in slightly; remove pin. Adjust location of waist, if desired; tack pearl cotton in place at center front and back.

4 Align two arm pieces, right sides together; pin. Stitch, using ¼" (6 mm) seam allowance; leave 1½" (3.8 cm) opening at upper back side. Stuff with fiberfill; slipstitch opening closed. Repeat for other arm. Stitch arms to body at desired location, using buttons, pearl cotton, and doll needle.

5 Thread long hand needle with 28" (71 cm) length of orange or gold thread; knot ends together. Roll felt triangle tightly from short side to narrow point; keep base even. Secure thread on base end; push needle through rolled felt at base.

6 Wrap thread around roll one-and-a-half times; take small stitch through roll. Wrap thread in opposite direction of first wrap. Continue until length is secure. Catching felt at tip, slip needle into roll at tip and come out at base; knot. Insert needle into head at desired nose location; gently squeeze head to bring needle out at back. Pull firmly to sink nose slightly into fabric; knot thread and trim tails.

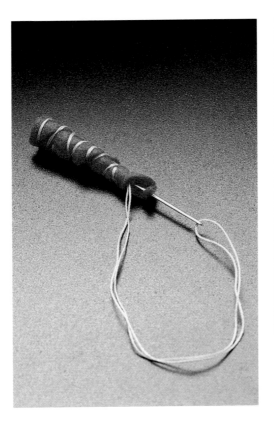

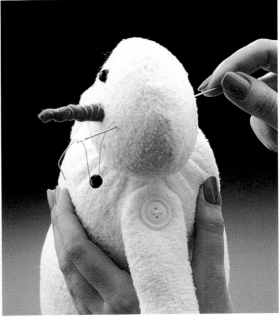

7 Sew large beads slightly above nose, for eyes, using doll needle; pull firmly to sink beads slightly into fabric. Knot at head back. Sew small beads below nose, for mouth. Apply cosmetic blush to cheeks lightly.

HOW TO DRESS MR. FROST

1 Turn under ½" (1.3 cm) on long sides of front bib; topstitch, using decorative thread, if desired. Turn under ⅜" (1 cm) on long sides of pocket, if using denim rectangle; repeat on short sides. Center pocket on bib just below original hemmed edge; pin. Topstitch pocket bottom and sides; stitch small triangles at upper corners for reinforcement stitching, if desired.

2 Pin short sides of pants rectangle right sides together; stitch, using ½" (1.3 cm) seam allowance. Press seam allowance open. Finish lower edge, if desired. Zigzag over topstitching thread ¼" (6 mm) from lower edge of pants, wrong side up; avoid piercing thread with needle. Leave topstitching thread tails. Pull tails to gather, leaving 1" (2.5 cm) opening; knot tails.

(Continued)

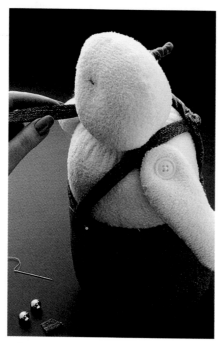

3 Turn pants right side out. Turn under ½" (1.3 cm) along upper edge. Pin pants to bibs, placing original pants seam at bib center; lap bib about ⅜" (1 cm). Topstitch upper pants edge, securing bib.

4 Turn under ⅜" (1 cm) on both long sides of straps; topstitch down center. Secure straps to upper corners of bib, using buttons. Insert body into pants; cross straps at center back. Trim straps ¾" (2 cm) below upper edge of pants; secure straps to pants, using buttons.

5 Wrap scarf around neck. Secure embellishments to hat as desired; set hat on head. Hand-stitch basket, bucket, or firewood tote to hand. Embellish further as desired.

HOW TO DRESS MRS. FROST

1 Lap eyelet trim binding over apron skirt sides and bottom; stitch. Baste upper edge; pull thread to gather edge to about 5" (12.5 cm). Fold bib in half crosswise, right sides together; stitch sides, using ¼" (6 mm) seam allowance. Turn; press flat. Stitch trim to upper edge of bib. Lap skirt upper edge over bib, matching centers; baste.

2 Fold waist tie in half lengthwise, right sides together. Stitch long side, using ¼" (6 mm) seam allowance. Turn; press flat. Repeat for neck strap. Lap waist tie over skirt upper edge, matching centers; topstitch to secure skirt, bib, and tie. Secure one neck strap end behind bib upper corner, using button. Position apron on body; tie waist at back. Wrap neck strap around neck; trim to desired length, and secure. Embellish as desired.

MORE IDEAS FOR SNOWMEN

Dress the snowmen in formal attire. *Make their bodies as for Mr. and Mrs. Frost, substituting a satin or moiré, if desired. Recycle an old pair of dress slacks to create the gentleman's pants; use the pants hem at the waist to eliminate topstitching. Add satin ribbon tuxedo stripes down the legs, if desired. Purchase decorative ribbon or braid for suspenders. Give him a bow tie of satin ribbon and a rayon frog*

cummerbund. Place a bottle of bubbly in his silver bucket. Add a ribbon muffler over his shoulders.

Use a slightly longer piece of satin, taffeta, or a sheer organdy for the lady's backless dress; finish the edges to prevent raveling. Select a decorative ribbon or lace to edge the dress.

91

SHARE
THE JOY

Encourage the artist in the young and not-as-young when making cards that reflect holiday traditions. Use these simple one-of-a-kind works of art to greet friends far away or use them as party invitations, place cards, gift tags, ornaments, and thank-you notes.

Find design inspiration in holiday books, dishes, ornaments, and fabrics. Trace cookie cutters and stencils for the simplest cutout motifs. Tear papers for delightful deckle-edged designs. Mix and match the styling variations and enjoy making each unique card.

Select card stock or cover-weight papers at art and stationery stores. Discover unlimited choices for decorative papers, including solids, geometric or marbleized prints, papers with bits of glitter or pine, even wrapping papers and candy bar foils.

Mail cards in envelopes that meet postal regulations, available at stationery or paper supply stores.

MATERIALS

* Card stock or heavyweight stationery; scissors.
* Table knife; straightedge.
* Decorative paper as desired.
* Scissors with decorative-edge blades, optional.
* Spray adhesive or craft glue.
* Decorative pens, optional.
* Envelopes, optional.

For cut cards:

* Tracing paper, graphite paper, cookie cutters, optional.
* Mat knife; cutting surface.

HOW TO MAKE A CARD

1 Subtract ¼" (6 mm) from envelope dimensions to determine the card size; decide location of opening. For side-opening card, cut card stock to determined height with twice the determined width. For bottom-opening card, cut card stock to determined width with twice the determined height.

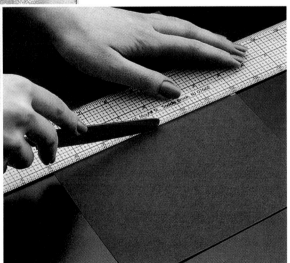

2 Lightly mark wrong side of card at centers of sides to be folded, using pencil. Align straightedge at marks; score foldline, using table knife.

3 Create card design, using one of the methods on page 96. Cut or tear decorative paper slightly smaller than card; use scissors with decorative-edge blades, if desired. Secure paper to inside of card, using adhesive; smooth out any bubbles. Write holiday message, using decorative pens, if desired.

HOW TO MAKE A CUTOUT CARD

1 Make card as on page 95, steps 1 and 2. Mark areas of card to be cut away on wrong side of card front, using graphite paper or tracing around cookie cutter. Mark mirror image of letters and directional designs.

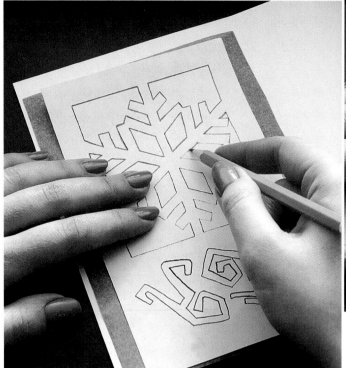

2 Using mat knife, cut background from design, leaving silhouette attached at several points as for snowflake. Or, remove entire shapes as for letters. Fold card; complete as on page 95, step 3.

HOW TO MAKE A TORN PAPER CARD

1 Make card as on page 95, steps 1 and 2. Tear general shapes of chosen design motif from colored papers; ignore small details to capture main features of shape. Arrange pieces on card; secure each piece, using glue. Complete card as on page 95, step 3.

CARD VARIATIONS

Fold card twice *so ends meet or lap.*

Use two papers on inside of card. *Cut or punch holes in front liner to reveal a design's second color—the back liner.*

Fold card front smaller than back (called a short fold). *Place part of the total design "inside."*

97

HOSTESS GIFTS: BOTTLES & JARS

When you give these unique hostess gifts, the lovely containers eliminate the need for further wrapping. Just decorate jars and bottles of food, oils, or wine to reflect the gift itself. Here are a few ideas to get you started.

Apple cider with cinnamon sticks. *Secure a bundle of cinnamon sticks with a rubber band. Tie narrow ribbon over the band, adding a small ornament or holiday charm at the bow. Suspend the bundle on the side of a decorative bottle filled with apple cider, and tie a large bow around the neck.*

Dressed-up wine. *Attach a spray of gold holly, faux grapes, or berries to a bottle of wine, using wire. Hide the wire beneath a large velvet bow with tails.*

Olive oil with pasta. *Fill a tall, decorative bottle with olive oil. Secure a package of pasta to the side of the bottle, using large rubber bands. Tie wide decorative ribbon over the bands. Hang garlic bulbs or dried red peppers with jingle bells from the bottle's neck, using narrow ribbon. Top it off with a festive bow.*

Mixed nut jar. *Select a large jar, and paint the cover gold. Fill the jar with mixed nuts. Lightly brush assorted nutshells with gold paint. Cover the lid with gold holly, loops of ribbon, and the nuts, using hot glue.*

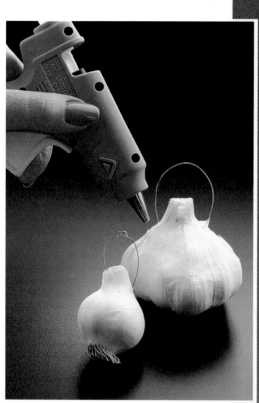

Secure loops of wire to garlic cloves or pepper pods, using hot glue. Or pierce items with needle just below stem and insert wire through hole. Twist ends to form loop.

Secure wired items at various heights, tying narrow ribbon through the wire loops. Accent with jingle bells.

Secure cascading nuts to looped 24-gauge wire, using hot glue.

Create personalized labels with decorative papers, using rub-on transfer letters. Cut labels ½" (1.3 cm) larger than existing bottle labels, using scissors with decorative-edge blades. Cut small shapes, using paper punches. Spray adhesive on label; position as desired. Smooth out any air bubbles.

101

MITTEN GIFT BAGS

These small gift bags are so delightful when hung on Christmas tree branches, you may want to hang several pairs! Tuck special gifts inside or fill them with wrapped candies.

Select nonwoven fabrics that do not ravel, for fast and easy sewing without seam finishing. Choose from a variety of polar fleece, felt, or synthetic suede fabrics in solids, subtle sculpted textures, and multicolored prints. Cut single layers of fabric with scissors or a rotary cutter to avoid shifting layers.

Choose woven fabrics, if desired, and finish the mitten seams and upper edge to prevent raveling. Vary the look with embossed velvets, flannels, or corduroys.

Purchase a boa of marabou feathers, the very soft, fine down of storks, at fabric and costume supply stores. Or use a narrow strip of knit fur fabric for the mitten's trim.

HOW TO MAKE A MITTEN BAG

MATERIALS

* ¼ yd. (0.25 m) fabric.

* Scissors; rotary cutter and cutting surface, optional.

* ¼ yd. (0.25 m) marabou feathers or 2" × 9" (5 × 23 cm) fur fabric, for trim.

* ¼ yd. (0.25 m) satin ribbon, ⅛" to ¼" (3 to 6 mm) wide, for hanger.

1 Cut two mirror-image pieces for mitten palm and mitten back, using pattern on page 308. Place palm on back, right sides together, aligning raw edges; pin. Stitch, using ¼" (6 mm) seam allowances; pivot at each side of thumb, and leave upper edge open. Finish seam, using zigzag stitch, if desired. Clip seam allowance to pivot points above and below thumb. Turn mitten right side out.

2 Place marabou trim on outside of mitten with core about ⅜" (1 cm) from upper edge. Whipstitch core to mitten, starting at outer wrist seam; avoid trapping feathers beneath stitches. Cut excess trim. Or hand-stitch fur strip near mitten edge.

3 Fold 9" (23 cm) ribbon in half; secure ends to seam allowance of outer wrist. Wrap small items in tissue or iridescent cellophane, if desired; hang from tree branch.

PAINTED SANTA GIFT BOXES & BAGS

These merry gift boxes and bags repeat the three-dimensional design of the patchwork Santa tree skirt (page 42) and wall quilt (page 66). Set them under the tree or throughout the house, filled with holiday mementos or treats. Or gift a friend and share the merriment of the holiday season.

Choose from a variety of unpainted wood, papier mâché, or heavy paperboard square boxes. Or select a papier mâché gift bag, available in craft stores. Paint the simple design quickly. Add a precut wood oval nose to designs 4½" to 8" (11.5 to 20.5 cm) square, or cut smaller noses to desired size from thin balsa wood. Shape Santa's spectacles around a small sturdy cylinder such as a nail polish bottle. Replace plain bag handles with festive wired ribbon handles tied in a bow.

MATERIALS

* Unpainted container.

* Acrylic sealer.

* Graphite paper; straightedge; painter's masking tape, optional.

* One 1¼" (3.2 cm) wooden oval, or 1/16" (1.5 mm) balsa wood and mat knife; craft glue.

* Acrylic paints; green, red, white, black, as desired for face.

* Texturizing medium, optional.

* 12" (30.5 cm) 24-gauge brass wire, for glasses; firm cylinder.

* Acrylic spray sealer.

* One brass jingle bell.

* 2 yd. (1.85 m) gold wired ribbon, ½" (1.3 cm) wide, for gift bag.

HOW TO MAKE A SANTA FACE PATTERN

 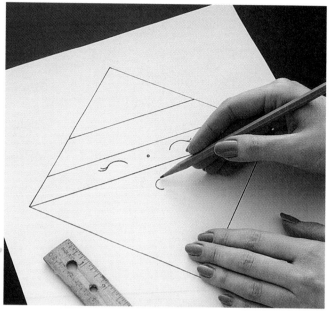

1 Trace box lid on paper. Draw diagonal line from corner to corner. Draw two lines parallel to first line, 7/8" and 2" (2.2 and 5 cm) above it. The small triangle at the top is the hat; below the hat is the trim, face, and beard. Adjust lines to suit box size.

2 Mark nose position at center of face. Draw two 3/4" (2 cm) arcs, for eyes; start each 3/4" (2 cm) from center. Add two short lines, as shown, for lashes. Draw 3/8" (1 cm) circle 1/2" (1.3 cm) from face, directly below nose position, for mouth.

HOW TO MAKE A SANTA BOX

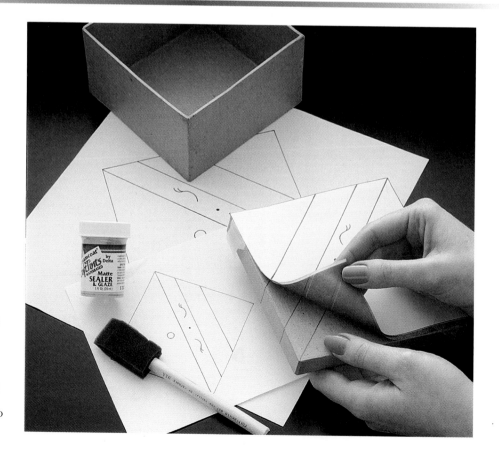

1 Apply acrylic sealer to box; allow to dry. Make pattern as shown above. Transfer pattern to box lid, using graphite paper; extend lines onto sides of lid.

2 Cut small nose from balsa wood, using mat knife, if desired. Paint box bottom, hat, face, and nose; allow to dry. Apply painter's masking tape along edge of hat and face, if desired. Paint trim and beard. Apply texturizing medium, if desired. Remove tape; allow paint to dry. Paint mouth.

3 Make wire spectacles, following steps 6 to 8 on pages 46 and 47. Attach nose at center mark and secure spectacles over nose, using glue. Paint eyes; allow to dry overnight. Spray container with two coats acrylic sealer, following manufacturer's directions. Glue jingle bell to tip of hat.

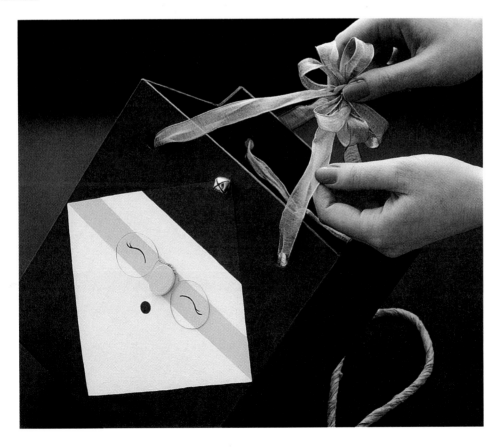

For gift bag, remove bag handles, if any. Follow steps 1 to 3. Cut ribbon in half, and thread through bag's holes; tie in bow.

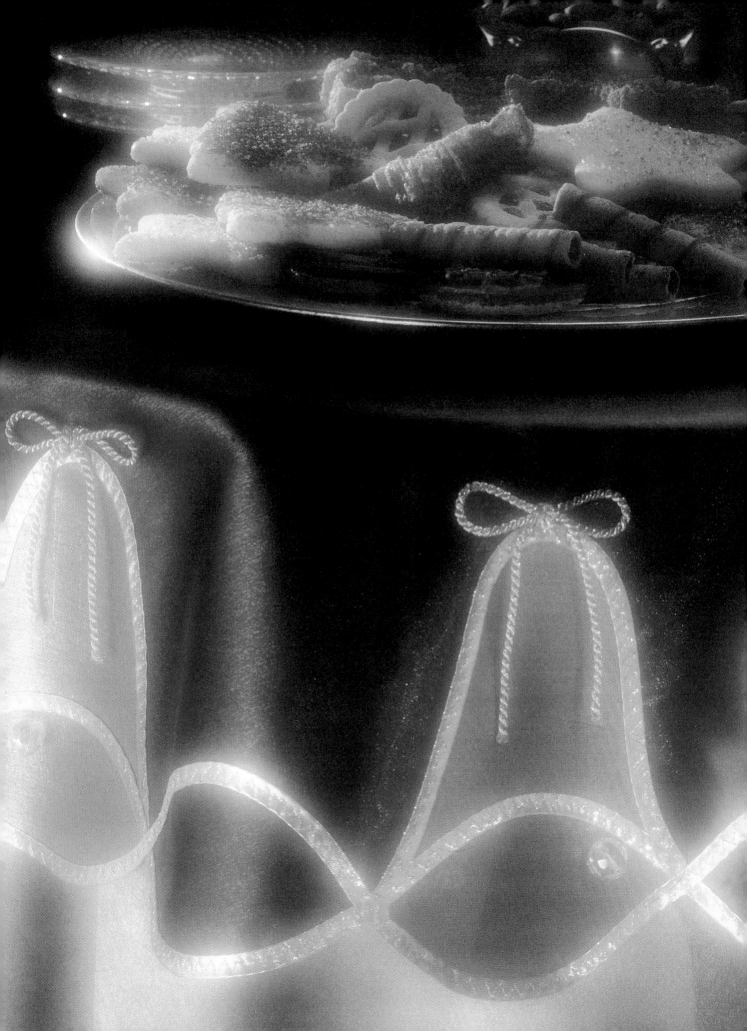

HOLIDAY TABLE LINENS

TABLE LINEN BASICS

Dress tables with special holiday linens to create a festive mood in your home. Make custom Christmas tablecloths to fit tables of any shape or size. Place a single table runner beneath a centerpiece to adorn a dining table. Cross two runners in the center of the table, or place one on each side beneath place settings. Coordinate linens from the dining table to the buffet and beyond. For a seasonal accent, use a simple table topper over year-round linens. Delight your guests with Christmas coasters at the table, with the appetizers, or in front of a cozy fire.

Determine the desired sizes of linens after measuring across the tabletop in both directions. Add twice the desired drop length, or overhang, to the measurements for a tablecloth; drop lengths range from 8" (20.5 cm) to floor length, but most are between 10" and 15" (25.5 and 38 cm). Decide if table runners, usually 12" to 18" (30.5 to 46 cm) wide, will rest entirely on the table, or if they will drop over the sides. Choose a placemat size that complements your table and place settings; a popular size is 18" × 12" (46 × 30.5 cm). Make napkins in a generous size, such as 15" (38 cm) square for luncheon napkins or 20" (51 cm) square for elegant dinner napkins.

Consider a wide variety of fabrics. To avoid or minimize seams in large cloths, choose wide decorator fabrics. Many have stain-resistant finishes, though laundering the fabrics may remove the finishes. Preshrink samples of elegant, dry-clean-only fabrics, such as crisp silk, to discover a pleasing change in the drape and appearance of the fabric; linens made of pre-washed fabrics are easy to care for.

Select from a variety of techniques to finish the edges of table linens, including easy fringed hems, serged edges, and mitered hems. Apply mitered banding to expand the width of fabrics too narrow for the desired drop length, or as an attractive edge for fabrics, like sheers, that may be difficult to hem. For a decorative edge on round linens, apply a contrasting bias binding.

Wide mitered band (opposite) *in a Christmas print extends the tablecloth to the desired drop length. Matching napkins are finished with a serged edge. Fringed edges work well for evenly woven fabrics like this plaid (top, right). Mitered hems (middle, right) provide a neat finish for many fabric types. Bias binding (bottom, right) molds smoothly over curved edges.*

HOW TO CUT A ROUND TABLECLOTH

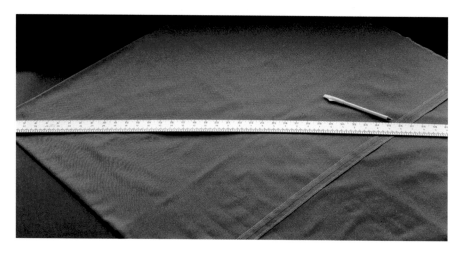

Measure the diameter of the round table; add twice the drop length, to determine the finished measurement. Cut a square of fabric at least 1" (2.5 cm) larger than this size; piece two fabric widths together, if necessary, and press seam open. Fold square of fabric in half lengthwise and again crosswise; pin layers together. Divide desired finished measurement by two and add ½" (1.3 cm), to determine radius of cut circle. Mark an arc, using a straight-edge and pencil, measuring from the folded center of fabric, a distance equal to radius. Cut on marked line through all layers.

HOW TO CUT AN OVAL TABLECLOTH

Measure length and width of table at longest points; add twice the drop length. Cut a rectangle of fabric at least 1" (2.5 cm) larger than this size; piece fabric widths together, if necessary, and press seams open. Place fabric on table, centered length-wise and crosswise; weight fabric down. Measure and mark around tablecloth an amount equal to desired drop length plus ½" (1.3 cm). Cut on marked line.

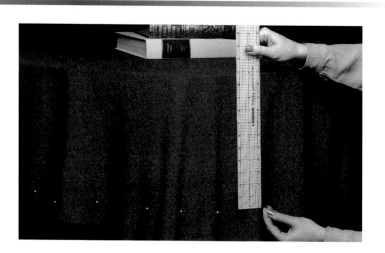

HOW TO SEW A MITERED BAND

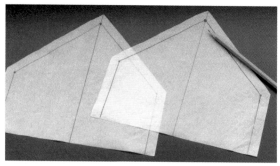

1 Determine finished size of tablecloth, placemat, or table topper, and plan finished dimensions of inner fabric and band; pattern provided (page 311) works for band widths of 1" to 4" (2.5 to 10 cm), in ½" (1.3 cm) increments. Trace pattern for desired band width, taking care to cut on cutting line; transfer seamlines and dots. Make duplicate pattern for opposite end.

2 Stabilize band fabric with lightweight fusible inter-facing, if necessary. Mark cutting lines for band on lengthwise grain of fabric, with lines a distance apart equal to twice the finished width plus 1" (2.5 cm). Place pattern pieces at ends of marked band, aligning cutting lines; space small dots (arrows) a distance apart equal to finished measurement of inner fabric. Distance between large dots at points should equal desired finished length of band. Cut out band; transfer dots. Repeat for each side.

3 Cut inner fabric to determined size plus 1" (2.5 cm) in each direction for seam allowances. Mark dot ½" (1.3 cm) from each corner of cloth, using fabric marker or pin.

4 Pin two adjacent band pieces right sides together; match dots at one end. Stitch ½" (1.3 cm) seam allowance between small dots; pivot at large dot. Trim seam allowances to ¼" (6 mm); trim at pivot point, as shown. Press seam open. Repeat for all corners.

5 Press under ½" (1.3 cm) on one continuous edge of band. Pin right side of other raw edge to wrong side of inner fabric; match dots and align edges. Stitch ½" (1.3 cm) seam on each side, pivoting at each corner dot.

6 Press seam toward band. Turn band to right side of tablecloth, so inner fold covers seam; pin. Edgestitch close to inner fold.

HOW TO SEW A FRINGED HEM

1 Mark fabric at desired size plus two times the desired width of fringe. Pull lengthwise and crosswise threads to ensure a straight, even fringe; cut along pulled threads. Pull threads to mark desired top of fringe.

2 Stitch narrow zigzag just above pulled thread, stitching into empty space with right-hand swing of needle. If fringe is more than ½" (1.3 cm) long, clip frequently on grainline up to stitching. Pull out threads to fringe edge.

HOW TO SERGE A HEM

1 Rectangular or square linens. Cut fabric 1" (2.5 cm) longer and wider than desired finished size. Set serger for balanced 3-thread overlock stitch, threading both loopers with texturized nylon for best coverage; use untexturized thread in needle. Set stitch width at 4 to 5 mm; set stitch length at 1 mm. Stitch along one side of fabric, holding tail chain taut as you begin; trim away ½" (1.3 cm) with serger blades. Leave long tail chains at ends. Repeat for adjacent side.

2 Stitch remaining two sides of fabric as in step 1. Thread tail chain through eye of tapestry needle, and weave needle under overlock stitches for 1" (2.5 cm); cut off remaining length of tail chain. Or apply liquid fray preventer to stitches at corners; allow to dry, and cut off entire tail chain.

1 Round or oval linens. Cut fabric 1" (2.5 cm) larger than desired finished size. Set serger as in step 1, above. Clip in ½" (1.3 cm) at edge; trim seam allowance for about 2" (5 cm).

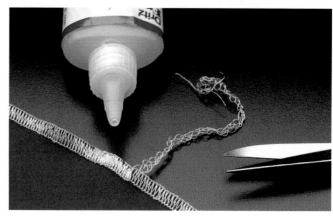

2 Clear thread from stitch fingers; insert fabric under presser foot with cut edge next to blade. Stitch around outer edge, trimming ½" (1.3 cm) with serger blade. Stop stitching when needle reaches previous stitches.

3 Disengage upper knife. Stitch over previous stitches for 1" (2.5 cm). Lift presser foot, and clear stitch fingers; turn fabric so it is behind needle. Stitch off edge of fabric, leaving long tail chain. Apply liquid fray preventer to chain; allow to dry. Trim chain close to stitches.

HOW TO SEW A MITERED HEM

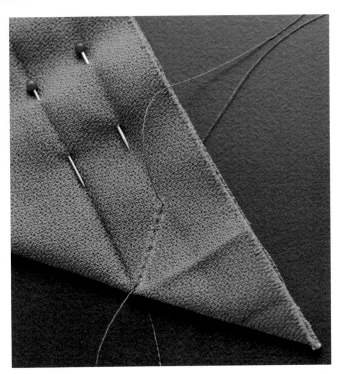

1 Cut fabric to desired finished size plus two times hem width plus 1" (2.5 cm); use a minimum ½" (1.3 cm) hem. For example, cut 22" (56 cm) square for a 20" (51 cm) napkin with a ½" (1.3 cm) hem. Press under an amount equal to hem width plus ½" (1.3 cm) on each side; press under ½" (1.3 cm) on raw edges.

2 Open out hem width at corner. Fold diagonally through corner, right sides together, matching foldlines of adjacent sides; pin. Draw perpendicular line, using fabric marker, from outer fold to point where inner pressed fold intersects diagonal fold. Stitch on marked line. Repeat at remaining corners.

3 Trim seam allowances to ¼" (6 mm); taper close to folds. Press seams open. Turn corners right side out, using point turner. Turn under raw edge on inner foldline. Press and pin.

4 Edgestitch inner fold to secure hem. Edgestitch again near outer edge, if desired.

HOW TO MAKE A CONTINUOUS BIAS STRIP

1 Trim selvages from large square of fabric. Mark crosswise grain edges with one pin; mark lengthwise grain edges with two pins. Fold fabric in half diagonally. Cut on fold to divide square into two triangles.

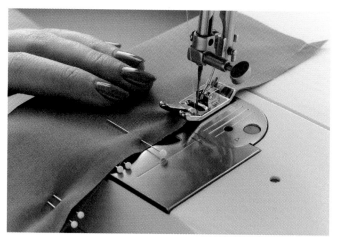

2 Stitch lengthwise edges together in ¼" (6 mm) seam, right sides together. Allow points to extend ¼" (6 mm), so edges meet exactly at seamline. Press seam open.

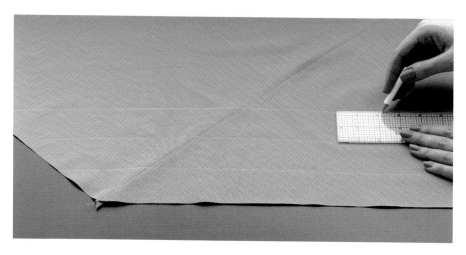

3 Mark cutting lines 2" (5 cm) apart, parallel to bias edges. Begin at one edge and work across fabric; cut off any excess at opposite edge.

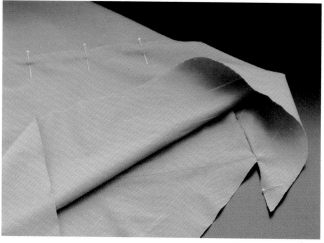

4 Pin crosswise grain edges together with one edge extending beyond other edge the marked width of one bias strip. Remaining lines should match, with last strip width extending off opposite end. Stitch ¼" (6 mm) seam, forming slightly twisted tube; press seam allowances open.

5 Cut fabric on the marked line, forming one continuous bias strip.

HOW TO SEW BIAS BINDING ON A CONTINUOUS CURVE

1 Feed bias strip into 1" (2.5 cm) bias tape maker, using pin to get it started. Raw edges will fold toward center as strip is pulled through bias tape maker; press folds. With iron resting on tape, gently slide bias tape maker over more of strip; press, but do not stretch bias binding. Continue down length of strip.

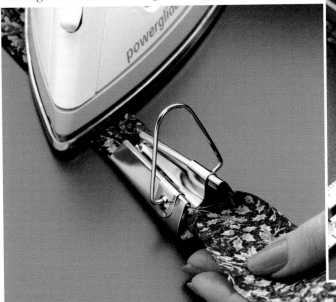

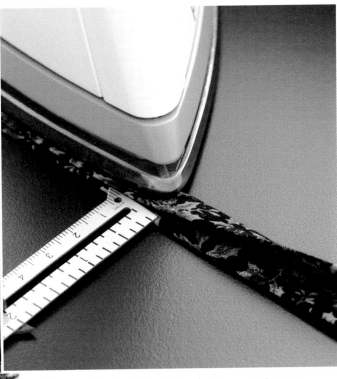

2 Press binding in half lengthwise, encasing raw edges and offsetting one edge by ⅛" (3 mm).

3 Align narrower raw edge of binding to tablecloth; fold end under ½" (1.3 cm). Stitch in well of fold around entire cloth; overlap binding ½" (1.3 cm). Press seam allowance toward binding.

4 Fold binding over cut edge of tablecloth to wrong side; binding on wrong side should overlap stitching line ⅛" (3 mm). Pin; press-shape binding to fit without puckering. Stitch in the ditch of the seam from the right side, catching the binding on the wrong side.

METALLIC APPLIQUÉ LINENS

Brighten your tables with the glimmer of metallic appliqués on padded linens. Stitch a coordinated set that includes a table runner, placemats, and coasters.

Lamé fabric with lightweight knit backing is easy to handle and offers dramatic effects. Choices include gold, silver, copper, and bright holiday colors and patterns. Design ideas may include the stellar theme, shown here, or other simple Christmas shapes, such as ornament balls, bells, or holly leaves.

Purchase paper-backed fusible web for a quick way to cut perfect appliqués. Use a low-temperature iron setting to apply the shapes easily and to avoid damaging the metallic lamé. Add a soft dimensional look and improve the durability of the appliqués by stitching around them with a satin stitch.

MATERIALS

* Solid-colored fabric, for background and lining.
* Batting.
* Knit-backed metallic lamé fabric, for appliqués and binding.
* Paper-backed fusible web.
* Tear-away stabilizer.
* Decorative thread, for satin stitching.

CUTTING DIRECTIONS

Cut solid-colored fabric, lining, and batting to the desired finished size, as determined on page 111.

Cut continuous 2" (5 cm) bias strip (page 116) equal in length to the total circumference of all linens plus waste allowance.

HOW TO MAKE APPLIQUÉ LINENS

1 Draw or transfer appliqué shapes onto paper backing of fusible web. For directional shapes, draw mirror images of desired finished shapes. Apply paper-backed fusible web to wrong side of appliqué fabrics, following the manufacturer's directions; use a low-temperature heat setting when pressing lamé. Cut out appliqués.

2 Remove paper backing. Arrange appliqués as desired on solid-colored fabric, fusible side down; consider how location of place setting and table accessories may affect position of appliqués. Fuse appliqués, using press cloth and low-temperature heat setting.

3 Place the fleece over wrong side of lining; place the background fabric over fleece, right side up. Align all edges; pin and baste layers together a scant ½" (1.3 cm) from edges.

4 Place tear-away stabilizer under lining, behind appliqués. Stitch around each appliqué, using satin stitch (short narrow zigzag).

5 Prepare bias binding as on page 117, steps 1 and 2. Align narrower raw edge of binding to one side of layered piece; cut binding end straight across. Stitch in well of fold to opposite end; cut binding even with end. Repeat for opposite side.

6 Fold binding over cut edge to wrong side; binding on wrong side should overlap stitching line ⅛" (3 mm). Pin. Stitch in the ditch of the seam from right side, catching binding on the wrong side.

7 Repeat step 5 for remaining sides, but trim ends of binding to extend ½" (1.3 cm) beyond finished edges.

8 Turn binding toward outer edge; fold ½" (1.3 cm) ends of binding over finished edge. Finish as in step 6.

PAPER-PIECED PLACEMATS

Paper foundation piecing is a quilting technique in which a simple pattern ensures the fast and easy stitching of seemingly intricate designs. These paper-pieced placemats are a beautiful way to dress the table with the traditional symbols of a decorated tree, a wrapped gift, and a wreath.

Strips of fabric, placed under the pattern along its design lines, are secured by stitching along the lines. Each consecutive piece is added after folding the fabric into position, and you can watch the designs develop as you sew. The pieced designs, joined in a column at the side of each mat, create placemats with a height of 12¾" (32.4 cm).

Most lightweight to mediumweight fabrics are appropriate for these placemats. Luxurious fabrics such as velveteen or brocade will provide elegance. Traditional cotton calicos and small holiday prints will lend a more casual feeling. Chintz, satins, and metallics will make bright contemporary placemats, or they can be used to add spirited accents within an individual design.

Prewashing fabrics will guarantee easy care. It may also change the appearance of the fabric or remove the easy-care finishes found on many decorator fabrics. Always prewash fabric samples, checking for colorfastness, if you want to launder the linens.

Small embellishments, such as decorative cords, embroidery stitches, and small beads, can be added to each design to form a pretty bow or to imitate ornaments. Channel quilting, easy-to-sew parallel rows of straight machine stitching, gives the placemats added dimension.

123

HOW TO MAKE A PAPER-PIECED PLACEMAT

MATERIALS

* Paper pattern.
* Fabric scraps or ⅛ yd. (0.15 m) of each design fabric.
* Lightweight fusible knit interfacing to back tissue lamé, optional.
* ⅞ yd. (0.8 m) fabric, for four placemat fronts.
* ⅞ yd. (0.8 m) lining fabric, for four placemat backs.
* ⅞ yd (0.8 m) polyester fleece.
* Fabric marker; straightedge.
* Embellishments as desired.

CUTTING DIRECTIONS

Apply interfacing to wrong side of tissue lamé, if using.

Cut fabric rectangles at least ½" (1.3 cm) larger than each section of the design.

Cut four 14" × 14" (35.5 × 35.5 cm) front pieces.

Cut four 14" × 18½" (35.5 × 47.3 cm) rectangles from lining and polyester fleece.

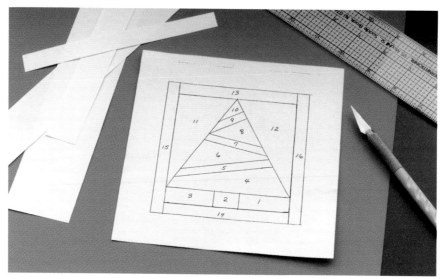

1 Trace paper foundation patterns (pages 314 and 315) onto paper, or photo-copy the designs. Trim each design 1" (2.5 cm) from outer edges of pattern.

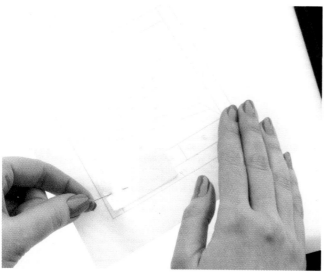

2 Center and pin the wrong side of fabric for Area 1 to back of pattern; hold pattern up to the light to help position the fabric so its edges extend at least ¼" (6 mm) beyond Area 1 design lines.

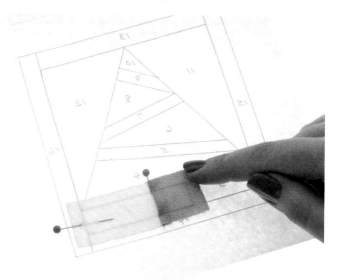

3 Place Area 2 fabric piece over Area 1 fabric piece, right sides together, aligning raw edges between Areas 1 and 2. Pin along shared design line; fold Area 2 fabric down and hold pattern up to light to confirm fabric extends at least ¼" (6 mm) beyond entire area. Adjust position of second fabric, if necessary.

4 Unfold fabric. Stitch, paper side up, along shared design line; extend stitching one or two stitches beyond line at both ends. Trim seam allowance to ¼" (6 mm), if necessary. Fold Area 2 fabric right side up; pin.

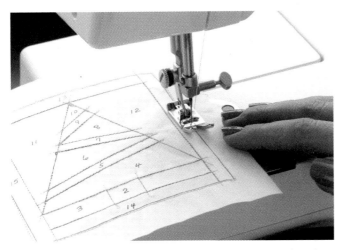

5 Repeat steps 3 and 4 for each consecutive area. Stitch around entire pattern, just outside outer design line. Trim excess fabric ¼" (6 mm) beyond outer lines. For gift box, insert ribbon at marked positions on pattern as block is pieced together. Attach bow to completed block.

6 Repeat steps 1 to 5 for each design. Remove paper. Arrange designs in column. Stitch adjoining seams, right sides together, using ¼" (6 mm) seam allowance. Stitch column to left side of placemat front. Press seam allowances to one side.

7 Mark two horizontal stitching lines across front, extending from seamlines between designs; use fabric marker and straightedge. Place front and lining pieces over fleece, right sides together; align all edges, and pin. Stitch ¼" (6 mm) seam allowance all around; leave 5" (12.5 cm) opening on bottom edge.

8 Trim corners diagonally. Turn and press; slipstitch opening closed. Pin-baste layers together as shown. Stitch in the ditch between pieced blocks and solid fabric. Stitch along marked lines and between pieced blocks. Hand-stitch embellishments as desired.

SILK RIBBON EMBROIDERED LINENS

The delicate beauty of silk-ribbon embroidery can be used to embellish purchased or sewn linens for special table decorations. A traditional needle art, ribbon embroidery may enhance a Victorian decorating style, enrich a formal contemporary elegance, or soften a setting of rustic simplicity.

Look for solid-colored linens that will complement the embroidery. Consider moirés, taffetas, or linens with Battenberg lace edges for a Victorian effect. Select satin or velveteen cloths for simple elegance. Choose coarse linen or lightweight wool fabric for a casual approach.

Chenille needles have a long eye, to accommodate the ribbons, and a sharp point. The higher the number, the finer the needle, so choose needle sizes 20 to 24 according to the weight of the purchased linen.

Develop a design to fit your linens, using any of the stitches shown here and on pages 128 to 131. Repeat partial or whole motifs to fill large areas, and rotate or trace mirror images of patterns to create symmetry.

Embroider poinsettias using the deceptively easy Japanese ribbon stitch. Make a series of French knots to form the centers of the blossoms.

Use the classic featherstitch to create evergreen motifs like wreaths, garlands, and trees. Decorate the greens with juniper berries or small ornaments made of French knots, or form pinecones with the decorative Cretan stitch. Add bows and wrap ribbon tails amid the greens, using the coral stitch.

MATERIALS

For poinsettias:

❋ 7 mm green silk ribbon.

❋ 7 mm white, rose, or red silk ribbon.

❋ 4 mm gold silk ribbon.

For evergreen motifs:

❋ 2 mm green silk ribbon.

❋ 2 mm brown silk ribbon, for cones and sprigs.

❋ 2 mm teal silk ribbon, optional, for juniper berries.

❋ 4 mm silk ribbon, optional, for bow and tails.

❋ Chenille needle, size 20, 22, or 24.

Thread chenille needle with a length of ribbon no longer than 18" (46 cm) to avoid excessive abrasion. Prevent ribbon from falling off needle by threading needle and taking a stitch through ribbon near one end.

Leave 3" (7.5 cm) tail on underside of cloth. Pierce tail with needle as first stitch is pulled to underside. Pierce tail again with second and third stitches. Clip tail close to last secure point.

Secure ribbon end by slipping needle under two stitches on underside. Wrap ribbon back over stitches, piercing twice through ribbon. Hand-tack tail with matching thread. Clip tail close to last secure point.

Use an awl to make a hole in closely woven or heavy linens so wider ribbons can be easily pulled to other side of cloth without damage.

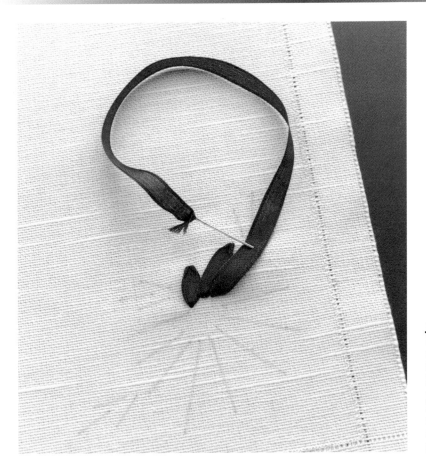

Japanese ribbon stitch.
Bring needle up from
underside. Smooth ribbon
flat in direction of stitch.
Insert needle at end of stitch,
piercing center of ribbon.
Pull needle through to
underside of fabric until
ribbon curls at tip; take care
not to pull ribbon too tight.

1 **French knot.** Bring needle up from underside. Holding the needle parallel to fabric near the exit point, wrap ribbon once or twice around needle, taking care to keep ribbon smooth.

2 Insert needle very close to exit point, holding ribbon in place close to wrapped needle. Hold ribbon while pulling needle through to underside of fabric, releasing ribbon as it disappears. Ribbon forms soft knot.

(Continued)

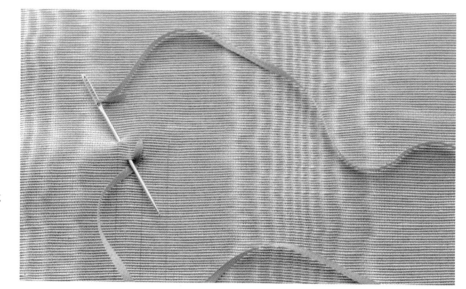

1 Featherstitch. Draw three faint, parallel lines, evenly spaced on fabric. Push the needle through fabric from underside on center line. Working toward yourself, insert needle into an outer line and exit at an angle below and halfway between first two points. Cross over ribbon with needle while pulling it through, forming loose U; keep ribbon from twisting.

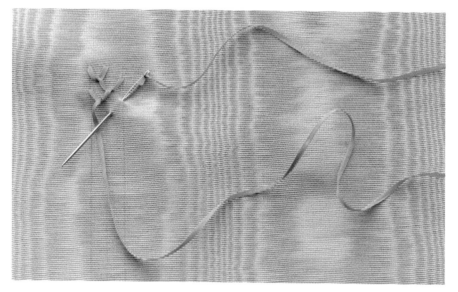

2 Take next stitch from opposite outer line. Repeat continuously, alternating from side to side. Secure last stitch with short straight stitch.

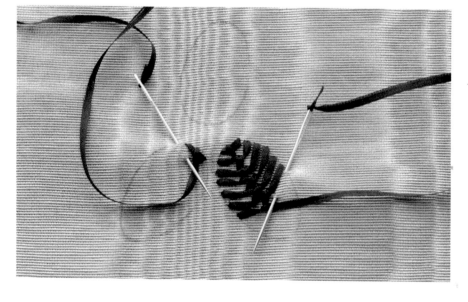

Decorative Cretan stitch. Draw faint oval on fabric. Push needle through fabric from underside, slightly to one side of center, at top of oval. Insert needle into line on opposite side, and return to surface halfway between exit and entry points. Cross over ribbon with needle while pulling it through. Alternate stitches from side to side, keeping ribbon smooth.

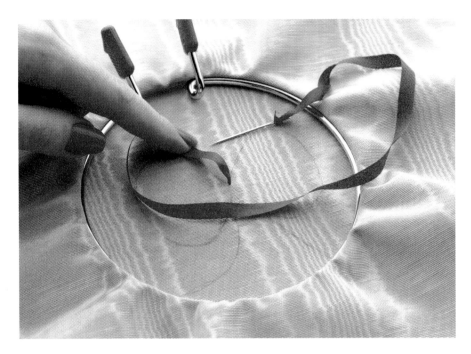

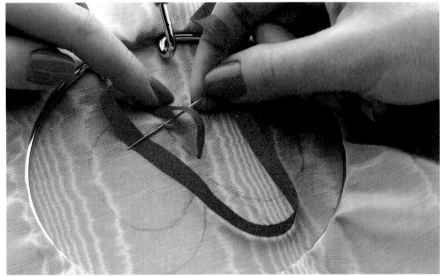

1 **Coral stitch.** Push the needle through fabric from underside. Smooth ribbon flat. Make gentle arch, and hold ribbon in place.

2 Take tiny stitch under ribbon arch; pass needle over ribbon tail while pulling ribbon through fabric. Gradually release ribbon arch, forming soft knot.

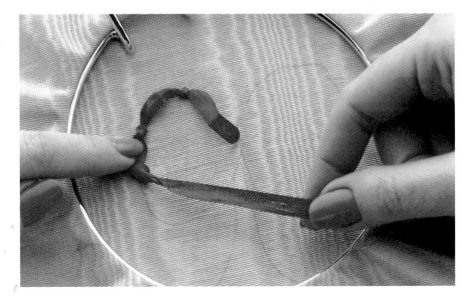

3 Smooth ribbon and make arch as in step 1; secure with knot as in step 2. Continue, following desired path; vary distance between knots, and flatten or raise segments as desired.

HOLIDAY BELLS
TABLE TOPPER

Create a unique holiday bells table topper with a stained glass look, using an innovative fusible bias tape as the "leading" in the design. The bias tape is very flexible, and molds easily over curves.

Select fabrics in two colors for the topper and bells. Layer the bell fabric over the topper fabric in the store to be sure you like the effect. Top each bell with a gold bow, and give it a gold button clapper.

MATERIALS

* 1 yd. (0.95 m) fabric, for table topper.
* 3/8 yd. (0.35 m) fabric, for bells.
* Liquid fray preventer.
* Paper-backed fusible web.
* 11 yd. (10.12 m) fusible gold bias tape.
* 12 gold buttons.
* 4 yd. (3.7 m) narrow gold ribbon.

HOW TO MAKE A HOLIDAY BELLS TABLE TOPPER

1 Cut a tissue paper pattern of a quarter circle with an 18" (46 cm) radius. Fold pattern in half, then into thirds, keeping curved outer edges aligned; crease.

2 Trace and cut out bell pattern (page 310). Trace lower edge onto folded tissue as shown. Cut tissue through all layers.

3 Fold the topper fabric in half lengthwise and crosswise. Pin the pattern over the folded fabric, aligning sides and center point. Trim the fabric through all layers along outer shaped edge. Seal the outer shaped edge, using liquid fray preventer.

4 Trace bell pattern twelve times onto paper-backed fusible web; apply to back of bell fabric, following manufacturer's directions. Remove paper backing, and fuse a bell to every other scallop, aligning the lower curved edges.

5 Fuse bias tape to top of bell, following manufacturer's directions; center tape over raw edge, and ease around curves. Trim ends even with scalloped edge. Repeat for each bell. Topstitch over tape, using multistitch-zigzag.

6 Fuse bias tape in continuous line along front rims of bells and connecting scallops, using bell shape as guide; lap tape slightly over raw edge. Lap ends. Topstitch over tape, using multistitch-zigzag.

7 Fuse bias tape in continuous line along back rims of bells and connecting upper curves, using bell shape as guide; lap ends. Topstitch over tape, using multistitch-zigzag.

8 Hand-stitch button in bottom of each bell, for clapper. Tie 12" (30.5 cm) lengths of ribbon into bows; hand-stitch bow at top of each bell.

PLACEMAT WITH SHEER INSERT

Accent an elegant holiday dinner with sophisticated placemats. Simply slip a sheer insert into a basic mitered-hem placemat in a color and style that complements your dinnerware.

Choose from a multitude of sheer fabrics for the insert. White, off-white, and iridescent shimmers are available year-round in bridal departments. Pastel sheers and jewel-tone brights are also found there. Elegant decorative sheers with shots of metallic threads are available during the holiday season. Look for solid-colored, mediumweight fabrics for the placemat to help set off the beauty of the sheer fabric.

The wide hem resembles a mitered border. These directions are for 12" × 18" (30.5 × 46 cm) finished mats that have a 1½" (3.8 cm) hem. The dimensions can be changed to suit your needs by following the directions for sewing a mitered hem on page 115.

HOW TO SEW A PLACEMAT
WITH A SHEER INSERT

MATERIALS for four placemats.

* 1 yd. (0.95 m) solid-colored (reversible) fabric, for backing and border hem.
* ¾ yd. (0.7 m) sheer fabric, for insert.

CUTTING DIRECTIONS

Cut solid-colored fabric 16" × 22" (40.5 × 56 cm).
Cut sheer fabric 11¾" × 17¾" (30 × 44.9 cm).

1 Press a 2" (5 cm) hem on each side of place-mat; press under ½" (1.3 cm) along raw edges, leaving 1½" (3.8 cm) hem. Make mitered corners as on page 115, steps 2 and 3.

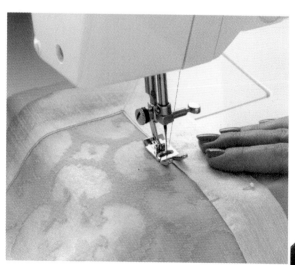

2 Tuck insert under hem; align edges near outer folds. Pin and edgestitch placemat as on page 115, step 4.

IDEAS FOR
PLACEMATS
WITH INSERTS

Use two coordinating print fabrics (above). Stitch purchased piping along the inside edge of the mitered border; glue-baste under inner edges before stitching. Use a zipper foot or piping foot.

Insert lace fabric (far right) over a bold color, highlighting the intricate lace pattern.

Purchase crocheted snowflakes (below), and hand-sew or glue, using washable craft glue, to inner area before inserting sheer.

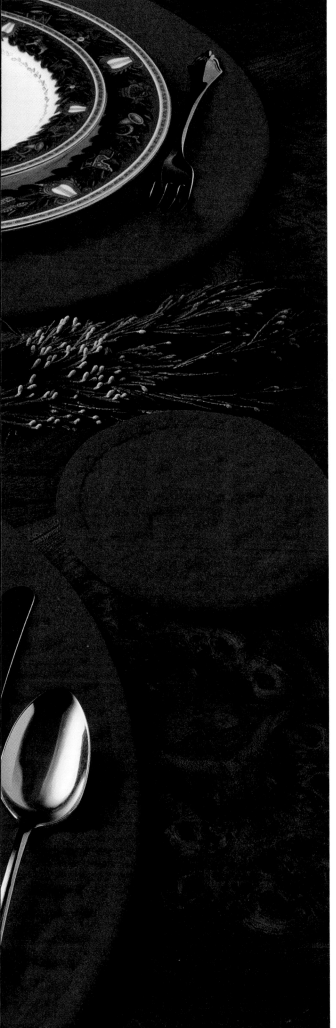

TEXTURIZED TABLE LINENS

Round coasters and placemats are a delightful way to frame dinner and glassware without crowding the holiday table. Create these beautifully textured linens quickly, using easy grid stitching and bias binding techniques. The trick is in using unlaundered cotton flannel for interlining. After construction, the pieces are machine washed and dried, causing the flannel to shrink and develop a wonderful crinkled surface texture.

Select washable fabrics, but don't be afraid to use traditional special-care fabrics such as cotton velveteen or silk taffeta, if you want an elegant effect. Machine wash and dry the outer fabrics only. Consider special decorative threads, such as rayon embroidery thread or a metallic thread, for a little extra holiday glitter. And relax, knowing you can toss them in the wash for super-easy care.

The directions that follow are for 15" (38 cm) round placemats and 4½" (11.5 cm) round coasters. However, the basic techniques can be used for round, oval, or rectangular placemats or toppers in any size.

MATERIALS

* 3 yd. (2.75 m) decorative fabric, for four placemats and coasters.
* 1 yd. (0.95 m) 100 percent cotton flannel, for interlining.
* Straightedge.
* Water-soluble marking pen.
* Paper, 16" (40.5 cm) square and 5" (12.5 cm) square.
* Fabric glue.

CUTTING DIRECTIONS

Preshrink the decorative fabric only.

Cut eight 16" (40.5 cm) squares and eight 5" (12.5 cm) squares from the decorative fabric.

Cut four 16" (40.5 cm) squares and four 5" (12.5 cm) squares from the flannel.

Cut a continuous bias strip equal in length to the total circumference of all linens (page 116); cut a 1" (2.5 cm) strip for lightweight fabric or a 1⅛" (2.8 cm) strip for heavier fabric, such as velveteen.

1 Mark a 1" (2.5 cm) grid on the right side of one decorative fabric square, using straightedge and water-soluble marker. Place flannel square on wrong side of unmarked decorative square. Place marked square on flannel, right side up. Align the edges and pin at 4" to 6" (10 to 15 cm) intervals.

2 Stitch layers together along grid lines; stitch two center lines first, using medium-length multistitch-zigzag, and work toward sides. Edge-finish all sides, using zigzag stitch or serger. Launder squares; dry in hot dryer with damp towel. Press lightly, if necessary.

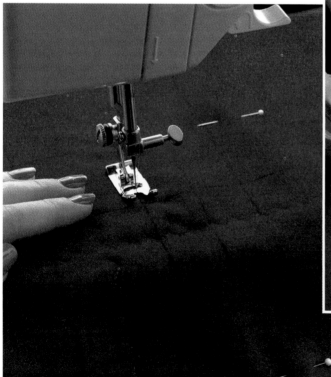

3 Quarter-fold paper squares. Mark a 7½" (19.3 cm) arc from folded center of larger paper; mark a 2¼" (6 cm) arc on smaller paper. Cut on marked lines through all layers. Use patterns to cut placemats and coasters.

4 Trim end of bias strip at a slight angle. Align raw edge of strip with edge of texturized layers, right sides together. Stitch scant ¼" (6 mm) seam allowance; avoid stretching bias as you sew. Trim excess strip about ½" (1.3 cm) beyond where you started sewing.

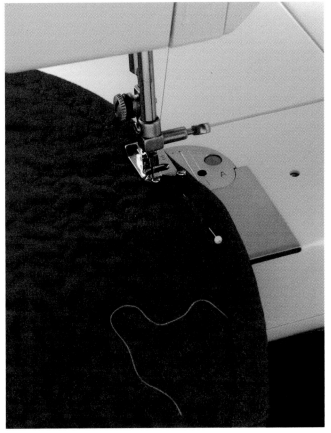

5 Press strip away from center, and wrap it around the raw edges. Shape strip to follow curve, using steam iron to ease raw edge on underside; pin. Glue end of binding strip in place.

6 Secure binding, using multistitch-zigzag; stitch from underside, allowing the far left stitch of the zigzag pattern to stitch just past the raw edge.

EASY PAINTED
PLACEMATS

Make quick and easy Christmas placemats from gesso-primed painter's canvas. Available at art supply stores, a half yard (0.5 m) of canvas 52" (132 cm) wide is enough to make four rectangular placemats. Because the surface is already primed, you merely paint Christmas designs using acrylic craft paints. Freeform designs, like those shown, require only minimal brush strokes. Copy these designs, if you wish, or develop simple designs of your own. A final coat of acrylic varnish seals the design and makes daily cleanup a breeze.

MATERIALS

* ½ yd. (0.5 m) gesso-primed painter's canvas, 52" (132 cm) wide.

* Acrylic craft paints; artist's brushes or household paintbushes in desired sizes.

* Acrylic varnish.

HOW TO MAKE PAINTED PLACEMATS

1 Measure and mark off four placemats about 13" × 17" (33 × 43 cm) on right side of canvas. Paint over lines to create simple borders; allow to dry. Cut out placemats.

2 Paint simple designs, using paintbrushes in desired sizes. Allow to dry. Apply acrylic varnish.

PLACEMAT TABLE RUNNER

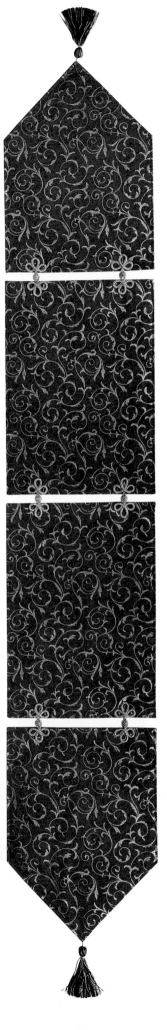

This innovative table runner adapts simply to the various needs of your holiday season. Join four 18" (46 cm) sections, using elegant frog closures or buttons and bows, for a 72" (183 cm) table runner. Remove the center sections and use them as placemats for a quiet dinner for two; leave the end sections joined for a short runner. Or create additional rectangular sections, as desired, for a longer runner and more place settings.

Select fabrics according to the feeling you wish to convey; jacquards or tapestries provide elegance; metallics are striking; cotton prints may add a touch of the country. Choose frog closures or buttons and ribbons to complement your fabric. Frogs are available in a variety of colors and metallics. Button styles range from plain to fun holiday shapes to metals and fancy jewels.

Metallic print fabric in the placemat table runner at right is connected with glimmering frogs. Ribbon-tied buttons on the star-spangled runner (opposite) are easily disconnected to set the table for two.

HOW TO MAKE A PLACEMAT TABLE RUNNER

MATERIALS

* ⅞ yd. (0.8 m) fabric, for front.
* ⅞ yd. (0.8 m) lining fabric.
* Polyester batting.
* Six frogs, or twelve buttons and 3 yd. (2.75 m) of ¼" (6 mm) ribbon.
* Two tassels.

CUTTING DIRECTIONS

Cut four 19" × 14" (48.5 × 35.5 cm) rectangles from each fabric and batting.

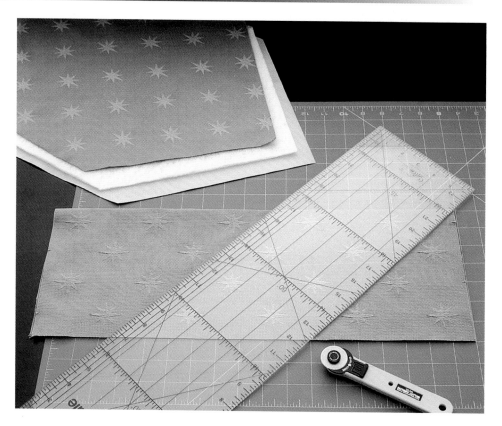

1 Fold one front rectangle in half lengthwise. Mark point 7" (18 cm) from corner on long cut side; align straightedge from end of fold to mark, as shown, and cut. Repeat with second front rectangle, two lining rectangles, and two batting rectangles, for two end sections.

2 Place one front end on one batting end, right side up. Position tassel at point so cord loop extends beyond cut edges; secure with pins. Place one lining end on front, right side down, aligning all raw edges; pin.

3 Stitch ½" (1.3 cm) seams around all sides, leaving 5" (12.5 cm) opening on short side; pivot each side of tassel cord, and stitch straight across point.

5 Repeat steps 2 to 4 for remaining end section and two rectangular sections; omit tassel on rectangular sections. Press; tuck seam allowances in at openings. Slipstitch openings closed. Topstitch 1/4" (6 mm) from all edges.

4 Trim batting close to stitching; trim 1/2" (1.3 cm) batting at opening. Trim seam allowances at corners; press seam allowances open. Turn right side out.

6 **Buttons and ribbon.** Stitch two buttons on each short side, 2³/4" (7 cm) from corners. Cut six 18" (46 cm) lengths of ribbon. Wrap ribbon in figure eight around two adjacent buttons; tie bow.

6 **Frogs.** Position two loops on short side of one end and both center sections, 2³/4" (7 cm) from corners; position frog buttons on adjacent sections, as shown. Secure frogs with hand stitches.

149

CENTERPIECES & CANDLELIGHT

CASCADING FRUITS & ROSES

Make an elegant statement with this cascading pedestal arrangement of roses, ivy leaves, and glittering fruits. Arrange the stems in a crystal stand so the fruits sweep through the ivy.

Purchase assorted fruits in clusters and on long stems; decorate them with a fine glitter, such as DecoArt™ Glamour Dust™. Cut individual blossoms from rose stems and place them at the top of the arrangement. Accent the arrangement with clusters of fragile, dried pepper berries, available in several colors.

HOW TO MAKE A FRUITS & ROSES ARRANGEMENT

MATERIALS

* Three different artificial fruit stems, such as lime, pear, and miniature orange.
* Grape clusters.
* Craft glue; flat paintbrush, about ⅜" (1 cm) wide.
* Fine glitter; sheet of paper.
* Floral Styrofoam®, 4" × 4" × 1½" (10 × 10 × 3.8 cm); serrated knife.

* Crystal compote or cake stand.
* Floral adhesive clay, floral stem wire, floral tape; wire cutter.
* Crystal marbles.
* One ivy plant with long stems.
* Pepper berries in desired color; hot glue gun, optional.
* Artificial rose stems with assorted blossoms.

1 Dilute craft glue slightly with water. Brush glue on fruit surface. Sprinkle fruit with fine glitter while glue is wet; shake excess glitter onto paper. Apply glue and glitter to all fruits; pour excess glitter back into bottle as necessary. Allow fruit to dry.

2 Trim Styrofoam block to sit level in compote, using serrated knife; trim height to level of compote rim. Secure foam to bowl of compote, using floral adhesive clay. Pour marbles around foam. Insert ivy into center of foam; arrange stems around compote as desired.

(Continued)

153

3 Break pepper berry stems about 1½" (3.8 cm) from berries. Wrap stem wires to berry stems, using floral tape; stretch tape slightly. Make several clusters. Glue broken clusters together, if necessary, using hot glue. Trim wire stems to various lengths, from 8" (20.5 cm) to 24" (61 cm) as desired.

4 Insert two fruit stems near side of foam top; insert third stem near other side. Insert one short berry stem on each side. Insert long berry stem on side with one fruit stem. Bend stems to follow curve of ivy stems; conceal stems, using ivy.

5 Cut stems of large and medium roses to 5" (12.5 cm); if stem is shorter than 5" (12.5 cm), extend stems as in step 3. Insert large rose at center, facing up; insert medium roses at center right, facing sides. Bend or trim taller stems so they fall below visual lines of dinner guests.

6 Cut two rosebud stems to 3" (7.5 cm), one to 6" (15 cm), and one or two to 15" (38 cm); extend stems as in step 3, if necessary. Insert short stems in front of medium roses; insert medium stem near large rose; insert long stems into sides.

VARIATIONS FOR THE FRUITS & ROSES ARRANGEMENT

7 Drape grape clusters over compote rim sides. Secure any rose leaves trimmed from floral stems to wire stems; insert as desired to fill gaps. Trim longest elements, if desired.

Secure moss-covered foam to top of decorative pedestal, about 5" × 14" (12.5 × 35.5 cm) tall. Trim longer stems, if desired; add additional fruit stem if you wish to view the arrangement from all sides. Weave decorative ribbon throughout stems.

Use a shallow bowl or ceramic urn, and place it at the end of the mantel. Gild leaves and fruits lightly, using wax-based paint. Drape stems partway across the mantel while allowing others to cascade down the fireplace side. Substitute rose leaves for blossoms and berries at back; scatter gilded nutshells among leaves.

FRESH ADVENT WREATH

Advent wreaths originated in the winter folk traditions of pre-Christian Europe when people gathered evergreens and lit fires as a sign of hope for the coming spring and renewed light. Making an Advent wreath has become a family tradition for many Christians, and the circle of greens and candles continues to be a symbol of everlasting hope and light.

Pine and fir evergreens and various specialty greens, such as cedar and boxwood, are available during the holiday season at garden centers. Most green sprigs release a wonderful fragrance; an assortment of needle lengths and colors will add rich texture and visual appeal to your wreath. Some specialty greens, such as holly, mistletoe, and juniper, add lovely symbolic accents, but they are poisonous and should be used with caution near children and food, or replaced with silk greens.

Most evergreens will last about two or three weeks when inserted into saturated fresh floral foam. Flowers will last at least two weeks if watered every other day; long-lasting florals, such as anthuriums, carnations, or orchids, will look fresh even longer. Several tips to prolong the freshness of the wreath are shown on page 159.

Four candles, one for each week of Advent, are placed amid the circle of greens; some families choose to add a fifth candle in the center of the wreath to light on Christmas Day. Typically, three candles are violet or dark blue, one is rose, and the optional one is white, but all white or all violet candles are also appropriate.

The most common embellishment of an Advent wreath is a ribbon, intertwined among the greens as a symbol of longing expectation. Glorious metallics, satins, and sheers are available, or a strip of soft linen may remind a family of a baby's swaddling clothes.

A round platter, a circle of glass, or a mirror may be used to protect your table from the moisture of the floral foam.

HOW TO MAKE A FRESH ADVENT WREATH

MATERIALS

* 12" (30.5 cm) foam wreath form for fresh flowers.
* Sheet moss; floral pins.
* Four spiked candle cups.
* Assorted greens, 4" to 6" (10 to 15 cm) long.

* Spray bottle and commercial plant protector or floral preservative, optional.
* 1 yd. (0.95 m) ribbon.
* Four or five candles, as on page 157.

1 Soak foam wreath form in water until saturated; dampen the sheet moss. Cover wreath form with sheet moss; secure with floral pins.

2 Insert candle cups into foam, spacing them evenly. Push greens into foam, starting with longest needles and distributing evenly; cut small opening in moss with knife, if necessary. Secure long branch tips with floral pins.

3 Insert any floral stems into foam, spacing them evenly. Mist wreath with water. Wind ribbon through greens. Insert candles into candle cups.

158

TIPS FOR A LONGER-LASTING ARRANGEMENT

Misting. Apply commercial plant protector, following product guidelines; a clear, glossy film will minimize moisture loss. Or spritz arrangements daily with water and a floral preservative.

Regular watering. Place wreath on drainboard, and pour at least 1 cup (250 mL) water into foam, as if watering a houseplant. Allow water to soak in.

Bath. Revive some flowers and most foliage by submerging them in cool water for about five minutes; pull limp elements from foam, revive, and replace.

Greens. Cut sprigs of greenery to lengths of 5" to 8" (12.5 to 20.5 cm); trim away any needles near the ends of the sprigs.

Florals. Gently scrape about 1" (2.5 cm) of stem end to enable it to absorb water quickly and efficiently.

Poinsettias. Cut leaf cluster from plant, leaving 4" (10 cm) stem. Singe cut end, using candle flame, until sap bubbles and turns black. Place stem in water for about four hours.

Fragrant and exotic. *Fresh gardenias and seeded eucalyptus share the spotlight in this very formal and sweetly scented table wreath.*

Crimson and white. *Stunning red poinsettias are accented by fluffy white carnations to make a festive and long-lasting Christmas centerpiece.*

Wassail cheer. *Plump fruits and cinnamon sticks nestle amid fresh spruce and juniper sprigs in a wreath surrounding the punch bowl.*

MOLDED BEESWAX CANDLES

With their warm, inviting glow and mellow scent, beeswax candles are a year-round favorite decorating accessory. For Christmas entertaining, brighten your table with molded beeswax candles you make yourself. Using innovative products, including flexible polymer candle molds, beeswax pellets, and boiling bags, you can enjoy the art of pouring candles without messing up the kitchen or ruining cookware. Available in many styles and sizes from craft stores or by mail order, flexible polymer molds are durable and easy to use. The beautifully detailed candles can be enjoyed in their natural state or highlighted with acrylic paints, wax-based metallics, or pearlized powders.

MATERIALS

* Beeswax pellets.
* Boiling bag; clothespin.
* Large saucepan; water.
* Flexible polymer candle molds; aerosol mold release.
* Candle wicking, size 2/0; wicking needle or large-eyed darning needle.
* Large metal hairpin.
* Rubber bands.
* Freezer paper.
* Acrylic paints, wax-based metallics, or pearlized powders; small paintbrush, for embellishing, optional.

HOW TO MAKE A MOLDED BEESWAX CANDLE

1 Pour beeswax pellets into melting bag. Roll top down, and secure with clothespin. Submerge in pan of boiling water.

2 Spray inner surface of polymer mold with light layer of mold release. Insert candle wicking into mold, using wicking needle or large-eyed darning needle. Pull wicking taut; secure through large metal hairpin, centered across opening of candle mold.

3 Wrap rubber bands around mold; check seam of mold for proper alignment. Place mold, open end up, on work surface covered with freezer paper.

4 Remove boiling bag from water when wax has melted; towel off any dripping water. Remove clothespin; slowly pour beeswax into candle mold, filling to top.

5 Allow beeswax to cool completely; cooling time may vary from 2 to 6 hours, depending on size of mold. Remove rubber bands; remove candle from mold, pulling wicking into position for the next candle.

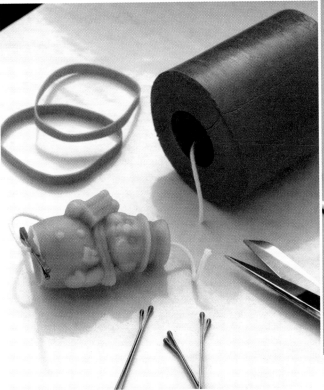

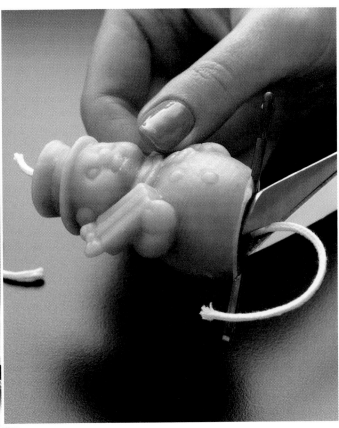

6 Cut wicking ½" (1.3 cm) above top of candle. Cut wicking at base of candle, removing hairpin.

7 Heat a disposable metal pie pan on stovetop burner. Press bottom of candle on heated pan; this melts wax on bottom, leveling candle and sealing wick.

8 Embellish candle, if desired, using acrylic paints (snowman), wax-based metallics (angel), or pearlized powders (tree).

BEESWAX ORNAMENTS & GARLANDS

Molded beeswax ornaments, a nostalgic memento of the Christmas season, are versatile as candle accents, napkin ring favors for dinner party guests, or a unique garland for a tabletop display. Beeswax is simply melted in boiling bags and poured into intricately detailed flexible polymer molds. The molds are available separately or in multiple sets, enabling you to pour several ornaments at a time. When cooled, the ornaments can be trimmed with ribbons, berries, sprigs of greenery, or dried flowers. They can also be painted with acrylic paints or accented with pearlized powders or wax-based metallics.

MATERIALS

* Beeswax pellets.
* Boiling bag; clothespin.
* Large saucepan; water.
* Flexible polymer ornament molds.
* Freezer paper.

* 9" (23 cm) length of ribbon or cord, for each hanger, if making individual ornaments.
* 1 yd. (0.95 m) narrow decorative cord in desired length, for garland.

* Embellishments, such as narrow ribbons, berries, sprigs of greenery, or dried flowers.
* Acrylic paints, wax-based metallics, or pearlized powders; small paintbrush.

HOW TO MAKE MOLDED BEESWAX ORNAMENTS

1 Cover work surface with freezer paper, shiny side up. Place molds on freezer paper. Knot ends of ribbon or cord together, for hangers.

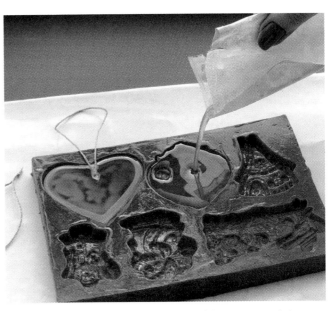

2 Melt and pour wax as on page 164, steps 1 and 4. Insert knotted end of hanger into beeswax at top of each mold, working quickly before wax hardens. Allow to cool.

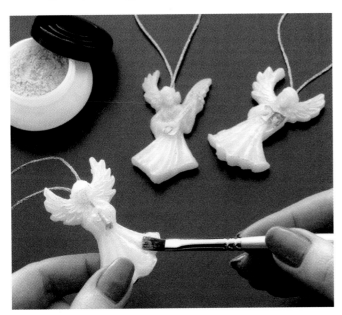

3 Remove cooled ornaments from molds. Paint or apply pearlized powders as desired.

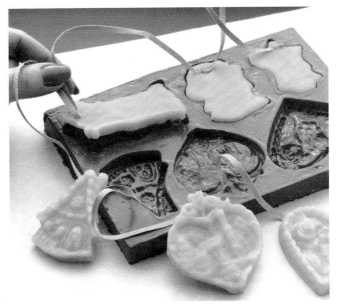

Garland. Tie knots at each end of 1 yd. (0.95 m) of narrow decorative cord; tie four knots evenly spaced between ends. Pour melted wax into molds. Quickly insert one knot into beeswax at top of each mold; allow to cool. Remove garland from molds; embellish as desired.

EMBELLISHING PURCHASED CANDLES

Decorative candles can be pretty costly, but there are some simple ways to dress up plain candles for the holidays, using craft supplies you may have around the house.

Metallic accents. *Brush metallic paint onto crumpled plastic wrap, using foam applicator. Apply paint to candle surface, using pouncing motion, for a glimmering contemporary look. Apply two or three metallic colors in multiple layers, allowing candle to dry between applications.*

Wax appliqués. *Melt the back of molded wax ornament (page 166), using tip of hot glue gun. Press onto sides of pillar candle.*

Stripes. *Mask off stripes with masking tape, for a candy cane effect. Apply thin layer of acrylic craft paint, using*

sponge pouncer or makeup sponge. Remove tape before paint is completely dry.

Snow-capped pinecones. *Cut pinecones in half, using nippers. Adhere them to the candle surface, using hot glue gun. Touch the tips with artificial snow or white acrylic paint. Sprinkle with fine glitter while wet, if desired.*

Snowflakes. *Create flexible, removable snowflake motifs, using stained glass paint (page 172). Apply self-stick motifs to candle surface.*

PAINTED GLASS CANDLEHOLDERS

Decorate glass hurricanes and other smooth glass candleholders with craft paints to enhance the flickering glow of the light. Stencil frosted designs to imitate etched glass. Or create colorful holiday motifs that are easy to remove from the glass at the end of the season.

Clean and dry the glass thoroughly before applying the paint or painted motif because dirt, grease, and fingerprints will affect the results.

Purchase special air-dry frost-effect paints at craft stores. Mix colors to obtain a wider palette, including pastels and dark tones. Choose flexible vinyl stencils because they cling well to glass. If you want to decorate a shaped hurricane or bowl, look for small designs so the stencil will adhere without rippling.

Make removable paint motifs or simulate traditional stained glass, using specialty paints designed for this purpose. Find simple designs in stained glass pattern books, or create your own. When your glass has strong curves, choose designs with "extensions" that can shift without distortion, such as a snowflake. If it is awkward to work directly on the glass, paint the design on a sheet of flexible plastic. It can then be peeled off and applied to the glass.

MATERIALS

For frosted glass:

* Surface conditioner for glass paints.
* Foam brushes; artist's brushes.
* Frost-effect paint.
* Flexible vinyl stencils.
* Masking tape, optional.

For removable paint motifs:

* Flexible plastic sheet for painting motifs and stained glass designs.
* Stained glass paint.
* Simulated liquid leading, optional.
* Toothpicks.
* Isopropyl alcohol; lint-free cloth.

HOW TO FROST GLASS

1 Wash glass well in hot, soapy water; dry. Apply surface conditioner, using brush. Allow to dry.

2 Position stencil at desired location. Press all design edges of stencil firmly to ensure proper adhesion; slash edge of stencil as necessary to fit curved surface. Stir paint well; do not shake. Apply paint, using dry brush. Allow to dry.

171

HOW TO MAKE A REMOVABLE PAINT MOTIF

1 Trace or draw design on paper; tape to cardboard. Tape plastic sheet over design. Apply paint to plastic along design lines; squeeze bottle with even pressure, and keep tip above surface. Stop squeezing bottle near the end of the design line, and lower tip to surface at end.

2 Apply paint in design area. Make sure paint connects with outline to prevent weak spots; use toothpick to fill corners and edges as necessary (paint appears milky when wet). Sprinkle with fine glitter, if desired. Allow to dry flat at least 24 hours.

3 Wash glass well in hot, soapy water. Wipe surface, using isopropyl alcohol and lint-free cloth. Peel motif from board. Press motif to glass, working from design center to edges.

HOW TO MAKE A FAUX STAINED GLASS MOTIF

1 Tape design under flexible plastic, and use leading to outline design as in step 1, opposite. Allow leading to dry at least 8 hours. Trim irregularities from leading, using a mat knife. Reapply leading as necessary. Allow to dry another 16 hours.

2 Apply paint next to leading in a design area; make sure paint seals with leading as in step 2, opposite. Apply paint within design area, working back and forth. Spread paint evenly, and remove bubbles, using toothpick. A few bubbles may be left to give an authentic stained-glass look. Repeat for all design areas.

3 Allow paint to dry, following manufacturer's recommendations. Apply additional coats to intensify colors, if desired. Cure 24 hours. Clean glass; peel and press motif to glass as in step 3, opposite.

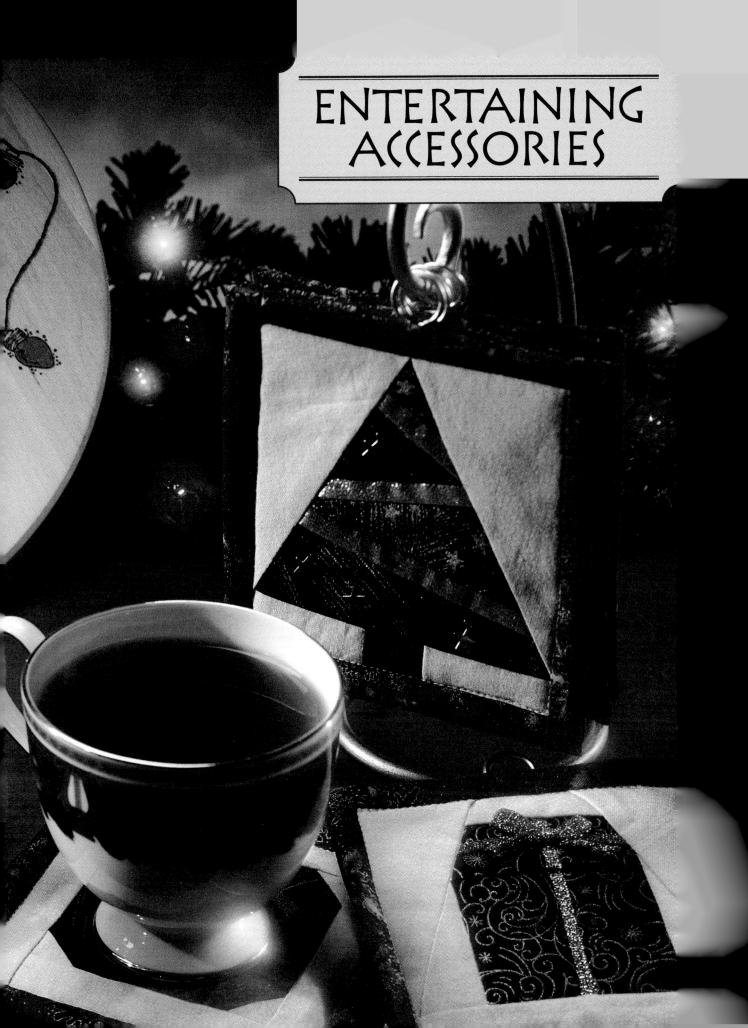

WOODBURNING DESIGNS

Combine the timeless charm of woodburning with other tested and true techniques, such as stenciling and rubber stamping; then add color with oil color pencils, to create unique wood serving trays, trivets, or chargers. The simple skills of tracing and coloring that you learned in grade school are the foundation for creating these beautiful works of art.

The best results are achieved on fine-quality wood products, such as basswood trays, plates, and plaques from Walnut Hollow. Basswood has a fine texture and uniform golden color, and it burns easily.

Select either stencils or rubber stamps in Christmas motifs, depending on the look you prefer. Stencil designs have the characteristic "bridges" or borders around all the design areas, whereas stamped designs do not. Unlike traditional stenciled designs, the stencil is merely traced with a pencil; the color is filled in with oil color pencils. If stamping, select stamps that provide outlines only of the designs, without filled-in spaces. Use ink pads designed for art stamping; bright or pastel colors are easiest to see when burning. Test your stamp on paper before applying it to the wood.

Select a woodburning pen with interchangeable points, such as the one from Walnut Hollow. You can use the Universal point, which comes with the pen, for many different effects, but there are specialized points that make the techniques easier. For beginners, the Mini Flow point works best for fine lines and small dots. The Flow point works well for burning curves, larger dots, and shading.

MATERIALS

* Basswood tray, plate, or plaque.
* Extra-fine sandpaper; soft rag.
* Woodburner; Flow point and Mini Flow point or Universal point.
* Scrap wood, for testing.
* Rubber stamp; ink pads, for stamped designs.
* Stencils; #2 pencil, for stencil-style designs.
* Oil color pencils; pencil sharpener.
* Workable fixative; clear wood sealer.

HOW TO WOODBURN & COLOR THE DESIGN

1 Sand the entire wood piece, using extra-fine sandpaper. Wipe with soft cloth. Transfer design, using stencil or rubber stamp method (opposite).

2 Attach Mini Flow point or Universal point; heat woodburner. Hold woodburner lightly as you would hold large pencil. Burn lines over marked lines, pulling woodburner toward you. Follow woodburning tips and techniques on page 180.

3 Erase any pencil lines, using artist's eraser. Or lightly sand away stamped lines. Color design, using oil color pencils; follow coloring tips and techniques on page 181.

4 Spray colored areas with workable fixative; allow to dry. Apply two thin coats of water-base varnish over entire project; allow to dry between coats.

Stencil method.
Place stencil over desired area; secure with masking tape. Trace all design areas with #2 pencil.

1 Rubber stamp method. Place wood faceup on surface where it won't easily slide. Hold stamp faceup in one hand; gently pat it with ink pad, transferring color. Take care to ink only raised areas, avoiding background. Test stamp on paper.

2 Reink stamp, if necessary. Hold stamp, facedown, parallel to wood surface. Press stamp firmly onto wood, applying enough pressure to transfer all raised areas. Rock stamp slightly from front to back and from side to side. Reink stamp each time you apply design in other areas.

Exercise safety precautions. Avoid touching the end of the woodburner or its stand. Never leave the woodburner unattended.

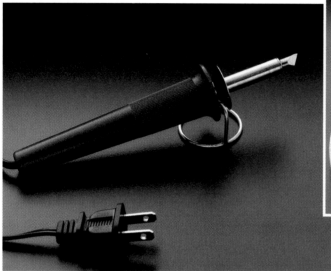

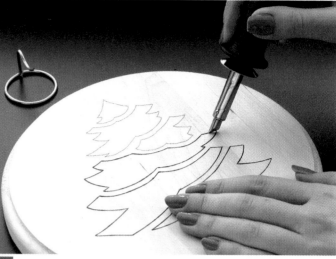

Always draw the point toward you at a slow, steady pace; hold pen lightly, letting point float over surface of wood. For darker lines, move the point slower; do not press harder. Turn the wood to work at various angles.

Mini Flow point. Burn fine lines over marked design lines. Stipple areas of tiny dots, for shading; the closer the dots, the darker the shading will appear. Hold in place longer for larger dots. Gradually burn dots farther apart to lighten shading.

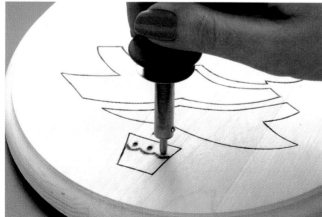

Flow point. Burn bold lines over marked designs. Burn large dots for design details.

Universal point. Use the sharp tip for burning fine lines or small dots. Burn bolder lines by drawing the blade edge against the wood; angle slightly to one side for wider lines. Test the point, holding it at different angles.

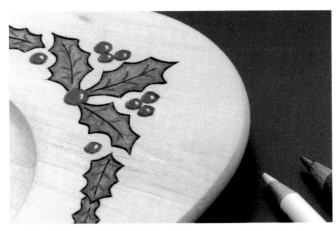

Highlights. Apply highlight colors first, using medium to heavy pressure. These may be white, pastel shades, or colors with very light values, such as yellow or cream. Avoid coloring into these highlight areas with other colors.

Blending. Color an entire area lightly, using various pencils to develop shaping, highlights, and shadows. Blend each color into the next, so that you are unable to tell where one color stops and the next begins. Then color over the entire area, using a light to medium color and applying heavy pressure.

Shading. Woodburning creates most of the shading, especially for stamped designs. To add additional shading, use pencils with darker values of same color, as for French horn and ribbon. Or first color lightly using similar value of the complementary color; then color over it with the intended color for that area. For instance, red, the complementary color to green, is colored in the deepest recesses of the holly leaves before coloring over with green. Avoid using black for shading, as this tends to make colors look dull.

Flat color. Develop flat graphic color, by filling each design area completely and evenly with only one color, using heavy pressure. This creates a dramatic look, and requires no highlighting, shading, or blending of colors.

Workable fixative seals the color, but allows you to add more color, if you wish. Reds sometimes tend to "run" when sprayed with fixative. If this occurs, allow the area to dry; carefully sand away color run, and then spray again.

HOOKED RUG TRIVET

The art of rug hooking, a classic American craft, is used to make these delightfully rustic Christmas trivets. With their primitive designs and coarse texture, they add a touch of nostalgia to the festivities. Useful as well as decorative, rug-hooked trivets are perfect for homespun country table decor, a traditional family buffet, or propped on a shelf as a seasonal memento.

In rug hooking, narrow wool strips are pulled into short loops through a foundation fabric, called monk's cloth, to create a design. The supplies are minimal, available at fiber-art or craft stores, and through mail-order suppliers. Wool fabrics should be lightweight and closely woven, either remnants or discarded garments. Solid colors as well as small plaids, herringbones, or tweeds may be used. In general, the amount required is about five times the size of the design area to be covered. The wool is machine washed and dried before cutting, to shrink it slightly and tighten the weave. Select one of the designs on pages 312 and 313, or draw your own, taking inspiration from Christmas cards, wrapping paper, or children's coloring books.

182

MATERIALS

* Lightweight, closely woven wool fabrics.
* Rotary cutter and cutting mat, or sharp scissors; quilting ruler.
* Cotton monk's cloth, for foundation.
* Heat transfer pencil and tracing paper.
* Wooden quilting hoop.
* Rug hook.
* ⅛" (3 mm) plywood.
* Staple gun; short staples.
* Felt square; craft glue.

TIPS FOR RUG HOOKING

Outline a design area first by hooking a row of loops around it, then fill in the area with loops. Complete one design area before moving to next.

Complete all design areas; then fill in the background.

Pull up a loop in every other hole of the monk's cloth in each row of hooking. Skip a hole between rows, so that loops will not become too dense.

Vary the direction of the rows within each design area to add a textural effect or to add interest to a background color.

HOW TO PREPARE THE WOOL

1 Machine wash wool fabrics in warm water with mild detergent; machine dry. Press. Cut wool into 9" × 12" (23 × 30.5 cm) pieces, following grainlines.

2 Cut lengthwise strips, ¼" (6 mm) wide, from each piece, using rotary cutter, cutting mat, and quilting ruler, for ease.

HOW TO HOOK THE DESIGN

1 Trace design onto tracing paper, using heat transfer pencil. Place design facedown over foundation; transfer design, following manufacturer's directions. Cut foundation at least 8" (20.5 cm) larger than design. Wrap outer edges with masking tape to prevent raveling.

2 Secure foundation in hoop, printed side up; fabric should be very taut. Hold rug hook in palm of hand, above design, with hook turned up. Hold wool strip between thumb and forefinger of opposite hand; this hand will be held beneath the frame and will guide wool strip, making sure it does not twist.

3 Push hook down through foundation, and catch wool strip in hook. Pull end of wool strip to right side, to height of about 1" (2.5 cm).

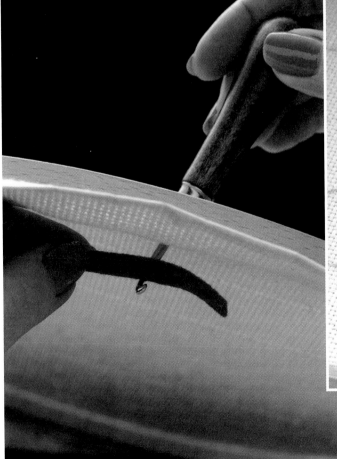

4 Insert the hook into next hole; pull up loop about ¼" (6 mm) above surface. Continue hooking the strip, pulling all loops to same height. Evenly space loops, with no gaps between them, and do not twist wool strip.

(Continued)

5 Pull end of strip through to right side of foundation; reinsert hook in same opening to begin hooking second strip.

6 Clip ends of strips even with loops when each design area is completed, taking care not to clip loops. Complete design with two rows of hooking completely around outer edge.

HOW TO COMPLETE THE TRIVET

1 Remove hooked design from hoop; place facedown on ironing surface. Cover with dampened press cloth, and steam press. Allow to dry.

2 Cut wooden base to finished design size, using jigsaw. Cut felt to same size.

3 Place hooked design facedown on work surface; place base over design. Wrap excess fabric over base; staple. Work from top to bottom and side to side, pulling edges taut, so outer rows of loops stand at edge of wood. Clip, overlap, and trim fabric as necessary, for smoothness.

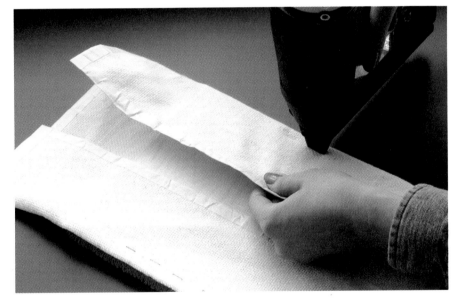

4 Glue felt over base back, aligning to trivet edges. Glue ¼" (6 mm) strip of matching wool or felt to narrow edge, covering foundation fabric.

TREE TRIVET

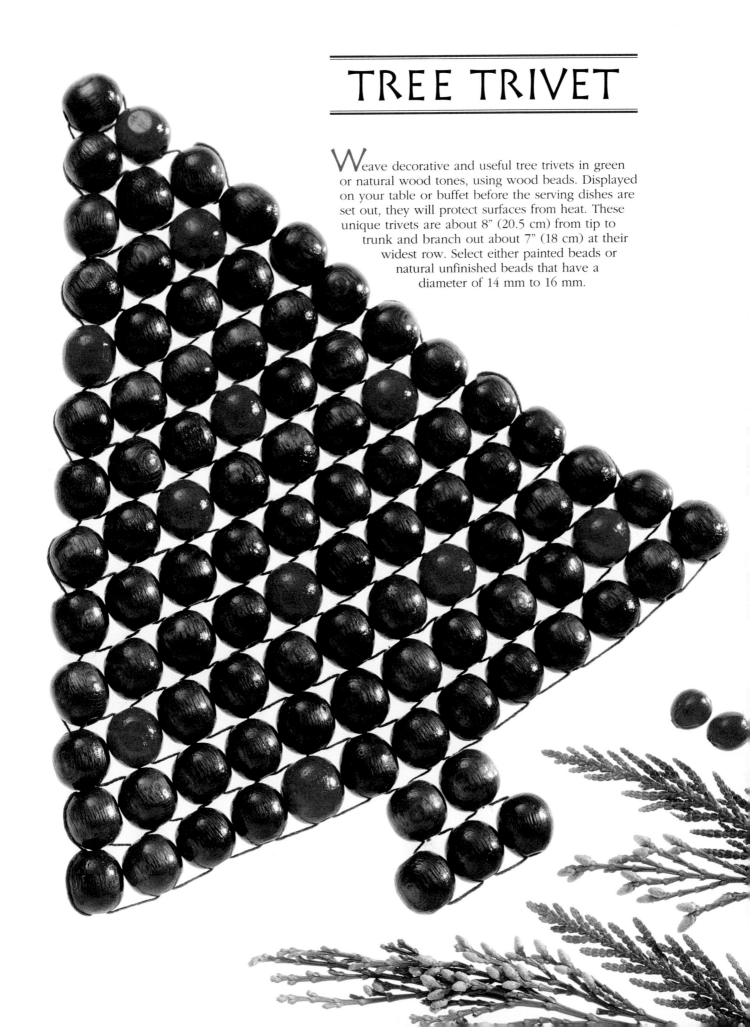

Weave decorative and useful tree trivets in green or natural wood tones, using wood beads. Displayed on your table or buffet before the serving dishes are set out, they will protect surfaces from heat. These unique trivets are about 8" (20.5 cm) from tip to trunk and branch out about 7" (18 cm) at their widest row. Select either painted beads or natural unfinished beads that have a diameter of 14 mm to 16 mm.

HOW TO MAKE A TREE TRIVET

MATERIALS

* Wood beads, painted or unfinished; ninety-six 14 mm beads or seventy-one 16 mm beads.
* Sturdy cotton cording, in green or white.
* Two large-eyed needles.
* Green fabric dye, optional.

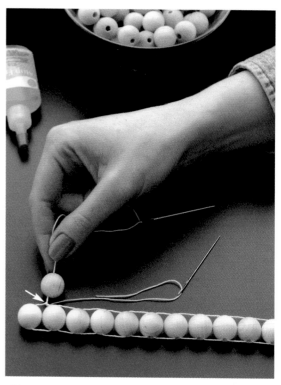

1 Thread 1 yd. (0.95 m) of cording with a large-eyed needle at each end. Weave row of eleven 16 mm beads or thirteen 14 mm beads together, following diagram; pull cording firmly between beads.

2 Knot cording ends securely above last two beads (arrow). Seal knot with glue. Thread one tail through new bead, pulling knot inside bead; trim other tail.

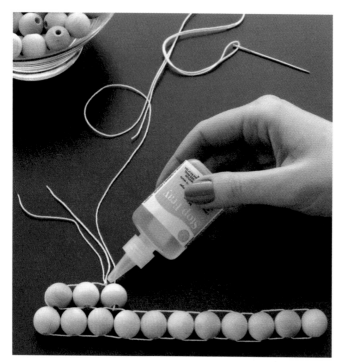

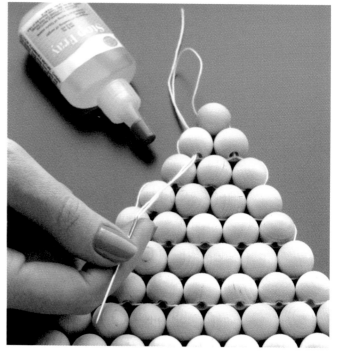

3 Weave ten more rows of 16 mm beads or twelve more rows of 14 mm beads, following diagram; wrap cording over cording in previous row with each bead. Add more cording as necessary; seal knot, and hide inside bead.

4 Secure single bead for top row so hole is horizontal. Thread needle through adjacent bead of previous row. Knot cording; seal knot with glue. Maneuver cording to hide knot inside bead.

5 Thread needle with 12" (30.5 cm) cording. Thread three beads onto cording; pass needle through first bead again in opposite direction. Secure to cording of first row between center and next bead; seal and hide knot. Attach remaining two beads to complete trunk, following diagram.

6 Dip entire trivet into green fabric dye, if desired, following manufacturer's directions. Allow to dry.

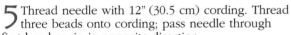

tail

knot

knot

tail

Start here

knot   knot

NAPKIN RINGS

Beautiful napkin rings are the finishing touch to your holiday table decor. When you make them yourself, you can afford to get fancy, even for large parties. With careful selection of materials, the napkin rings carry the theme of the party and echo elements used in other decorations, such as centerpieces, table linens, or buffet table decor.

Fabric-covered napkin rings, made from short lengths of PVC pipe, are embellished with decorative cording and braid. A miter box helps to ensure even, accurate cutting of the PVC pipe. Any nontransparent fabrics are suitable, from light decorative silks to heavy brocades.

Brushed metal napkin rings are fashioned from sheet metal, available at craft and hardware stores. Select

aluminum, brass, or copper. An 8" × 10" (20.5 × 25.5 cm) sheet is enough for ten napkin rings.

Decorative ribbons are gathered into miniature wreaths, perfect for holding napkins. Select from a wide variety of satin, sheer, nylon-edged, or wire-edged ribbons.

Beaded napkin rings can take on many different looks, depending on the type and size of beads you use. Select metallic beads for a glimmering accent, or select wooden beads for country charm. Catch the sparkle of Christmas lights in clear faceted beads, or wrap your napkins with elegant pearls. Both of the beaded napkin rings shown are woven together following the same basic technique, called a twill pattern. Additional rows are used to make wide bands with smaller beads.

HOW TO MAKE A FABRIC-COVERED NAPKIN RING

MATERIALS

* 6" (15 cm) PVC pipe 1½" to 1¾" (3.8 to 4.5 cm) in diameter, for four rings.

* Miter box and saw; medium-grit sandpaper.

* ⅛ yd. (0.15 m) fabric.

* Clothespins, optional.

* ⅔ yd. (0.63 m) ribbon, ½" to 1" (1.3 to 2.5 cm) wide, for four rings.

* Decorative trim.

* Fabric or craft glue; small bowl; 1" (2.5 cm) foam brush.

1 Mark 1⅛" (2.8 cm) from end of PVC pipe. Cut through pipe at mark, using miter box and saw. Sand edges of ring smooth.

(continued)

2 Measure outer circumference of ring. Cut 2½" (6.5 cm) bias fabric strip the length of circumference plus ¼" (6 mm).

3 Dilute glue with water. Apply glue to inner surface and edges, and in a narrow band across outside of ring, using brush. Center end of fabric strip on glue band; apply glue to underside of other end. Pull fabric around ring, and lap ends. Wrap fabric to inside; smooth. Allow to dry.

4 Measure inner circumference of ring; cut ribbon to this length. Apply diluted glue to wrong side of ribbon. Secure ribbon to inside of ring, covering raw fabric edges. Seal cut ends of trim. Decorate napkin ring as desired.

HOW TO MAKE A BRUSHED METAL NAPKIN RING

MATERIALS

* Sheet metal, medium weight, such as brass #252.
* Craft scissors or tin snips.
* Sandpaper, medium-grit and extra-fine-grit.
* Fine steel wool, optional.

* Dowel or other cylindrical object, 1¼" to 1½" (3.2 to 3.8 cm) in diameter.
* Pliers and soft cloth, optional.

 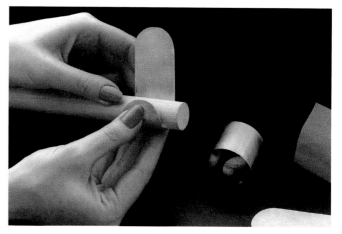

1 Trace pattern (page 314); cut out. Trace around pattern on craft metal, using pencil. Cut out, using scissors or tin snips. Smooth cut edges, using medium-grit sandpaper.

2 Scuff surface in circular motion, using extra-fine-grit sandpaper or steel wool. Wrap metal around dowel. Use pliers to shape rounded ends, if necessary; protect metal with cloth.

HOW TO MAKE A WREATH NAPKIN RING

MATERIALS

* 1 yd. (0.95 m) decorative ribbon, 1¼" (3.2 cm) wide.
* 1 yd. (0.95 m) decorative ribbon, ½" to ⅝" (1.3 to 1.5 cm) wide.
* ⅞ yd. (0.8 m) ribbon, up to ⅜" (1 cm) wide, for bow.
* Safety pin.

1 Fold ⅜" (1 cm) under on each end of decorative ribbons. Center narrow ribbon on wide ribbon, wrong sides together; pin. Edgestitch both long sides of narrow ribbon.

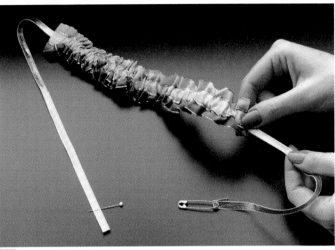

2 Insert narrow ribbon for bow through channel between ribbons, using safety pin. Gather decorative ribbon on narrow ribbon, forming ring; tie knot and bow in narrow ribbon. Trim ribbon tails as desired.

HOW TO MAKE A BEADED NAPKIN RING

MATERIALS

* Beads, of desired size and type, such as metal, wood, pearl, or faceted acrylic; eighteen ½" (1.3 cm) beads, twenty-one ⁷⁄₁₆" (1.2 cm) beads, or about eighty ³⁄₁₆" (4.5 mm) beads.
* Cording, such as #5 pearl cotton, in desired color; two large-eyed needles.

1 **Three-row.** Thread 1 yd. (0.95 m) of cording with a large-eyed needle at each end. Weave the beads together, following diagram A, page 196; continue to length of 5" to 5½" (12.5 to 14 cm).

2 Thread one needle through first bead; knot ends securely, forming ring. Seal knot with dot of glue. Maneuver cording to hide knot inside bead; trim tails.

(Continued)

HOW TO MAKE A BEADED NAPKIN RING (CONTINUED)

1 Five-row. Follow steps 1 and 2 on page 195. Thread another yd. (0.95 m) of cording with a large-eyed needle at each end. Weave beads onto the ring, following diagram B; thread cording through bead of outside row with each addition.

2 Continue around the ring. Thread one needle through first bead in new row; knot ends securely. Seal knot with dot of glue. Maneuver cording to hide knot inside bead; trim tails.

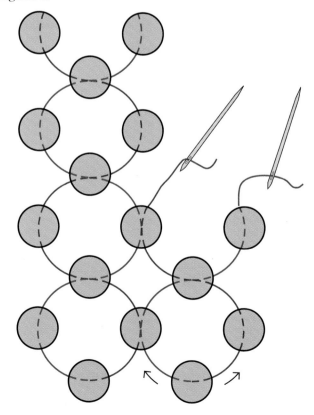

DIAGRAMS FOR BEADED NAPKIN RINGS

Diagram A

Diagram B

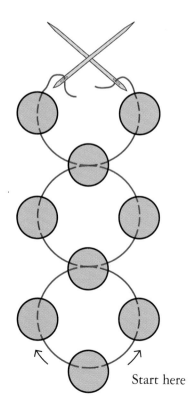

Start here

MORE
IDEAS FOR
NAPKIN
RINGS

Shape 30" (76 cm) of wire garland *into a spiral, and wrap it around a circular napkin rolled in the shape of a Christmas tree.*

Secure a beeswax ornament *(page 166) around a napkin with wired ribbon or decorative cord.*

String jingle bells *on jewelry wire; join ends, forming a ring.*

SCENTED COASTERS

Fill these lovely stenciled coasters with spices to add a soft holiday scent to the room. Tantalizing aromas grow whenever you place a warm mug on the coaster, and the multiple layers help protect tables from the heat.

To maximize the effect and the durability of the painted design, select solid fabrics that are at least fifty percent cotton or linen. Avoid fabrics with polished or protective finishes, and always prewash fabrics to remove sizing.

Purchase precut stencils at craft stores. Use undiluted fabric paints or mix craft acrylic paints with a textile medium. Work on a hard surface, using sandpaper to keep the fabric from slipping. If only one stencil is used for a multicolored design, cover areas not in use with masking tape.

Try different blends of whole cloves, whole allspice, star anise, cinnamon sticks, nutmeg, orange peel, or lemon peel to fill these 4½" (11.5 cm) coasters. Shatter large pieces, like the cinnamon sticks, with pliers. When the fragrances begin to fade, roll a can across the coaster to lightly crush the spices and release fresh scents.

MATERIALS

* ¼ yd. (0.25 m) solid fabric, for six coaster fronts.

* ¼ yd. (0.25 m) fabric, for six coaster backs.

* ⅓ yd. (0.32 m) polyester fleece.

* Sandpaper, 7" (18 cm) square.

* Masking tape.

* Precut stencil.

* Fabric paints or craft acrylic paints and textile medium.

* Stencil brushes, one for each paint color, or sponge pouncers.

* Disposable plates; paper towel.

* ¾ cup (175 g) assorted spice blend, as desired.

CUTTING DIRECTIONS

Cut six 5½" (14 cm) squares from solid fabric.

Cut six 5½" (14 cm) squares from back fabric.

Cut six 5½" × 11" (14 × 28 cm) rectangles from polyester fleece.

1 Secure sandpaper to hard surface, using tape. Center solid fabric square over sandpaper. Mask areas of stencil, if desired, using tape. Tape stencil in position over fabric. Wrap tape around bristles of stencil brush, ¼" (6 mm) from end.

2 Pour paint puddle onto plate; mix two parts acrylic paint with one part textile medium, if necessary. Dip brush tip into paint. Blot brush on paper towel in a circular motion until bristles are nearly dry.

3 Hold brush perpendicular to fabric, and apply paint in largest part of design, using up-and-down pouncing motion. For shaded effect, apply paint more heavily along stencil edges, leaving centers light. Apply paint to all areas of one color; allow to dry. Apply additional colors. Heat-set paint, following manufacturer's directions.

Alternate method. Apply dry formula stencil paint, following manufacturer's directions. Use sponge pouncer instead of stencil brush, if desired.

HOW TO MAKE A SCENTED COASTER

1 Fold fleece in half, forming square. Align back and front of coaster, right sides together; place over fleece. Pin aligned layers together.

2 Stitch ½" (1.3 cm) seam allowance all around, leaving 3" (7.5 cm) opening on one side. Trim corners diagonally; trim fleece close to stitching. Turn; press.

3 Pour ⅛ cup (25 g) spice blend between two fleece layers. Fold seam allowances in; slipstitch opening closed. Topstitch about ⅛" (3 mm) from outer edges.

PAPER-PIECED COASTERS

Keep a set of quilted holiday coasters close at hand to add holiday charm to any gathering. Three intricate designs are easily sewn from patterns (pages 314 and 315), using the popular paper-piecing method of construction. A small ring sewn to the center of each coaster's upper edge enables you to hang the six coasters on an ornament stand when not in use. Add small, fairly flat embellishments, such as tiny bows, beads, or charms.

MATERIALS

* Paper patterns (pages 314 and 315); copy two of each design.
* Fabric scraps or 1/8 yd. (0.15 m) of each design fabric.
* Lightweight fusible knit interfacing, optional.
* 1/4 yd. (0.25 m) polyester fleece.
* 1/4 yd. (0.25 m) lining fabric, for six coasters.
* Six brass rings, 1/2" (1.3 cm) in diameter.
* Large ornament stand.

CUTTING DIRECTIONS

Apply interfacing to the wrong side of tissue lamé, if using.

Cut fabric rectangles at least 1/2" (1.3 cm) larger than each section of the design.

Cut six 4¾" (12 cm) squares from lining and batting.

HOW TO MAKE A PAPER-PIECED COASTER

1 Make pieced holiday design as on pages 124 and 125, steps 1 to 5. Place design and lining, right sides together, on batting; align all edges, and pin. Stitch 1/4" (6 mm) seam allowance all around; leave 2" (5 cm) opening on the bottom edge.

2 Trim batting close to stitching. Trim corners diagonally. Turn; press. Slipstitch opening closed. Stitch in the ditch of outer border. Sew ring on back, at center top. Hand-stitch additional embellishments to designs as desired.

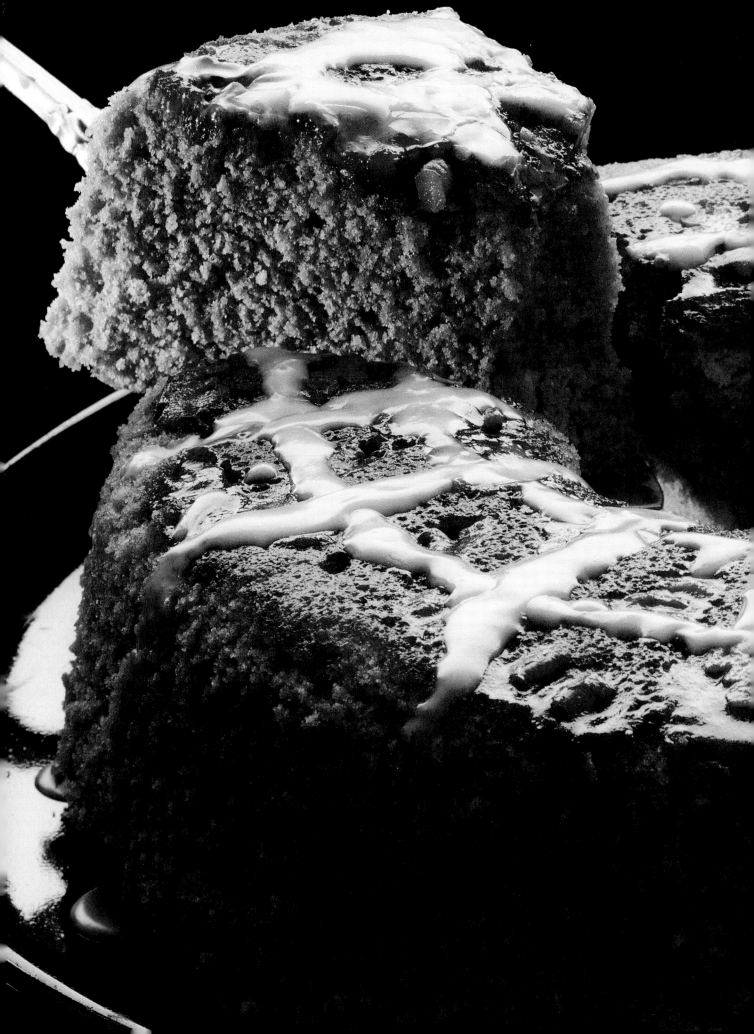

EGG DISHES

BAKED ◄ FRENCH TOAST

- ½ cup (125 mL) maple syrup
- 8 slices French bread (3-inch/7 cm diameter), 1 inch (2.5 cm) thick
- ½ cup (125 mL) skim milk
- 2 eggs, beaten
- 1 teaspoon (5 mL) vanilla
- ½ teaspoon (2 mL) ground cinnamon
- ¼ teaspoon (1 mL) ground allspice
- Dash cardamom
- 2 cups (500 mL) sliced fresh strawberries
- Powdered sugar

4 servings

1 Spray 12 × 8-inch (3 L) baking dish with nonstick vegetable cooking spray. Pour syrup into dish, tilting dish to coat bottom. Arrange bread in single layer in dish.

2 Combine milk, eggs, vanilla, cinnamon, allspice and cardamom in 2-cup (500 mL) measure. Whisk to blend. Pour milk mixture evenly over bread, coating bread completely. Cover dish with plastic wrap, pressing wrap directly onto bread. Refrigerate overnight.

3 Heat oven to 350°F (180°C). Remove and discard plastic wrap. Bake for 30 to 38 minutes, or until surface appears dry and edges are crisp. Spoon strawberries evenly over each serving of toast. Lightly dust toast with powdered sugar. Serve immediately.

PARTY QUICHE

Crust:
- ⅓ cup (75 mL) vegetable shortening
- 1 tablespoon (15 mL) butter or margarine
- 1¼ cups (300 mL) all-purpose flour
- ½ teaspoon (2 mL) salt
- 2 to 3 tablespoons (25 to 50 mL) cold water with 2 drops yellow food coloring
- 1 egg, separated
- ½ teaspoon (2 mL) water

Filling:
- 10 slices bacon, chopped
- 4 eggs
- 1 can (12 oz./354 g) evaporated milk
- ½ teaspoon (2 mL) salt
- ⅛ teaspoon (0.5 mL) cayenne
- 1 cup (250 mL) shredded Swiss cheese
- ⅓ cup (75 mL) chopped green onion

8 servings

1 In medium mixing bowl, cut shortening and butter into flour and salt until particles resemble small peas. Sprinkle with water mixture, 1 tablespoon (15 mL) at a time, stirring with fork until dough forms a ball. Roll out 12-inch (30 cm) square on floured surface.

2 Gently place in 10-inch (3 L) square casserole. Crimp edges and ease dough halfway up sides of casserole. Prick with fork. Microwave at High for 3 to 6 minutes, or until crust is dry.

3 Combine egg yolk and ½ teaspoon (2 mL) water. Brush crust with yolk mixture. Microwave at High for 30 to 60 seconds, or until yolk is set. Set crust aside.

4 In 2-quart (2 L) casserole, microwave bacon at High for 6 to 9 minutes, or until crisp, stirring 2 or 3 times. Remove bacon to paper towel with slotted spoon. Discard fat.

5 In the same casserole, combine reserved egg white and the 4 eggs, evaporated milk, salt and cayenne. Blend thoroughly. Reduce power to 50% (Medium). Microwave for 4 to 6 minutes, or until very hot but not set, stirring with wire whip every 1 to 2 minutes during cooking time.

6 Layer cheese, bacon and green onion in crust. Pour in egg mixture. Cover with wax paper. Place in microwave on inverted pie plate or dinner plate. Reduce power to 30% (Medium Low). Microwave for 20 to 28 minutes, or just until set, rotating 3 or 4 times during cooking time. Let stand for 10 minutes.

Helpful Hint: *This quiche can be prepared up to 24 hours ahead. Cover and refrigerate. To serve, cut into 16 pieces and place on platter. Cover with wax paper. Microwave at 50% (Medium) for 3 to 6 minutes, or until heated, rearranging pieces once.*

PUFFY OMELET

- 4 eggs
- ¼ cup (50 mL) milk
- ¼ teaspoon (1 mL) salt
- ¼ teaspoon (1 mL) baking powder
- ⅛ teaspoon (0.5 mL) pepper
- 1 tablespoon (15 mL) butter or margarine
- One or more of the following fillings: shredded cheese; crumbled crisp bacon; sliced cooked mushrooms; chopped fully cooked ham; chopped green pepper; sliced green onion; sautéed onion slices; chopped tomato; diced, cooked potato; shredded chipped beef; chopped cooked shrimp.

2 to 4 servings

1 Separate eggs. Place whites in medium mixing bowl and yolks in small mixing bowl. Beat whites until stiff but not dry. Set aside.

2 Blend milk, salt, baking powder and pepper into egg yolks. Fold yolk mixture gently into beaten egg whites, using rubber spatula. Set aside.

3 Melt butter in 9-inch (1 L) pie plate at High for 45 seconds to 1 minute. Add egg mixture.

4 Microwave at 50% (Medium) for 3 to 5 minutes, or until partially set, lifting edges 2 or 3 times during cooking, so uncooked portions spread evenly. Microwave at 50% (Medium) for 2 to 5 minutes, or until set.

5 Sprinkle with desired fillings. Loosen omelet with spatula and fold in half. Gently slide onto serving plate.

BREADS

CRAN-PINEAPPLE BREAD

- ½ cup (125 mL) unbleached all-purpose flour
- ½ cup (125 mL) whole wheat flour
- ⅓ cup (75 mL) yellow cornmeal
- 1 teaspoon (5 mL) baking soda

- ¼ teaspoon (1 mL) ground allspice
- ¼ teaspoon (1 mL) ground mace
- 1 can (8 oz./220 g) crushed pineapple, drained
- ½ cup (125 mL) chopped fresh cranberries

- ¼ cup (50 mL) dark molasses
- ¼ cup (50 mL) butter or margarine, cut up
- 1 egg
- 2 tablespoons (25 mL) chopped raisins

16 to 20 servings

1 Line bottom of 2-cup (500 mL) measure with circle of wax paper. Set aside. In medium mixing bowl, combine all ingredients. Beat at high speed of electric mixer for 1 minute, scraping bowl frequently. Pour half the batter (about 1⅓ cups/325 mL) into prepared measure. Cover with vented plastic wrap.

2 Microwave at 50% (Medium) for 6 to 10 minutes, or until center springs back when touched lightly and no uncooked batter remains on the sides, rotating measure ½ turn after every 3 minutes. Let stand on counter for 5 to 10 minutes. Loosen edges of bread using knife or spatula. Invert onto wire rack.

3 Repeat for second loaf. Cool completely. Cut two ⅜-inch (8 mm) slices from small end of each loaf. Set aside. Cut remainder of each loaf into 4 slices. Cut large slices in half.

APPLESAUCE-
◀ SPICE LOAF

- 1⅓ cups (325 mL) all-purpose flour
- ¾ cup (175 mL) sugar
- 1 teaspoon (5 mL) baking soda
- 1 teaspoon (5 mL) salt
- 1 teaspoon (5 mL) ground cinnamon
- ¼ teaspoon (1 mL) ground nutmeg
- ¼ teaspoon (1 mL) ground cloves
- ¼ cup (50 mL) vegetable shortening
- ¾ cup (175 mL) applesauce
- ½ cup (125 mL) chopped nuts or raisins
- 2 eggs
- ¼ cup (50 mL) milk
- 2 teaspoons (10 mL) vinegar or lemon juice

16 servings

1 In large mixing bowl, combine all ingredients. Beat at low speed of electric mixer for 15 seconds. Beat at medium speed for 2 minutes.

2 Spread batter in 9 × 5-inch (2 L) loaf dish lined on bottom with wax paper. Shield ends of dish with 2-inch (5 cm) strips of foil.

3 Center loaf dish on inverted saucer in microwave. Microwave at 50% (Medium) for 9 minutes, rotating ¼ turn every 3 minutes.

4 Remove foil. Increase power to High. Microwave for 3 to 5 minutes, rotating every 2 minutes.

5 If using clear glass dish, check for doneness by looking through bottom. (No unbaked batter should appear in center.) Let stand for 5 to 10 minutes before removing from dish.

Helpful Hint: *If quick bread loaves are uncooked in center, return to loaf dish. Set on inverted saucer in microwave. Microwave at High for 1 to 2 minutes.*

DATE-NUT BREAD

- 1 cup (250 mL) dates, cut in half
- 1 teaspoon (5 mL) baking soda
- ¾ cup (175 mL) boiling water
- ¾ cup (175 mL) packed brown sugar
- 1 tablespoon (15 mL) grated orange peel (optional)
- ¼ cup (50 mL) vegetable

- shortening
- 1 egg
- 1½ cups (375 mL) all-purpose flour
- 1 teaspoon (5 mL) salt
- ½ cup (125 mL) chopped nuts

16 servings

1 In small mixing bowl, combine dates, baking soda and water. Let stand for about 10 minutes. In large mixing bowl, mix sugar, peel, shortening and egg. Stir in date mixture, the flour, salt and nuts.

2 Spread batter in 9 × 5-inch (2 L) loaf baking dish lined on bottom with wax paper. Shield ends of dish with 2-inch (5 cm) strips of foil.

3 Center loaf dish on inverted saucer in microwave. Microwave at 50% (Medium) for 8 minutes, rotating ¼ turn every 2 minutes. Remove foil. Increase power to High. Microwave for 2 to 6 minutes. If using clear glass dish, check for doneness by looking through bottom. (No unbaked batter should appear in center.) Let stand for 5 to 10 minutes before removing from dish.

APRICOT BREAD ▶

- 1 cup (250 mL) all-purpose flour
- ¾ cup (175 mL) whole wheat flour
- ½ cup (125 mL) packed brown sugar
- 1½ teaspoons (7 mL) baking soda
- ¼ teaspoon (1 mL) ground cardamom
- 1 cup (250 mL) buttermilk
- 1 egg, beaten
- 2 tablespoons (25 mL) vegetable oil
- ½ cup (125 mL) Grape Nuts® cereal
- ½ cup (125 mL) chopped dried apricots

16 servings

1 Heat oven to 350°F (180°C). Spray 8½ × 4½-inch (1.5 L) loaf pan with nonstick vegetable cooking spray. Dust lightly with all-purpose flour. Set aside.

2 In large mixing bowl, combine flours, sugar, baking soda and cardamom. Add buttermilk, egg and oil. Beat at low speed of electric mixer just until blended, scraping sides of bowl frequently. Fold in cereal and apricots.

3 Pour mixture into prepared pan. Bake for 45 to 50 minutes, or until wooden pick inserted in center comes out clean. Let stand for 10 minutes. Remove loaf from pan. Cool completely on wire rack before slicing.

BANANA BREAD

- 1 cup (250 mL) sugar
- ¼ cup (50 mL) butter or margarine, softened
- ¼ cup (50 mL) applesauce
- 4 egg whites
- 2 very ripe medium bananas, mashed (1 cup/250 mL)
- 1 teaspoon (5 mL) vanilla
- 1½ cups (375 mL) all-purpose flour
- ½ cup (125 mL) whole wheat flour
- 1 teaspoon (5 mL) baking powder
- ½ teaspoon (2 mL) baking soda
- ¼ teaspoon (1 mL) salt

16 servings

1 Heat oven to 350°F (180°C). Spray 9 × 5-inch (2 L) loaf pan with nonstick vegetable cooking spray. Set aside. In large mixing bowl, combine sugar, butter and applesauce. Beat at medium speed of electric mixer until light and fluffy. Gradually beat in egg whites. Stir in bananas and vanilla. Add flours, baking powder, baking soda and salt. Beat at low speed until smooth batter forms.

2 Pour batter into prepared pan. Bake for 1 hour to 1 hour 10 minutes, or until wooden pick inserted in center comes out clean. Cool 10 minutes in pan. Turn loaf out onto wire rack. Cool completely.

▲ CINNAMON-NUT LOAF ❄ FREEZE AHEAD

Topping:
- ⅓ cup (75 mL) packed brown sugar
- ¼ cup (50 mL) butter or margarine
- 1 teaspoon (5 mL) ground cinnamon
- ½ cup (125 mL) chopped walnuts or pecans

Cake:
- 2¾ cups (675 mL) all-purpose flour
- 1 cup (250 mL) packed brown sugar
- 2 teaspoons (10 mL) ground cinnamon
- 1 teaspoon (5 mL) baking powder
- 1 teaspoon (5 mL) baking soda

- ½ teaspoon (2 mL) salt
- 2 cups (500 mL) buttermilk
- ½ cup (125 mL) vegetable shortening
- ½ cup (125 mL) honey
- ¼ cup (50 mL) butter or margarine, softened
- 2 eggs

Glaze:
- 2 to 4 teaspoons (10 to 20 mL) half-and-half
- ⅔ cup (150 mL) powdered sugar

2 loaves, 16 servings each

1 Line bottom of two 9 × 5-inch (2 L) loaf dishes with wax paper. In small bowl, combine all topping ingredients except nuts. Microwave at High for 1 to 2 minutes, or until mixture is bubbly, stirring 1 or 2 times. Stir in nuts. Divide equally and spread in loaf dishes.

2 In large mixing bowl, combine all cake ingredients. Beat at low speed of electric mixer for 30 seconds, scraping bowl constantly.

3 Beat at medium speed for 2 minutes, scraping bowl occasionally. Divide batter equally in prepared loaf dishes. Shield ends

of dishes with 2-inch (5 cm) strips of foil.

4 Place one loaf at a time on inverted saucer in microwave. Microwave at 50% (Medium) for 6 minutes, rotating 1 or 2 times. Remove foil. Increase power to High. Microwave for 2 to 6 minutes, or until no unbaked batter can be seen through bottom of dish, rotating 1 or 2 times. Let stand on counter for 10 minutes. Loosen edges; invert on wire rack. Cool. Wrap, label and freeze no longer than 1 month.

5 To serve, unwrap and place on plate. Microwave at 50%

(Medium) for 1½ to 3½ minutes, or until wooden pick can be easily inserted. Let stand for 5 minutes. For glaze, stir half-and-half into powdered sugar until of desired consistency. Drizzle over loaves.

Cinnamon-Nut Coffee Cake

Line bottom of two ring dishes with wax paper. Continue as directed with loaves, microwaving one coffee cake at a time. Cool and freeze as directed. To serve, defrost ring cake as directed for loaf, except increase microwaving time to 3½ to 5 minutes. Glaze as directed above.

(See photo, page 205)

◀ BRANDIED APPLE LOAF ❄ FREEZE AHEAD

- Graham cracker crumbs
- ¼ cup (50 mL) brandy
- 2 cups (500 mL) peeled and chopped apple
- ½ cup (125 mL) raisins
- ½ cup (125 mL) chopped walnuts
- 1½ cups (375 mL) all-purpose flour
- 1½ cups (375 mL) whole wheat flour
- ¾ teaspoon (4 mL) baking soda
- ¾ teaspoon (4 mL) baking powder
- ½ teaspoon (2 mL) salt
- ¾ cup (175 mL) packed dark brown sugar
- ½ cup (125 mL) vegetable shortening
- ¾ cup (175 mL) apple juice
- 2 eggs
- ¼ cup (50 mL) butter or margarine, softened

2 loaves, 16 servings each

1 Generously grease two 8 × 4-inch (1.5 L) loaf dishes. Coat bottom and sides of each dish with graham cracker crumbs. Place brandy in small bowl. Microwave at High for 30 to 45 seconds, or until warm. Stir in apple, raisins and walnuts. Set aside.

2 In large mixing bowl, combine remaining ingredients. Beat at medium speed of electric mixer for 3 minutes, or until blended, scraping bowl constantly. Stir in apple mixture. Spread equally in dishes. Shield ends of dishes with 2-inch (5 cm) strips of foil.

3 Place one loaf at a time in oven on inverted saucer. Microwave at 50% (Medium) for 6 minutes. Remove foil. Increase power to High. Microwave for 2 to 6 minutes, or until top springs back when touched lightly and no unbaked batter appears through bottom of dish. Let stand on counter for 5 to 10 minutes. Loosen edges. Invert on wire rack; cool. Wrap each loaf. Label and freeze no longer than 1 month.

4 To serve, unwrap and place one loaf on plate. Microwave at 50% (Medium) for 3½ to 5½ minutes, or until wooden pick can be easily inserted in center. Let stand for 5 minutes.

PINWHEEL BREAD SPREAD ▲

- ½ cup (125 mL) butter or margarine, softened
- 1 pkg. (3 oz./85 g) cream cheese, softened
- 1 cup (250 mL) powdered sugar
- ¼ cup (50 mL) chocolate fudge topping
- Chocolate shot (optional)

One 6-inch (15 cm) roll

1 In small mixing bowl, blend butter and cream cheese. Reserve ¼ cup (50 mL) of mixture in separate bowl. Add powdered sugar to larger portion of butter mixture. Mix until smooth.

2 Line baking sheet with wax paper. Spread cream cheese and sugar mixture on baking sheet, forming 6 × 9-inch (15 × 23 cm) rectangle, about ¼ inch (5 mm) thick. Chill 15 minutes.

3 Blend topping into reserved ¼ cup (50 mL) butter mixture. Spread fudge mixture evenly over chilled sugar layer. Chill 1 hour to firm.

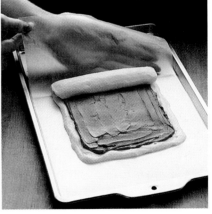

4 Starting on short side, lift paper and roll until layer begins to roll tightly, enclosing fudge layer. Lift and peel back paper while rolling, until roll is complete. Sprinkle with chocolate shot. Chill at least 2 hours before slicing. Store covered in refrigerator no longer than 2 weeks. Slice to serve.

Mocha Spread: *Follow recipe above, except blend 1 teaspoon (5 mL) instant coffee with 1 teaspoon (5 mL) hot water and add to fudge-butter mixture.*

BEVERAGES

PINK ZINGER PUNCH

- 1 can (8 oz./220 g) unsweetened pineapple slices, drained (reserve juice)
- 1 quart (1 L) strawberry-apple juice, well chilled
- 2 cups (500 mL) red-colored herbal tea, well chilled
- 2 cups (500 mL) sparkling water, well chilled

8 to 10 servings

1 Cut pineapple rings into quarters and freeze on a baking sheet.

2 At serving time, combine reserved pineapple juice, strawberry-apple juice, tea and sparkling water in a punch bowl. Stir gently. Add frozen pineapple before serving.

Helpful Hint: *Other fruits, such as strawberries or apple slices, can be frozen and added to punch before serving.*

HOT BLOODY MARY

- 1¾ cups (425 mL) tomato juice
- 2 teaspoons (10 mL) lemon juice
- ¾ teaspoon (4 mL) Worcestershire sauce
- ¼ teaspoon (1 mL) celery salt
- ⅛ teaspoon (0.5 mL) red pepper sauce
- 2 tablespoons (25 mL) vodka
- Freshly ground pepper
- Celery stalks

2 servings

1 In 4-cup (1 L) measure, combine tomato juice, lemon juice, Worcestershire sauce, celery salt and red pepper sauce. Cover with plastic wrap. Microwave at High for 3 to 4½ minutes, or until mixture is hot, stirring once.

2 Stir in vodka. Divide evenly between 2 mugs. Garnish each drink with pepper and celery stalk.

MEXICAN HOT CHOCOLATE

- ⅔ cup (150 mL) sugar
- ½ cup (125 mL) unsweetened cocoa
- 2 teaspoons (10 mL) ground cinnamon
- ½ cup (125 mL) hot water
- 4 cups (1 L) milk
- 1 teaspoon (5 mL) vanilla extract
- Prepared whipped topping
- Sliced almonds

4 to 6 servings

1 In 6-cup (1.5 L) measure, combine sugar, cocoa and cinnamon. Add hot water. Mix well. Cover. Microwave at High for 1 to 2 minutes or until mixture is hot, stirring once. Blend in milk.

2 Cover. Microwave at High for 7 to 10 minutes, or until mixture is hot but not boiling, stirring 2 or 3 times. Add vanilla. Serve hot, topped with whipped topping and almonds.

HOT PINEAPPLE PUNCH

- 1 can (46 oz./1,360 mL) pineapple juice
- 1 small orange, thinly sliced
- ¼ cup (50 mL) butter or margarine
- 1 to tablespoons (15 to 25 mL) sugar
- 1 teaspoon (5 mL) rum extract
- ½ teaspoon (2 mL) ground cardamom
- Toasted coconut (optional)

10 to 12 servings

1 In 8-cup (2 L) measure, combine all ingredients, except coconut. Cover with plastic wrap. Microwave at High for 10 to 15 minutes, or until mixture is hot, stirring once or twice.

2 Sprinkle each serving with toasted coconut before serving.

APPETIZERS

FINGER FOOD

STUFFED MUSHROOMS *(Opposite, right)*

Per Recipe

- 8 oz. fresh mushrooms, cleaned and stems removed (reserve)

Classic

- Chopped mushroom stems
- 1 small onion, finely chopped
- 2 tablespoons (25 mL) butter or margarine
- 1 tablespoon (15 mL) snipped fresh parsley
- 1/3 cup (75 mL) seasoned dry bread crumbs
- 1/4 teaspoon (1 mL) salt
- 1/8 teaspoon (0.5 mL) garlic powder

Place mushroom stems, onion and butter in small bowl. Microwave at High for 1½ to 2½ minutes, or until mushrooms are tender. Stir in remaining ingredients. Spoon filling into mushrooms.

Spinach

- 1 pkg. (12 oz./336 g) frozen spinach soufflé
- 1/4 cup (50 mL) shredded Cheddar cheese
- 1/4 cup (50 mL) seasoned dry bread crumbs
- 1/4 teaspoon (1 mL) dried thyme leaves
- 1/4 teaspoon (1 mL) salt

Unwrap frozen soufflé and cut in half with sharp knife. Rewrap one half and return to freezer. In small bowl, microwave remaining soufflé half at 50% (Medium) for 2 to 5 minutes, or until defrosted, stirring once. Mix in remaining ingredients. Spoon filling into mushroom caps.

Ham & Cream Cheese

- Chopped mushroom stems
- 1 pkg. (3 oz./85 g) cream cheese, softened
- 1/2 cup (125 mL) finely chopped fully cooked ham
- 1/4 cup (50 mL) chopped almonds

Place mushroom stems in small bowl. Cover with plastic wrap. Microwave at High for 1½ to 2 minutes. Add cream cheese and microwave at High for 15 to 30 seconds, or until softened, before adding remaining ingredients. Spoon filling into mushroom caps.

About 12 servings

To Microwave Stuffed Mushrooms:

Arrange stuffed mushrooms on paper-towel-lined plate, with larger mushrooms toward outside. Microwave at High for 1½ to 3½ minutes, or until hot, rotating plate twice.

BARBECUED MEATBALLS

- 1/4 lb. (110 g) ground beef
- 1 tablespoon (15 mL) seasoned bread crumbs
- 1/2 teaspoon (2 mL) dried parsley flakes
- 1/2 teaspoon (2 mL) dried minced onion
- 1/8 teaspoon (0.5 mL) salt
- 1/8 teaspoon (0.5 mL) pepper
- 1/2 teaspoon (2 mL) lemon juice
- 1/2 cup (125 mL) barbecue sauce, divided

1 In small mixing bowl, mix ground beef, bread crumbs, parsley flakes, minced onion, salt, pepper, lemon juice and 2 teaspoons (10 mL) barbecue sauce. Shape by heaping teaspoonfuls into 10 meatballs.

2 Place in 8-inch (2 L) square dish. Add remaining barbecue sauce. Cover with wax paper. Microwave at High for 2 to 3½ minutes, or until meatballs are firm and no longer pink inside, stirring sauce and rearranging meatballs after half the time. Skim fat before serving. Refrigerate leftover meatballs no longer than 2 days.

2 servings

COMPANY CANAPÉS *(Above, left)*

Per Recipe
- 24 crisp crackers

Hawaiian Chicken
- 3 slices cooked bacon, crumbled
- 1 can (5 oz./140 g) chunk chicken
- ¼ cup (50 mL) drained crushed pineapple
- ¼ cup (50 mL) chopped walnuts
- ¼ teaspoon (1 mL) salt
- Dash pepper

Far-East Tuna
- 1 can (3¼ oz./92 g) tuna, drained
- 3 tablespoons (50 mL) mayonnaise
- 3 tablespoons (50 mL) finely chopped pecans
- 3 tablespoons (50 mL) drained crushed pineapple
- ⅛ teaspoon (0.5 mL) curry powder

Midwest Bacon & Cheese
- 6 slices cooked bacon, crumbled
- ½ cup (125 mL) shredded Cheddar cheese
- 3 tablespoons (50 mL) mayonnaise
- 1 teaspoon (5 mL) dried parsley flakes
- 1 teaspoon (5 mL) caraway or poppy seed (optional)

Seashore Crab
- 1 pkg. (3 oz./85 g) cream cheese, softened
- 1 can (6 oz./170 g) crab meat, drained and rinsed, cartilage removed
- 2 teaspoons (10 mL) Worcestershire sauce
- ½ teaspoon (2 mL) lemon juice
- 2 tablespoons (15 mL) sliced green onion

2 dozen canapés

To Prepare Canapés:

In small bowl, combine ingredients. Spread one half of mixture evenly on 12 crisp crackers. Arrange on paper plate or paper-towel-lined plate. Microwave at High for 30 seconds to 1 minute, or until topping is hot, rotating plate once. Repeat with remaining mixture and crackers.

219

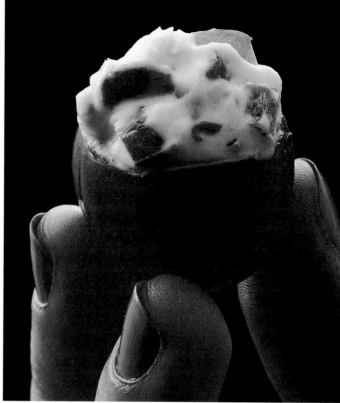

CHICKEN & BROCCOLI BITES

- 1 boneless, skinless whole chicken breast
- ⅓ cup (75 mL) teriyaki sauce
- 1 tablespoon (15 mL) vegetable oil
- ½ teaspoon (2 mL) grated orange peel
- ⅛ teaspoon (0.5 mL) ground cinnamon
- ⅛ teaspoon (0.5 mL) ground coriander
- ⅛ teaspoon (0.5 mL) pepper
- 12 oz. (330 g) fresh broccoli

4 servings

1 Pound chicken breast between 2 sheets of plastic wrap to about ¼-inch (5 mm) thickness. Cut into about 1¼-inch (3 cm) square pieces.

2 Place chicken pieces in small mixing bowl. Set aside. In 1-cup (250 mL) measure, combine teriyaki, oil, orange peel, cinnamon, coriander and pepper. Mix well. Pour over chicken pieces. Toss to coat. Cover and refrigerate at least 2 hours.

3 Drain chicken, discarding marinade. Arrange chicken pieces in single layer in 9-inch (2.5 L) square baking dish. Set aside.

4 Cut broccoli into flowerets. Skewer 1 broccoli floweret with wooden pick. Skewer chicken piece so broccoli portion is on top. Picks will stand upright. Cover dish with plastic wrap.

5 Microwave at High for 4½ to 6 minutes, or until chicken is firm and no longer pink in center and broccoli is tender-crisp, rearranging once.

CHEESY TOMATO PUFFS

- ¼ lb. (110 g) bacon, cut into ¼-in. (5 mm) widths
- 8 oz. (227 g) cream cheese
- 1 teaspoon (5 mL) baking powder
- ½ teaspoon (2 mL) minced onion
- 1 egg yolk
- ⅓ cup (75 mL) finely chopped green pepper
- 2 to 3 pints (1 to 1.5 L) firm cherry tomatoes

About 50 puffs

1 Microwave bacon in 2-quart (2 L) covered casserole at High for 9 minutes, or until crispy, stirring every 3 minutes. Drain well.

2 Place cream cheese in casserole with bacon; microwave at High for 30 seconds to soften. Add baking powder, onion and egg yolk to cheese and bacon. With electric mixer, cream contents of casserole until well blended and fluffy. Stir in green pepper.

3 Cut tops from tomatoes and scoop out seeds. Fill with cheese mixture. Place 10 to 12 close together in ring on large dinner or pie plate lined with paper towel. Place 3 or 4 in center of ring.

4 Microwave at 50% (Medium) for 1 to 2 minutes, or until cheese is just dry on surface, rotating ¼ turn every 30 seconds. Serve warm.

FETA & PEPPER APPETIZER PIZZAS ▶

- 1 tablespoon (15 mL) snipped fresh parsley
- 2 teaspoons (10 mL) olive oil
- 1 teaspoon (5 mL) dried basil leaves
- 1 clove garlic, minced
- ½ teaspoon (2 mL) dried rosemary leaves, crushed
- ½ cup (125 mL) green pepper strips (1 × ¼-inch/2.5 cm × 5 mm strips)
- ½ cup (125 mL) red pepper strips (1 × ¼-inch/2.5 cm × 5 mm strips)
- 2 tablespoons (25 mL) chopped onion
- 2 whole wheat pitas (4-inch/ 10 cm)
- 1 tablespoon (15 mL) feta cheese, crumbled

4 servings

1 In small bowl, combine parsley, oil, basil, garlic and rosemary. Mix well. Set aside.

2 In 1-quart (1 L) casserole, place peppers and onion. Cover. Microwave at High for 4 to 5 minutes, or until peppers are tender. Set aside.

3 Cut each pita in half crosswise to form 2 rounds. Toast pita halves. Place toasted halves on 10-inch (25 cm) round platter. Brush each evenly with parsley mixture. Spoon pepper mixture evenly onto pita halves. Sprinkle with feta cheese. Microwave at High for 30 seconds to 1 minute, or until cheese is melted and crisps are warm.

GARLIC-CHIVE POTATO CRISPS

- 1 russet potato
- 2 teaspoons (5 mL) snipped fresh chives
- ⅛ teaspoon (0.5 mL) garlic powder
- ⅛ teaspoon (0.5 mL) salt

About 24 crisps

1 Heat oven to 425°F (220°C). Spray 15½ × 10½-inch (40 × 25 cm) jelly roll pan with nonstick vegetable cooking spray. Set aside.

2 Using thin slicing blade of food processor or very sharp knife, cut potato into ⅛-inch (2.5 mm) slices. Place slices in bowl of ice water to prevent darkening. Let stand for 15 minutes.

3 Remove potato slices from water and blot dry with paper towels. Arrange slices in single layer on prepared pan.

4 Sprinkle chives, garlic powder and salt evenly over potato slices. Bake for 15 to 20 minutes, or until crisps are brown, rearranging twice during baking and removing as they brown. Place browned crisps on cooling rack. Cool completely.

CHICKEN-PINEAPPLE CANAPÉS ❄ FREEZE AHEAD

- 1½ lbs. (675 g) boneless, skinless chicken breasts
- ⅓ cup (75 mL) finely chopped celery
- ⅓ cup (75 mL) finely chopped green pepper
- 3 tablespoons (50 mL) finely chopped onion
- 1 tablespoon (15 mL) butter or margarine
- 1 pkg. (8 oz./227 g) cream cheese
- 1 can (8¼ oz./230 g) crushed pineapple, drained
- ⅓ cup (75 mL) chopped cashews
- 1 tablespoon (15 mL) snipped fresh parsley
- 1½ teaspoons (7 mL) lemon juice
- ¼ teaspoon (1 mL) salt
- Dash pepper
- 15 slices wheat and white bread
- Paprika (optional)

About 5 dozen canapés

1 Place chicken breasts in 1½-quart (1.5 L) casserole. Cover. Microwave at High for 8 to 10 minutes, or until chicken is no longer pink in center. Cool. Discard cooking liquid. Chop into small pieces.

2 In medium mixing bowl, combine celery, green pepper, onion and butter. Microwave at High for 2 to 4 minutes, or until vegetables are tender-crisp. Add cream cheese. Microwave at High for 20 to 30 seconds, or until cream cheese softens. Stir in chicken, pineapple, cashews, parsley, lemon juice, salt and pepper.

3 Trim crusts from bread. Spread filling on bread. With knife or small cookie cutter, cut each slice of bread into four shapes. Sprinkle with paprika. Freeze on tray until firm. Wrap, label and freeze no longer than 3 weeks.

4 To serve, unwrap 12 canapés; arrange in circle on large plate. Microwave at 50% (Medium) for 4½ to 6½ minutes, or until defrosted but still cold, rotating and rearranging canapés once. Let stand for 5 minutes. Repeat, as desired.

▲ HAM & SWISS CANAPÉS ❄ FREEZE AHEAD

- 1 container (8 oz./220 g) Swiss almond cheese food
- 1 can (4½ oz./127 g) deviled ham
- 1½ teaspoons (7 mL) chopped chives
- Dash cayenne
- 36 to 48 almond slices (optional)
- 36 to 48 crackers

3 to 4 dozen canapés

1 Place cheese food in small bowl or 1-quart (1 L) casserole. Microwave at High for 30 to 45 seconds, or until softened. Mix in deviled ham, chives and cayenne.

2 Using pastry bag and number 6 star tip, pipe canapé mixture onto wax-paper-lined tray, making rosettes about 1¼ inches (3 cm) in diameter. (If mixture is too soft, refrigerate until it reaches firmer consistency.) Top each rosette with almond slice. Freeze until firm. Package in freezer containers. Label and freeze no longer than 1 month.

3 To serve, remove 12 rosettes from container and center on 12 crackers. Arrange in circle on paper-towel-lined plate. Microwave at 30% (Medium Low) for 45 seconds to 2 minutes, or until rosettes are softened, rotating plate every 30 seconds. Let stand for 1 to 2 minutes. Repeat, as desired.

CHEESE & BASIL PEPPER SPIRALS

- 1 red bell pepper
- 2 oz. (60 g) cream cheese, softened
- ½ teaspoon (2 mL) dried basil leaves
- ⅛ teaspoon (0.5 mL) garlic powder
- Dash cayenne
- Melba rounds (optional)
- Cucumber slices (optional)

About 24 spirals

1 Place red pepper on baking sheet. Place under conventional broiler 4 to 5 inches (10 to 12 cm) from heat. Broil for 15 to 18 minutes, or until skin of pepper blisters and darkens, turning several times. (Skin may blacken in some areas.)

2 Place pepper in brown paper bag, using tongs. Roll top down tightly. Let pepper sweat for 15 minutes in bag. Remove pepper from bag. Using thin-bladed knife, peel off skin, working in sections from top to bottom.

3 Cut peeled pepper in half lengthwise. Remove core and seeds. Make tiny slits in bottom of each pepper half so halves lie flat. Place on paper towels. Gently pat dry. Set aside.

4 Place cheese in small bowl. Stir in basil, garlic powder and cayenne. Divide cream cheese mixture in half.

5 Place each pepper half on sheet of plastic wrap. Spread each pepper half evenly with cheese mixture. Starting with longer side, roll up peppers, jelly roll style, using plastic wrap to lift and roll.

6 Wrap each roll-up in plastic wrap. Chill 2 hours, or until firm. Slice each roll-up into 12 spirals. Serve spirals on melba toast rounds or cucumber slices.

223

DIPS & SPREADS

BACON & HORSERADISH DIP

- 1 slice bacon
- 1 pkg. (3 oz./85 g) cream cheese
- 1 tablespoon (15 mL) yogurt or sour cream
- 2 teaspoons (10 mL) prepared horseradish
- 1 green onion, chopped

⅓ cup (75 mL) dip

1 Place bacon on paper-towel-lined plate. Microwave at High for 1 to 1½ minutes, or until brown. Crumble.

2 Place cream cheese in 10-ounce (300 mL) custard cup or small bowl. Reduce power to 50% (Medium). Microwave for 30 to 60 seconds, or until softened. Blend in yogurt, horseradish and green onion. Sprinkle with bacon. Refrigerate no longer than 2 days.

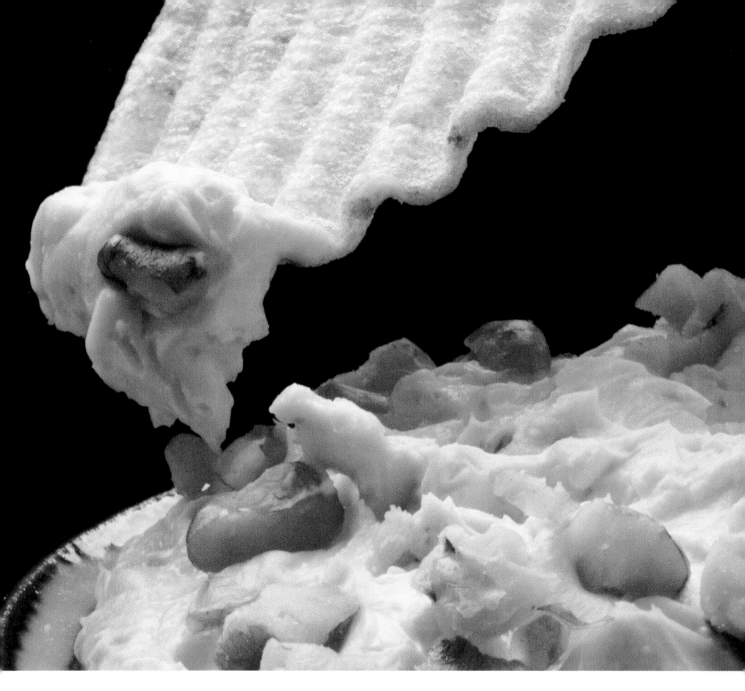

ONION DIP

- 1 pkg. (3 oz./85 g) cream cheese
- 1 tablespoon (15 mL) yogurt or sour cream
- ½ teaspoon (2 mL) dried onion flakes
- ¼ teaspoon (1 mL) instant beef bouillon granules
- 1 teaspoon (5 mL) water
- ¼ teaspoon (1 mL) Worcestershire sauce
- 1 tablespoon (15 mL) chopped walnuts or pecans

⅓ cup (75 mL) dip

1 Place cream cheese in 10-ounce (300 mL) custard cup or small bowl. Microwave at 50% (Medium) for 30 to 60 seconds, or until softened. Blend in yogurt.

2 In separate custard cup, mix onion flakes, bouillon granules and water. Cover with plastic wrap. Increase power to High. Microwave for 30 seconds, stirring to dissolve bouillon. Stir into cream cheese mixture. Add Worcestershire sauce. Sprinkle with chopped nuts. Serve hot or cold with chips, or celery and carrot sticks, if desired. Refrigerate dip no longer than 2 days.

Chili Dip: *Substitute 1 tablespoon (15 mL) chili sauce and ⅛ teaspoon (0.5 mL) chili powder for onion flakes, bouillon granules, water, Worcestershire sauce and nuts. Blend together. Chill or serve at room temperature.*

◄ CHUNKY SALSA

- 1 cup (250 mL) chopped onion
- 1 clove garlic, minced
- 1 can (15 oz./425 g) no-salt whole tomatoes, cut up
- 1 can (8 oz./227 g) no-salt tomato sauce
- 1 can (4.5 oz./127 g) diced green chilies, rinsed and drained
- 1 teaspoon (5 mL) ground cumin
- ½ teaspoon (2 mL) dried oregano leaves
- ¼ teaspoon (1 mL) dried crushed red pepper

26 servings,
2 tablespoons (25 mL) each

1 In 2-quart (2 L) casserole, combine onion and garlic. Cover. Microwave at High for 2 to 4 minutes, or until onion is tender-crisp.

2 Stir in remaining ingredients. Microwave, uncovered, at High for 8 to 11 minutes, or until hot and flavors are blended, stirring once or twice. Chill at least 4 hours before serving.

CHÈVRE & SUN-DRIED TOMATO PÂTÉ

- ¼ cup (50 mL) low-fat cottage cheese
- 2 oz. (60 g) chèvre (goat cheese)
- 3-oz. (90 g) jar sun-dried tomatoes, drained and chopped
- ⅛ teaspoon (0.5 mL) dried thyme
- 8 large slices French bread
- 2 tsp. (10 mL) minced parsley

8 servings

1 Drain cottage cheese and purée until smooth.

2 In medium mixing bowl, mix together cottage cheese, chèvre, tomatoes and thyme.

3 Lightly toast French bread. Spread with cheese-tomato mixture. Sprinkle with parsley before serving.

MEXICAN BEAN DIP

- ½ cup (125 mL) chopped onion
- ⅓ cup (75 mL) chopped green pepper
- 1 clove garlic, minced
- ½ teaspoon (2 mL) ground cumin
- ¼ teaspoon (1 mL) pepper
- 1 can (15 oz./425 g) garbanzo beans, rinsed and drained
- 2 tablespoons (25 mL) water
- ½ cup (125 mL) seeded and chopped fresh tomato

26 servings, 1 tablespoon (15 mL) each

1 In 1-quart (1 L) casserole, combine onion, green pepper, garlic, cumin and pepper. Stir. Cover. Microwave at High for 2 to 4½ minutes, or until tender, stirring once.

2 In food processor or blender, process vegetable mixture, beans and water until smooth. Return to casserole. Stir in tomato. Cover. Microwave at High for 2 to 3 minutes, or until hot, stirring once. Serve as a dip or spread.

PARMESAN-BACON SPREAD ❄ FREEZE AHEAD

- 12 slices bacon
- 1 cup (250 mL) unsalted butter
- 1 pkg. (8 oz./227 g) cream cheese
- ⅔ cup (150 mL) grated Parmesan cheese
- 3 tablespoons (50 mL) chopped green onion
- 8 to 10 drops red pepper sauce

2 spreads,
1¼ cups (300 mL) each

1 Place bacon in 2 to 3-quart (2 to 3 L) casserole. Microwave at High for 8 to 12 minutes, or until crisp. Drain on paper towels. Crumble; set aside.

2 In medium bowl, combine butter and cream cheese. Microwave at 50% (Medium) for 30 to 60 seconds, or until butter softens. Mix in crumbled bacon and remaining ingredients.

3 Line two small bowls with foil, flattening wrinkles. If desired, lightly butter foil and coat with additional Parmesan cheese and paprika. Spoon cheese-bacon mixture into foil. Press into bowls. Freeze until firm. Remove spreads from bowls. Wrap separately, label and freeze no longer than 1 month.

4 To serve, unwrap one package and place on plate. Microwave at 30% (Medium Low) for 1½ to 3 minutes, or until slightly defrosted, taking care not to melt edge, and rotating 2 or 3 times. Let stand for 10 to 15 minutes. Serve with crackers, if desired.

HERBED GARLIC & ALMOND SPREAD

- 1 cup (250 mL) fresh white bread crumbs
- ¼ cup (50 mL) lemon juice
- ½ cup (125 mL) blanched almonds
- 1 to 2 tablespoons (15 to 25 mL) minced garlic
- ¼ to ½ teaspoon (1 to 2 mL) salt
- ¼ cup (50 mL) olive oil
- 1 teaspoon (5 mL) prepared mustard or horseradish
- ¼ cup (50 mL) minced fresh parsley, cilantro or basil (optional)
- 8 to 10 slices whole-grain bread, toasted
- Tomato slices, cucumber slices and watercress

8 to 10 servings

1 Place bread crumbs in a small bowl. Sprinkle with lemon juice and let soak a few minutes, until juice is absorbed.

2 Meanwhile, combine almonds, garlic and salt in a food processor and grind to a coarse meal. Add lemon-soaked bread crumbs to mixture in food processor and process well.

3 Add oil a few teaspoons at a time, continuing to process. Add mustard or horseradish and fresh herbs. Blend until the mixture becomes a thick paste (adding water to thin, if necessary). To serve, spread on bread and top with tomato, cucumber and watercress.

Helpful Hint: *To blanch almonds, bring 2 cups (300 mL) water to a boil. Add almonds and simmer for 2 minutes, or until skins become soft. Drain in a strainer, then rinse with cold water. Squeeze almonds out of their skins and discard skins.*

INDIAN FRUIT DIP PLATTER ►

- 1 cup (250 mL) flaked coconut
- 2 pkgs. (8 oz./227 g each) cream cheese, cut into 1-inch (2.5 cm) cubes
- 1 teaspoon (5 mL) grated orange peel
- ¾ to 1 teaspoon (4 to 5 mL) curry powder
- ⅓ cup (75 mL) chutney
- ¼ cup (50 mL) raisins
- ¼ cup (50 mL) salted peanuts
- 2 pears, cored and cut into ¼-inch (5 mm) slices
- 2 red apples, cored and cut into ¼-inch (5 mm) slices
- 2 tablespoons (25 mL) lemon juice
- 1 tablespoon (15 mL) water

8 to 10 servings

1 Spread coconut in an even layer in 9-inch (1 L) pie plate. Microwave at High for 3 to 5 minutes, or just until coconut is golden brown, tossing with fork after every minute. Set aside.

2 Place cream cheese cubes in bottom of 12-inch (30 cm) round platter. Sprinkle with orange peel and curry powder. Microwave at 50% (Medium) for 1½ to 3 minutes, or until cream cheese softens. Blend mixture together.

3 Spread evenly to within 1 or 2 inches (2.5 to 5 cm) from edge of platter. Spread chutney over cream cheese. Top with coconut, raisin and peanuts. Set aside.

4 Combine lemon juice and water in medium mixing bowl. Add fruit; toss to coat. Drain well. Arrange fruit slices around outside edge of platter to serve.

HOT HAM-N-CHEESE CRACKERS ▲

- 1 pkg. (3 oz./85 g) cream cheese
- ⅓ cup (75 mL) finely chopped boiled ham
- ⅓ cup (75 mL) shredded Monterey Jack cheese
- 2 tablespoons (25 mL) finely chopped green pepper
- ⅛ teaspoon (0.5 mL) salt
- Dash pepper
- 24 wheat crackers

2 dozen appetizers

1 In small mixing bowl, microwave cream cheese at High for 15 to 30 seconds, or until softened. Mix in ham, Monterey Jack cheese, green pepper, onion salt and pepper.

2 Spread about 1 teaspoon (5 mL) of ham and cheese mixture on each cracker. Arrange 12 crackers on paper-towel-lined plate. Microwave at High for 45 seconds to 1½ minutes, or until cheese melts, rotating plate once. Repeat with remaining crackers.

CHEESE

PORT WINE CHEESE BALL ▶

- 1 pkg. (3 oz./85 g) cream cheese
- 1½ cups (375 mL) grated sharp Cheddar cheese
- 1 tablespoon (15 mL) port wine
- Paprika
- 1 stick cinnamon
- 1 bay leaf

1 cheese ball

1 Place cream cheese in medium bowl. Microwave at 50% (Medium) for 30 to 60 seconds, or until softened. Blend in Cheddar cheese and port wine. Shape into ball. Wrap in wax paper or plastic wrap. Chill until slightly set, about 1 hour.

2 Form into apple shape. Sprinkle with paprika. Insert cinnamon stick for stem and bay leaf for leaf. Serve with crackers, apple and pear slices, or grape clusters, if desired.

PARTY CHEESE BALL

- ½ teaspoon (2 mL) olive oil
- ⅓ cup (75 mL) finely chopped green pepper
- ⅓ cup (75 mL) finely chopped green onions
- 2 cups (500 mL) shredded Cheddar cheese
- 1 pkg. (8 oz./227 g) light cream cheese, softened
- 4 oz. (125 g) blue cheese, crumbled
- 2 tablespoons (25 mL) unsalted sunflower seeds
- 1 tablespoon (15 mL) diced pimiento, drained
- 2 to 3 teaspoons (10 to 15 mL) prepared horseradish
- 1 clove garlic, minced
- ½ cup (125 mL) chopped pecans

20 servings

1 In small nonstick skillet, heat oil over medium heat. Add green pepper and onions. Sauté for 2 to 4 minutes, or until vegetables are tender-crisp. Remove from heat.

2 In large bowl, combine vegetable mixture and remaining ingredients, except pecans. Shape mixture into a ball. Wrap ball in plastic wrap. Chill 2 to 3 hours, or until firm. Just before serving, unwrap ball and roll evenly in pecans. Serve cheese ball with assorted raw vegetables and crackers, if desired.

(See photo, page 217)

Helpful Hint: *Rolling ball in pecans just before serving keeps pecans from softening in the refrigerator.*

BLUE CHEESE LOG ❄ FREEZE AHEAD

- 2 teaspoons (10 mL) butter or margarine
- 3 tablespoons (50 mL) sesame seed
- 2 pkgs. (8 oz./85 g each) cream cheese
- 1 pkg. (4 oz./125 g) blue cheese
- 1 cup (250 mL) shredded Cheddar cheese
- 1 tablespoon (15 mL) dry sherry
- 1 tablespoon (15 mL) Worcestershire sauce
- ¼ teaspoon (1 mL) onion powder
- ⅛ teaspoon (0.5 mL) garlic powder

Two 6-inch (15 cm) logs

1 Melt butter in pie plate at High for 30 to 45 seconds. Stir in sesame seed to coat. Microwave at High for 5 to 10 minutes, or until light brown, stirring every other minute. Set aside.

2 In 2-quart (2 L) casserole, place cream cheese, blue cheese and Cheddar cheese. Reduce power to 50% (Medium). Microwave for 1 to 2½ minutes, or until cheeses soften. Add sherry, Worcestershire sauce, onion powder and garlic powder. Beat with electric mixer until fluffy. Cover and refrigerate 1 to 2 hours, or until mixture can be handled easily.

3 Divide chilled mixture in half. Using wax paper, shape each half into a 6-inch (15 cm) log. Roll each log in toasted sesame seed. Wrap separately, label and freeze no longer than 1 month.

4 To serve, unwrap one log and place on plate. Microwave at 30% (Medium Low) for 2 to 4 minutes, or until wooden pick can be easily inserted in center, rotating plate every minute. Let stand for 10 to 15 minutes. Serve with crackers, if desired.

◄ CHEESE BALL OR LOG

Crock Cheese (see below)

Optional Coatings:

- 1 cup (250 mL) finely chopped walnuts plus ¼ cup (50 mL) snipped fresh parsley
- 1 cup (250 mL) finely crushed corn chips
- ¼ cup (50 mL) sesame seed, toasted

2 cheese balls or logs

1 Prepare Crock Cheese as directed, except do not pack in crock.

2 Divide cheese mixture in half. Shape into two 3½-inch (8 cm) diameter balls or two 6-inch (15 cm) logs. Roll in one of the coatings. Refrigerate at least 3 hours, or until firm.

CROCK CHEESE

- 1 lb. (450 g) Cheddar, Colby or Monterey Jack cheese
- ½ cup (125 mL) butter or margarine
- 1 pkg. (3 oz./85 g) cream cheese
- 2 tablespoons (25 mL) finely chopped onion
- 1 to 2 tablespoons (15 to 25 mL) butter or margarine, melted

1½ lbs. (750 g) cheese

1 Cut cheese, butter and cream cheese into 1-inch (2.5 cm) pieces. Place in medium bowl. Microwave at 30% (Medium Low) for 1 to 3½ minutes, or until slightly softened, stirring and rotating bowl every 30 seconds. Watch carefully to avoid melting.

2 Mash the cheese and the butter pieces with a fork or pastry blender until smooth. Stir in onion.

3 Pack mixture into cheese crock, serving dish, cellophane-lined clay pot, mug or pitcher.

4 Pour melted butter over cheese to seal crock (⅛-inch/2.5 mm layer). Refrigerate cheese no longer than 2 weeks.

Port Wine Cheese: *Add ¼ cup (50 mL) port or sherry wine, 2 tablespoons (25 mL) snipped fresh parsley, ¼ teaspoon (1 mL) freshly ground pepper and ⅛ teaspoon (0.5 mL) garlic powder to the softened cheese and butter mixture. Continue as directed.*

Pepper Cheese: *Add 1 tablespoon (15 mL) finely chopped fresh or canned jalapeño pepper and ½ teaspoon (2 mL) dried crushed red pepper flakes to the softened cheese and butter mixture. Continue as directed.*

Pepperoni Cheese: *Add ⅓ cup (75 mL) finely chopped pepperoni to the softened cheese and butter mixture. Continue as directed.*

MAIN DISHES

POULTRY

◄ROASTED WILD TURKEY

- 1 whole dressed wild turkey (8 to 10 lbs./4 to 5 kg)
- Salt and pepper to taste
- 2 stalks celery, cut into 3-inch (7.5 cm) pieces
- 1 medium onion, quartered
- 3 tablespoons (50 mL) vegetable oil
- 1 tablespoon (15 mL) all-purpose flour

6 to 8 servings

1 Heat oven to 350°F (180°C). Season cavity of turkey with salt and pepper. Place celery and onion in cavity of turkey. Tuck tips of wings behind turkey's back. Truss legs with kitchen string. Brush entire turkey with oil.

2 Place flour in large oven cooking bag. Hold bag closed at top and shake to coat. Place cooking bag in 13 × 9-inch (3.5 L) roasting pan

3 Place turkey in cooking bag; secure bag with nylon tie. Insert meat thermometer into thickest part of thigh through top of bag. Make six ½-inch (1.5 cm) slits in top of bag.

4 Roast turkey for 2 to 2½ hours, or until internal temperature reads 185°F (85°C). Remove turkey from bag. Let stand, tented with foil, for 20 minutes before carving.

FRESH FRUIT-STUFFED TURKEY

- 3-lb. (1.5 kg) boneless turkey breast

Stuffing:
- ½ cup (125 mL) chopped apple
- ½ cup (125 mL) chopped pear
- ½ small orange, peeled and chopped
- ¼ cup (50 mL) raisins
- ½ teaspoon (2 mL) ground cinnamon
- ⅛ teaspoon (0.5 mL) ground allspice
- ⅓ cup (75 mL) corn bread stuffing mix
- 2 teaspoons (10 mL) packed brown sugar
- ¼ teaspoon (1 mL) ground cinnamon

6 to 8 servings

1 Carefully pull apart turkey breast, separating breast halves. Place turkey skin-side-down. If necessary, cut slightly so breast lies flat, being careful not to cut all the way through. Set aside.

2 In medium mixing bowl, combine all stuffing ingredients. Mix well. Pack stuffing mixture down center of turkey breast. Reassemble breast, enclosing stuffing. Tie securely with string.

3 In small mixing bowl, combine brown sugar and cinnamon. Rub breast with brown sugar mixture.

4 Place breast skin-side-up in cooking bag. Secure bag loosely with nylon tie or string. Place bag in 9-inch (2.5 L) square baking dish. Microwave at 70% (Medium High) for 30 to 40 minutes, or until temperature reads 175°F (80°C), rotating dish 2 or 3 times. Let stand for 10 minutes before slicing.

CRANBERRY-STUFFED TURKEY TENDERLOINS

- ¾ cup (175 mL) frozen chopped cranberries, divided
- ½ cup (125 mL) sliced fresh mushrooms
- ¼ cup (50 mL) finely chopped onion
- 2 tablespoons (25 mL) plus 1 teaspoon (5 mL) packed brown sugar, divided
- 1 tablespoon (15 mL) dried parsley flakes, divided
- ½ teaspoon (2 mL) grated orange peel, divided
- ¼ teaspoon (1 mL) salt, divided
- 1 tablespoon (15 mL) butter or margarine
- 2 turkey tenderloins (about ¾ lb./330 g each)
- ⅓ cup (75 mL) orange juice
- 2 teaspoons (10 mL) cornstarch

4 to 6 servings

1 Combine ½ cup (125 mL) cranberries, the mushrooms, onion, 2 tablespoons (25 mL) brown sugar, 2 teaspoons (10 mL) parsley, ¼ teaspoon (1 mL) orange peel, ⅛ teaspoon (0.5 mL) salt and the butter in 1-quart (1 L) casserole. Cover and microwave at High for 2 to 3 minutes, or until mushrooms are tender, stirring once. Set aside.

2 Slit each tenderloin lengthwise to within ½ inch (1.5 cm) of edge to form pocket. Fill each tenderloin with half of cranberry mixture. Arrange in 9-inch (2.5 L) square baking dish, with openings toward center. Cover with wax paper. Microwave at 70% (Medium High) for 15 to 21 minutes, or until turkey is firm and no longer pink, rotating dish twice. Remove tenderloins to platter. Cover with foil to keep warm. Reserve cooking liquid.

3 Place orange juice in 2-cup (500 mL) measure. Stir in cornstarch, remaining 1 teaspoon (5 mL) brown sugar, 1 teaspoon (5 mL) parsley, ¼ teaspoon (1 mL) orange peel and ⅛ teaspoon (0.5 mL) salt. Mix well. Blend in reserved cooking liquid. Stir in remaining ¼ cup (50 mL) cranberries. Microwave at High for 3 to 4½ minutes, or until sauce is thickened and translucent, stirring twice. Serve sauce over turkey.

TURKEY PATTIES WITH CRANBERRY-NUT CHUTNEY

Patties:

- 1 lb. (450 g) ground turkey, crumbled
- 1 cup (250 mL) herb-seasoned stuffing mix
- ¼ cup (50 mL) snipped fresh parsley
- ¼ teaspoon (1 mL) salt
- ⅛ teaspoon (0.5 mL) pepper
- 1 egg, beaten

Chutney:

- 1 cup (250 mL) whole-berry cranberry sauce
- 1 can (8 oz/220 g) crushed pineapple in juice, drained
- 1 tablespoon (15 mL) packed brown sugar
- ¼ teaspoon (1 mL) salt
- ¼ teaspoon (1 mL) ground cinnamon
- ⅛ teaspoon (0.5 mL) ground cloves
- 1 tablespoon (15 mL) cider vinegar
- ½ cup (125 mL) chopped pecans or walnuts

4 servings

1 Grease shallow baking pan. Set aside. Heat oven to 375°F (190°C). In medium mixing bowl, combine all patty ingredients. Shape mixture into 4 patties, about ½ inch (1.5 cm) thick. Arrange in prepared baking pan. Bake for 25 to 30 minutes, or until meat is firm and no longer pink.

2 In 4-cup (1 L) measure, combine remaining ingredients, except pecans. Microwave at High for 4 to 5 minutes, or until mixture boils, stirring once. Stir in pecans. Serve chutney with turkey patties.

239

CIDER-SAUCED TURKEY BREAST

- 1 tablespoon (15 mL) all-purpose flour
- 3-lb. (1.5 kg) boneless, skinless whole turkey breast
- 1 medium onion, cut into 8 wedges
- 1½ cups (375 mL) apple cider, divided
- ¼ teaspoon (1 mL) ground cardamom
- ¼ teaspoon (1 mL) salt
- 1 tablespoon (15 mL) packed brown sugar
- 2 teaspoons (10 mL) cornstarch
- ¼ teaspoon (1 mL) ground cinnamon
- 2 Rome apples (8 oz./220 g each) sliced crosswise into ¼-inch (5 mm) rounds, seeds removed

16 servings

1 Place flour in large oven cooking bag. Hold bag closed at top and shake to coat. Place turkey breast and onion in bag. In 1-cup (250 mL) measure, combine ½ cup (125 mL) cider, the cardamom and salt. Mix well. Pour over turkey breast and onion. Secure bag with nylon tie. Make six ½-inch (1.5 cm) slits in neck of bag below tie.

2 Place bag in 8-inch (2 L) square baking dish. Microwave at High for 5 minutes. Microwave at 50% (Medium) for 32 to 55 minutes longer, or until internal temperature registers 175°F (80°C) in several places, turning once. Let stand in bag for 10 minutes.

3 In 2-quart (2 L) casserole, combine sugar, cornstarch and cinnamon. Blend in remaining 1 cup (250 mL) cider. Add apples. Stir gently to coat. Cover. Microwave at High for 6 to 11 minutes, or until sauce is thickened and translucent and apples are tender, stirring twice. Serve turkey with apples and sauce.

RASPBERRY-GLAZED TURKEY TENDERLOIN SLICES

- 2 turkey tenderloins (6 to 8 oz./165 to 220 g each)
- Cayenne
- 1½ teaspoons (7 mL) cornstarch
- ⅓ cup (75 mL) raspberry jelly
- 2 tablespoons (25 mL) blush wine
- 1 tablespoon (15 mL) catsup
- 1 clove garlic, minced
- ½ teaspoon (2 mL) cream-style horseradish

4 servings

1 Place tenderloins in 8-inch (2 L) square baking dish. Sprinkle lightly with cayenne. Cover with plastic wrap. Microwave at 70% (Medium High) for 10 to 16 minutes, or until turkey is firm and no longer pink, rearranging twice. Set aside.

2 Place cornstarch in 2-cup (500 mL) measure. Blend in remaining ingredients. Microwave at High for 1½ to 3 minutes, or until sauce is thickened and translucent, stirring after every minute.

3 Slice each tenderloin diagonally into 10 pieces. Arrange 5 pieces on each individual serving plate. Spoon sauce over tenderloin slices. Garnish with fresh raspberries, if desired.

CORNISH HEN & VEGETABLE PLATTER

- 2 Cornish game hens (18 oz./ 500 g each)
- 1 tablespoon (15 mL) butter or margarine
- 3 tablespoons (50 mL) seasoned dry bread crumbs
- 2 tablespoons (25 mL) Italian dressing
- ¼ teaspoon (1 mL) brown bouquet sauce
- 1 medium red pepper, cut into 1½-inch (3.5 cm) chunks
- 1 medium green pepper, cut into 1½-inch (3.5 cm) chunks
- 1 medium yellow squash, cut into 1½-inch (3.5 cm) chunks
- 1 small onion, cut into 8 wedges
- 2 tablespoons (25 mL) butter or margarine, cut up

2 servings

1 Gently lift and loosen skin from breast area of each Cornish hen. Set aside. In small bowl, microwave butter at High for 45 seconds to 1 minute, or until melted. Add bread crumbs, stirring to coat. Place stuffing mixture under loosened skin of hens. Secure legs together with string. Place hens breast-sides-up on 12-inch (30 cm) round microwavable platter. Set aside.

2 In small bowl, combine Italian dressing and bouquet sauce. Mix well. Brush hens lightly with mixture. Microwave hens at High for 17 to 20 minutes, or until legs move freely and juices run clear, rearranging hens once or twice, and brushing with glaze after half the time. (If desired, blot platter with paper towels to absorb cooking liquids.) Cover hens with foil. Set aside.

3 Combine remaining ingredients in 1½-quart (1.5 L) casserole. Cover and microwave at High for 6 to 7 minutes, or until vegetables are tender-crisp, stirring once. To serve, arrange vegetables around Cornish hens.

(See photo, page 235)

▲ LIME & CUMIN CORNISH GAME HENS

- ¼ cup (50 mL) dark corn syrup
- ½ to 1 teaspoon (2 to 5 mL) grated lime peel
- 2 tablespoons (25 mL) lime juice
- 1 teaspoon (5 mL) ground cumin, divided

- 4 Cornish game hens (24 oz./ 675 g each)
- ½ teaspoon (2 mL) dried oregano leaves
- ¼ teaspoon (1 mL) salt
- ⅛ teaspoon (0.5 mL) pepper

8 servings

1 Combine syrup, peel, juice and ½ teaspoon (2 mL) cumin in small bowl. Set aside.

2 Secure legs of hens together with string. Place hens in large resealable food-storage bag. Pour syrup mixture over hens. Refrigerate at least 2 hours, turning bag over once.

3 Heat oven to 350°F (180°C). Remove hens from marinade and arrange breast-side-up on rack in shallow roasting pan. Discard marinade. In small bowl, combine remaining ½ teaspoon (2 mL) cumin and remaining ingredients. Rub hens with mixture.

4 Bake for 45 minutes to 1 hour, or until internal temperature in thickest portions of thighs reads 175°F (80°C). To serve, cut hens in half lengthwise. Remove skin, if desired.

GAME BIRDS

FRUITY GARLIC-ROASTED PHEASANT

- ½ cup (125 mL) brandy or cognac, divided
- ⅓ cup (75 mL) raisins
- ⅓ cup (75 mL) dried cranberries
- 1 whole dressed pheasant (1½ to 2¼ lbs./675 g to 1 kg), skin on
- 1 clove garlic, minced
- Salt and pepper to taste
- 2 sprigs fresh sage
- 8 whole cloves garlic, peeled
- 1¼ cups (300 mL) dry red wine, divided
- 1 teaspoon (5 mL) honey

3 to 4 servings

1 In small bowl, combine ⅓ cup (75 mL) brandy, the raisins and cranberries. Let soak for several hours or overnight.

2 Heat oven to 375°F (190°C). Rinse pheasant and pat dry with paper towels. Rub surface of pheasant with minced garlic. Sprinkle surface and cavity with salt and pepper. Place sage sprigs in pheasant cavity, and truss pheasant. Place pheasant in small roasting pan. Arrange whole garlic cloves around pheasant. Pour 1 cup (250 mL) red wine and raisin mixture into pan around pheasant.

3 Roast pheasant for 50 minutes to 1 hour, or until meat is tender and juices run clear, basting occasionally with pan juices. Remove pheasant from oven, draining any juices in cavity of bird into pan. Place pheasant on serving platter and keep warm.

4 Place roasting pan over medium-high heat. Add remaining ¼ cup (50 mL) red wine and remaining brandy to pan, scraping bottom of pan to remove any browned bits. Bring to a boil. Boil for 5 to 6 minutes, or until liquid is reduced to desired thickness. Whisk in honey. Spoon sauce around pheasant on platter.

Helpful Hint: *To speed-soak raisins and cranberries, cover the bowl containing the brandy and fruit with plastic wrap. Microwave at High for 1 minute. Let stand for 30 minutes.*

SAVORY POT PIE ▶

Single Pie Crust Pastry:
- 1 cup (250 mL) all-purpose flour
- ¼ teaspoon (1 mL) salt
- ½ cup (125 mL) vegetable shortening
- 2 to 4 tablespoons (25 to 50 mL) cold water

Filling:
- 2 tablespoons (25 mL) butter or margarine
- ½ cup (125 mL) water
- 1 cup (250 mL) thinly sliced carrot

- 1 medium potato, cut into ¼-inch (5 mm) cubes
- ½ cup (125 mL) thinly sliced celery
- ½ cup (125 mL) chopped onion
- ½ cup (125 mL) frozen peas
- 2½ to 3 cups (625 to 750 mL) cut-up cooked pheasant, partridge or turkey
- 1 recipe Easy Velouté Sauce or Wild Mushroom Sauce (see below)
- 1 egg yolk, beaten

4 to 6 servings

1 Heat oven to 375°F (190°C). To prepare pastry, combine flour and salt in medium mixing bowl. Cut shortening into flour until particles resemble coarse crumbs or small peas. Sprinkle with cold water while tossing with fork, until particles are just moist enough to cling together. Shape into ball. Wrap in plastic wrap and refrigerate.

2 In medium saucepan, combine butter and water. Heat until butter melts. Add carrot; cover and cook over medium heat for 3 minutes. Add potato; cover and cook for 5 minutes longer, stirring twice. Add celery, onion and peas; cover and cook for 3 minutes, stirring once. Drain vegetable mixture. In medium mixing bowl, combine vegetable mixture, cooked meat and prepared sauce; stir well to mix. Transfer mixture to 1½-quart (1.5 L) casserole.

3 On lightly floured surface, roll out pastry slightly larger than top of casserole. Carefully place pastry on top of casserole. Turn edge of pastry under; flute edge, if desired. Brush pastry with beaten egg yolk. Cut a small hole in center of pastry to allow steam to escape. Bake for 30 to 35 minutes, or until golden brown.

EASY VELOUTÉ SAUCE

- 2 tablespoons (25 mL) butter or margarine
- 2 tablespoons (25 mL) all-purpose flour
- ¼ teaspoon (1 mL) salt
- ¾ cup (175 mL) game bird stock or chicken broth
- ¼ cup (50 mL) whipping cream or half-and-half

About 1 cup (250 mL) sauce

1 In small saucepan, melt butter over medium-low heat. Whisk in flour, salt and pepper. Blend in stock and cream.

2 Cook over medium heat, stirring constantly, for 5 to 7 minutes, or until sauce thickens and bubbles. Serve sauce warm.

Helpful Hint: *Serve this sauce with birds or small game. Create your own sauce variations by adding fresh herbs.*

WILD MUSHROOM SAUCE

- ½ ounce dried morels or other mushrooms (about ⅔ cup/150 mL)
- 1 cup (250 mL) warm water
- 2 tablespoons (25 mL) butter or margarine
- 2 tablespoons (25 mL) all-purpose flour
- ¼ teaspoon (1 mL) salt
- Dash white pepper
- Dash ground nutmeg
- ¼ cup (50 mL) whipping cream or half-and-half

About 1½ cups (375 mL) sauce

1 Break mushrooms into pieces. In small mixing bowl, combine mushrooms and water; stir. Let rehydrate for 15 minutes. Remove mushrooms with slotted spoon; set aside. Reserve ¾ cup (175 mL) soaking liquid.

2 In small saucepan, melt butter over medium-low heat. Stir in flour, salt, pepper and nutmeg. Blend in cream, reserved mushrooms and liquid. Cook over medium heat for 5 to 7 minutes, or until sauce thickens and bubbles. Serve sauce warm.

◄ ROAST GOOSE

- 1 tablespoon (15 mL) all-purpose flour
- 1 whole dressed goose (about 8 lbs./3.5 kg), skin on
- 1 cup (250 mL) dry red wine
- 1 cup (250 mL) water
- 1 pkg. (1 oz./30 g) onion soup mix

6 to 8 servings

1 Heat oven to 350°F (180°C). Add flour to large oven cooking bag; shake to distribute. Place cooking bag in large roasting pan. Rinse goose and pat dry with paper towels. Place goose in oven cooking bag.

2 In small mixing bowl, combine wine, water and soup mix. Pour mixture over goose in bag. Secure bag with tie. Insert meat thermometer into thickest part of goose breast through top of the bag. Make six ½-inch (1.5 cm) slits in top of bag.

3 Roast goose for 1½ to 2 hours, or until internal temperature reads 185°F (85°C). Remove goose from bag. Let stand, tented with foil, for 10 minutes before carving.

CREAMED PHEASANT & BISCUITS

- 7 cups (1.75 L) water
- 1 whole dressed pheasant (1½ to 2¼ lbs./750 g to 1 kg)
- 1 medium carrot, cut into 1-inch (2.5 cm) lengths
- 1 stalk celery, cut into 1-inch (2.5 cm) lengths
- 1 small onion, cut into 8 wedges
- 6 peppercorns
- 1 bay leaf
- ½ cup (125 mL) all-purpose flour
- 1 cup (250 mL) milk
- Salt and pepper to taste
- 6 buttermilk biscuits

6 servings

1 In 4-quart (4 L) saucepan, combine water, pheasant, carrot, celery, onion, peppercorns and bay leaf. Bring to a boil over high heat. Cover. Reduce heat to medium-low. Simmer for 45 minutes to 1 hour, or until pheasant is tender.

2 Remove pheasant from pot; set aside to cool slightly. Strain stock through fine-mesh sieve. Discard vegetables and bay leaf. Set 2 cups (500 mL) of stock aside. Reserve remaining stock for future use. Remove pheasant meat from bones; discard bones. Coarsely shred meat. Set aside.

3 Return reserved 2 cups (500 mL) stock to saucepan. Bring to a simmer over medium heat. Place flour in small mixing bowl. Blend milk into flour. Whisk milk mixture into stock saucepan. Stir in pheasant. Cook for 3 to 4 minutes, or until bubbly, stirring constantly. Add salt and pepper to taste. Serve creamed pheasant over split biscuits.

TRADITIONAL ROAST DUCK WITH DRESSING

- 1 teaspoon (5 mL) salt
- 1 teaspoon (5 mL) caraway seed, crushed
- ¼ teaspoon (1 mL) freshly ground pepper
- 1 medium onion, quartered
- 2 tablespoons (25 mL) butter, melted
- 2 whole dressed puddle ducks (1¼ to 1½ lbs./625 to 750 g each), skin on

Dressing:
- 6 cups (1.5 L) cubed dry bread (½-inch/1.5 cm cubes)
- 3 tablespoons (50 mL) butter or margarine
- 8 oz. (250 g) fresh mushrooms, sliced (3 cups/750 mL)
- 1 stalk celery, sliced (½ cup/125 mL)
- 1 small onion, chopped (½ cup/125 mL)
- 2 to 3 teaspoons (10 to 15 mL) poultry seasoning
- ½ teaspoon (2 mL) salt
- ¼ teaspoon (1 mL) dried thyme leaves
- ¼ teaspoon (1 mL) freshly ground pepper
- ¼ cup (50 mL) ready-to-serve chicken broth

4 servings

1 Heat oven to 400°F (200°C). In small bowl, combine salt, caraway seed and ¼ teaspoon (1 mL) pepper. Sprinkle mixture evenly over surface and in cavities of ducks. Place ducks breast-side-up in 12 × 8-inch (3 L) baking dish. Bake for 1 hour to 1 hour 15 minutes. Let ducks stand for 10 minutes before cutting.

2 Meanwhile, place bread cubes in large mixing bowl. Set aside. In 10-inch (25 cm) skillet, melt butter over medium heat. Add mushrooms, celery and onion. Cook for 3 to 5 minutes, or until vegetables are tender-crisp, stirring occasionally. Add vegetables, poultry seasoning, salt, thyme and pepper to bread cubes. Stir to combine. Add broth. Toss just until moistened.

3 Spray 1½-quart (1.5 L) casserole with nonstick vegetable cooking spray. Spoon dressing into casserole. Cover and bake for 40 to 45 minutes, or until very hot. Serve dressing with ducks.

Helpful Hint: *If desired, uncover dressing during last 15 minutes of baking to brown top.*

PORK

HAM SLICES WITH SWEET POTATOES & APPLES

- 2 cups (500 mL) peeled, cubed sweet potatoes (½-inch/1.5 cm cubes)
- 2 tablespoons (25 mL) butter or margarine
- ⅓ cup (75 mL) orange marmalade
- 2 tablespoons (25 mL) apple juice or water
- ¼ teaspoon (1 mL) salt
- ⅛ teaspoon (0.5 mL) ground nutmeg
- 1 medium green apple, cored and thinly sliced
- 4 slices fully cooked ham (3 to 4 oz./90 to 125 g each)

4 servings

1 In 10-inch (25 cm) square casserole, combine sweet potatoes and butter. Cover. Microwave at High for 7 to 10 minutes, or until potatoes are tender, stirring once. Set aside.

2 In small mixing bowl, combine marmalade, juice, salt and nutmeg. Pour over potatoes. Add apple slices. Microwave at High, uncovered, for 4 to 8 minutes, or until apples are tender and sauce has thickened, stirring once. Place ham slices on microwavable platter. Spoon sweet potato mixture over top. Microwave at High, uncovered, for 2 to 3 minutes, or until hot.

FRUITED PORK ROAST

- ¾ cup (175 mL) packed brown sugar, divided
- ¾ cup (175 mL) dried apricot halves, cut in half
- ½ cup (125 mL) dried prunes, cut in half and pitted
- ¾ cup (175 mL) hot water
- ¼ cup (50 mL) plus 2 tablespoons (25 mL) frozen orange juice concentrate, defrosted and divided
- 1 small onion, sliced
- ½ teaspoon (2 mL) ground ginger
- ¼ teaspoon (1 mL) salt
- ⅛ teaspoon (0.5 mL) pepper
- 1 tablespoon (15 mL) butter or margarine
- 3-lb. (1.5 kg) boneless pork loin roast

6 to 8 servings

1 In 1-quart (1 L) casserole, combine ½ cup (125 mL) brown sugar, the apricots, prunes, water, ¼ cup (50 mL) orange concentrate, the onion, ginger, salt and pepper. Microwave at High for 8 to 12 minutes, or until fruit is softened, stirring every 4 minutes. Set aside.

2 In small bowl, melt butter at High for 30 to 45 seconds. Stir in remaining ¼ cup (50 mL) brown sugar and 2 tablespoons (25 mL) concentrate.

3 Place roast fat-side-down on roasting rack. Spread with butter mixture. Microwave at High for 5 minutes. Reduce power to 50% (Medium). Microwave for 20 minutes.

4 Turn roast over. Insert meat thermometer. Spoon half of sauce over top. Microwave at 50% (Medium) for 20 to 25 minutes, or until internal temperature reaches 165°F (72°C). Spoon on remaining sauce. Let stand, tented loosely with foil, for 10 minutes, or until internal temperature reaches 170°F (76°C), checking in several places.

▲ CHERRIED HAM STEAK

- 1½-lb. (675 g) well-trimmed fully cooked bone-in lean ham steak, ¾ inch (2 cm) thick
- 2 cups (500 mL) fresh whole bing, Lambert or Rainier cherries, pitted
- ⅓ cup (75 mL) sugar
- ¼ cup (50 mL) orange juice
- 1 teaspoon (5 mL) grated lime peel
- ¼ cup (50 mL) lime juice
- 1 tablespoon (15 mL) plus 1 teaspoon (5 mL) cornstarch

4 servings

1 Place ham steak in 10-inch (25 cm) square casserole. Set aside.

2 In medium mixing bowl, combine remaining ingredients. Pour mixture over ham steak. Cover and microwave at High for 10 to 15 minutes, or until sauce is thickened and translucent, stirring sauce and rotating dish twice. Garnish with additional grated lime peel, if desired.

GLAZED HAM & SWEET POTATOES

- 1 can (23 oz./645 g) sweet potatoes (or yams) in syrup, drained and cut into 1-inch (2.5 cm) cubes
- 1 to 1¼ lb. (450 to 560 g) fully cooked, boneless ham slices, ½ inch (1.5 cm) thick
- ¼ cup (50 mL) maple syrup
- ¼ cup (50 mL) packed brown sugar
- ¼ teaspoon (1 mL) dry mustard
- Dash cloves

4 servings

1 Arrange sweet potatoes around edges of 12 × 8-inch (3 L) dish. Place ham slices in center, overlapping slightly to fit dish.

2 Combine remaining ingredients to make glaze; pour half over ham and sweet potatoes. Cover and microwave at High for 4 minutes.

3 Pour remaining glaze over ham and sweet potatoes. Microwave, uncovered, at High for 4 to 7 minutes, or until ham is hot.

PORK & CANDIED YAMS ▶

- 2 cups (500 mL) thin strips of cooked pork
- 1 tablespoon (15 mL) all-purpose flour
- 1 cup (250 mL) finely chopped apple
- 1 can (23 oz./645 g) yams in syrup, drained and cut into 1-inch (2.5 cm) cubes
- 1 tablespoon (15 mL) butter or margarine
- ¼ cup (50 mL) packed brown sugar
- ⅓ cup (75 mL) coarsely chopped pecans

4 servings

1 In 1-quart (1 L) casserole, toss pork with flour. Top with apple, then yams. Dot with butter. Sprinkle with sugar and pecans. Cover.

2 Microwave at High for 8 to 11 minutes, or until apples are tender and casserole is heated through, rotating dish ½ turn after half the time.

HAM & CHEESE RING ▶

- 6 slices white bread
- ¼ cup (50 mL) chopped onion
- 2 cups (500 mL) cooked ham, cut into ½-inch (1.5 cm) cubes
- 1 cup (250 mL) shredded Cheddar cheese
- 4 eggs
- 1 cup (250 mL) milk
- ½ teaspoon (2 mL) salt
- ⅛ teaspoon (0.5 mL) pepper
- ⅛ teaspoon (0.5 mL) dry mustard
- 2 teaspoons (10 mL) parsley flakes

4 to 6 servings

1 Cut bread into ½-inch (1.5 cm) cubes. Place ¾ of cubes in bottom of ring mold. Top with onion, ham, cheese and remaining bread.

2 In small mixing bowl, blend together eggs, milk, salt, pepper and mustard. Pour over layers; sprinkle with parsley. Cover. Refrigerate overnight.

3 To serve, microwave, uncovered, at 50% (Medium) for 23 to 28 minutes, or until set, rotating ½ turn after half the time. Let stand for 5 minutes.

VEGETABLES

STUFFED VEGETABLE PLATTER

Filling:

- 4 oz. (125 g) cream cheese
- 1 tablespoon (15 mL) snipped drained oil-pack sun-dried tomatoes
- 1 tablespoon (15 mL) shredded fresh Parmesan cheese
- 1 tablespoon (15 mL) snipped fresh chives

Vegetables:

- Hollowed-out cherry tomatoes
- Whole mushrooms, stems removed
- Celery stalks, cut into 2-inch (5 cm) lengths
- Snow pea pods, opened
- Baby carrots, steamed and sliced lengthwise

4 servings

1 In small mixing bowl, microwave cream cheese at High for 30 to 45 seconds, or until softened, stirring once. Stir in sun-dried tomatoes, Parmesan cheese and chives.

2 Spoon or pipe cheese mixture into one or more of desired vegetables. Garnish with additional snipped fresh chives, if desired.

Helpful Hint: *Cut a lengthwise wedge into each carrot. Spoon or pipe cheese mixture into wedges. Trim with sprigs of fresh parsley to simulate carrot tops.*

STEAMED VEGETABLE PLATTER WITH HERBED HOLLANDAISE

- 8 oz. (220 g) asparagus spears, trimmed to 6-inch (15 cm) lengths
- 1 medium yellow squash, diagonally sliced (1 cup/250 mL)
- 1½ cups (375 mL) cauliflowerets
- 5 oz. (140 g) baby carrots (1 cup/ 250 mL)
- ¾ cup (175 mL) plus 2 tablespoons (25 mL) water, divided
- 1 pkg. (1¼ oz./38 g) hollandaise sauce mix
- 1 tablespoon (15 mL) vegetable oil
- 2 teaspoons (10 mL) snipped fresh tarragon leaves

4 servings

1 Arrange asparagus spears in center of oval microwavable serving platter. Surround asparagus with squash slices. Encircle squash with cauliflower. Arrange carrots on edge of platter. Sprinkle with 2 tablespoons (25 mL) water. Cover with plastic wrap. Microwave at High for 8 to 10 minutes, or until vegetables are tender-crisp, rotating platter once or twice. Pierce plastic wrap with tip of knife to release steam. Let stand, covered, for 5 minutes.

2 Place sauce mix in medium mixing bowl. Blend in remaining ¾ cup (175 mL) water and the oil until smooth. Microwave at High for 4 to 5 minutes, or until sauce is thickened, stirring every minute. Stir in tarragon leaves. Serve hollandaise with vegetables.

(See photo, page 253)

▲ SPICY GLAZED CARROTS

- 1 pkg. (16 oz./450 g) frozen crinkle-cut carrots
- ¼ cup (50 mL) apricot preserves
- 2 tablespoons (25 mL) water
- ¼ teaspoon (1 mL) chili powder
- ¼ teaspoon (1 mL) salt
- ⅛ teaspoon (0.5 mL) sugar
- Dash cayenne

1 Combine all ingredients in 2-quart (2 L) saucepan.

2 Cover and cook over medium heat for 12 to 17 minutes, or until carrots are tender-crisp, stirring occasionally.

6 servings

▲ BEETS WITH SWEET & SOUR APPLES

- 2 cups (500 mL) sliced peeled fresh beets (1/8-inch/ 2.5 mm slices)
- 3/4 cup (175 mL) water
- 2 teaspoons (10 mL) olive oil
- 1 small onion, sliced and separated
- 1 medium Granny Smith apple, chopped (1 cup/ 250 mL)
- 2 tablespoons (25 mL) packed brown sugar
- 1 teaspoon (5 mL) white wine vinegar

4 servings

1 In 2-quart (2 L) saucepan, combine beets and water. Cover and cook over high heat for 10 to 12 minutes, or until beets are tender, stirring occasionally. Drain.

2 Meanwhile, heat oil in 10-inch (25 cm) nonstick skillet over medium heat. Add onion. Cook for 5 to 7 minutes, or until onion is lightly browned, stirring frequently. Stir in apple and sugar. Cook for 1 1/2 to 3 minutes, or until apple is heated through, stirring frequently. Stir in vinegar. Remove from heat. Serve apple mixture over sliced beets.

SAUTÉED CELERY WITH TOASTED ALMONDS

- 8 stalks celery, cut diagonally into 1 to 1 1/2-inch (2.5 to 3.5 cm) pieces
- 1/3 cup (75 mL) chopped green onion
- 2 tablespoons (25 mL) butter or margarine
- Dash garlic powder
- Dash pepper
- 1/2 teaspoon (2 mL) sugar
- 1/4 teaspoon (1 mL) salt
- Toasted Almonds (below)

4 to 6 servings

1 In 1 1/2-quart (1.5 L) casserole, combine celery, onion, butter, garlic powder and pepper. Cover and microwave at High for 6 minutes, or until crisp-tender, stirring after 3 minutes.

2 Stir in sugar and salt. Mix in toasted almonds.

Toasted Almonds:

- 1 tablespoon (15 mL) butter
- 1/4 cup (50 mL) slivered almonds

In pie plate, melt butter at High for 45 to 60 seconds. Stir in almonds. Microwave at High for 3 1/2 to 4 1/2 minutes, or until lightly browned, stirring once. Let stand for 5 minutes (almonds will become darker as they stand).

SAGE PARSNIPS ▶ & APPLES

- 1 tablespoon (15 mL) butter or margarine
- 2 medium red cooking apples, cored and thickly sliced (2 cups/ 500 mL)
- 2 teaspoons (10 mL) olive oil
- 2 cups (500 mL) sliced peeled parsnips
- 1 small onion, sliced and separated into rings
- 1 clove garlic, minced
- 1 teaspoon (5 mL) fennel seed
- 1 cup (250 mL) apple juice
- 1 cup (250 mL) ready-to-serve chicken broth
- 1 tablespoon (15 mL) snipped fresh sage leaves
- 1 tablespoon (15 mL) Dijon mustard
- 1 tablespoon (15 mL) sugar

8 servings

1 Heat butter over medium heat in 10-inch (25 cm) nonstick skillet. Add apples. Cook for 8 to 10 minutes, or until apples are golden brown, stirring occasionally. Transfer apples to serving dish. Cover to keep warm.

2 In same skillet, heat oil over medium heat. Add parsnips, onion, garlic and fennel. Cook for 6 to 8 minutes, or until parsnips are lightly browned, stirring frequently. Add juice, broth and sage. Bring to a boil over medium-high heat. Reduce heat to low. Cover. Simmer for 10 minutes. Using slotted spoon, add parsnip mixture to apples. Cover to keep warm.

3 Add mustard and sugar to same skillet. Bring to a boil over medium-high heat. Boil for 5 to 7 minutes, or until sauce is reduced by half and looks glossy. Pour over apple and parsnip mixture. Toss to coat. Serve immediately.

GARLIC GREEN BEANS

- 2 tablespoons (25 mL) butter or margarine
- 1 clove garlic, minced
- ¼ teaspoon (1 mL) salt
- ⅛ teaspoon (0.5 mL) pepper
- 2 cups (500 mL) fresh green beans

4 servings

1 In 2-quart (2 L) casserole, microwave butter at High for 45 seconds to 1 minute, or until melted. Add garlic, salt and pepper. Mix well.

2 Add green beans. Toss to coat. Cover and microwave at High for 6 to 10 minutes, or until beans are tender-crisp, stirring once.

(See photo of this recipe with Raspberry-glazed Turkey Tenderloin slices, page 241)

SLICED TOMATOES WITH GOAT CHEESE DRESSING PLATTER

- 8 ripe tomatoes
- 2 oz. (50 g) chèvre (goat cheese), crumbled
- ½ cup (125 mL) loosely packed fresh basil leaves
- 2 tablespoons (25 mL) pine nuts, lightly toasted
- 2 tablespoons (25 mL) white wine vinegar
- 2 tablespoons (25 mL) olive oil
- Freshly ground black pepper

8 servings

1 Slice tomatoes and arrange on serving platter.

2 In blender, combine goat cheese, basil, pine nuts and vinegar. Blend until smooth. With motor running, slowly add oil in thin stream. Blend until dressing thickens, about 3 minutes.

3 Spoon dressing over tomatoes (about 1 tablespoon/15 mL per tomato). Sprinkle with pepper.

▲ SAUTÉED PEPPERS IN TARRAGON VINAIGRETTE

Sauce:
- 2 tablespoons (25 mL) lemon juice
- 1 tablespoon (15 mL) cider vinegar
- 1 teaspoon (5 mL) sugar
- 1 teaspoon (5 mL) cornstarch
- 1 teaspoon (5 mL) ground cumin
- ½ teaspoon (2 mL) dried tarragon leaves

- ½ teaspoon (2 mL) salt
- ¼ teaspoon (1 mL) paprika
- ⅛ teaspoon (0.5 mL) cayenne
- 2 cups (500 mL) chopped red pepper (1-inch/2.5 cm cubes)
- 2 cups (500 mL) chopped green pepper (1-inch/2.5 cm cubes)
- 1 teaspoon (5 mL) olive oil

6 servings

1 Combine sauce ingredients in 1-cup (250 mL) measure. Set aside.

2 In 12-inch (30 cm) nonstick skillet, combine peppers and oil. Cook over medium heat for 7 to 9½ minutes, or until peppers are tender-crisp, stirring frequently. Stir in sauce. Cook for additional 30 to 45 seconds, or until sauce is thickened and peppers are coated, stirring constantly.

TOMATO-CUCUMBER ASPIC

- 1 envelope (0.25 oz./8 g) unflavored gelatin
- ½ cup (125 mL) cold water
- 1 can (12 oz./330 g) tomato juice
- 1 tablespoon (15 mL) frozen apple juice concentrate
- ½ teaspoon (2 mL) low-sodium instant beef bouillon granules
- ⅛ teaspoon (0.5 mL) pepper
- 1 bay leaf
- 1 cup (250 mL) peeled, seeded and chopped cucumber
- 2 tablespoons (25 mL) sliced green onion

5 servings, ½ cup (125 mL) each

1 In 1-cup (250 mL) measure, soften gelatin in cold water. Set aside.

2 In 4-cup (1 L) measure, combine tomato juice, apple juice concentrate, bouillon, pepper and bay leaf.

3 Microwave at High for 2½ to 5 minutes, or until boiling. Remove and discard bay leaf. Add softened gelatin mixture. Stir until gelatin dissolves. Chill until thickened but not set, about 2 hours.

4 Fold in cucumber and onion. Spray 3 to 4-cup (750 mL to 1 L) mold with nonstick vegetable cooking spray. Pour into prepared mold. Chill until set, about 2 hours.

5 To serve, dip mold into warm water for 30 seconds. Loosen edges and unmold onto serving plate.

SPICY PUMPKIN SOUP

- 2 teaspoons (10 mL) olive oil
- 2 medium carrots, chopped (1 cup/250 mL)
- 1 small onion, chopped (½ cup/125 mL)
- 1 stalk celery, chopped (½ cup/125 mL)
- ¼ cup (50 mL) water
- 2 tablespoons (25 mL) packed brown sugar
- 2 teaspoons (10 mL) ground coriander
- 1 teaspoon (5 mL) ground cumin
- ½ teaspoon (2 mL) ground allspice
- 2½ cups (625 mL) ready-to-serve chicken broth
- 1 can (15 oz./425 g) pumpkin
- 1 medium russet potato, peeled and cut into ½-inch (1.5 cm) cubes (1 cup/250 mL)
- Plain nonfat or low-fat yogurt (optional)
- Toasted pumpkin seeds (optional)

1 In 4-quart (4 L) saucepan, heat oil over medium heat. Add carrots, onion, celery and water. Cook for 6 to 8 minutes, or until vegetables are tender, stirring occasionally.

2 Stir in sugar, coriander, cumin and allspice. Cook for 2 minutes, stirring constantly. Stir in broth, pumpkin and potato. Bring to a boil. Reduce heat to low. Cover and simmer for 20 minutes to blend flavors.

3 Place soup in food processor or blender. Process until smooth. Return soup to saucepan. Bring just to a simmer over medium-low heat, stirring frequently. Garnish each serving with dollop of yogurt and sprinkle with pumpkin seeds.

Helpful Hint: *To toast pumpkin seeds, spread them on a baking sheet, and bake at 325°F (160°C) for 15 to 20 minutes, or until golden brown, stirring occasionally.*

6 servings

FIVE-SPICE SQUASH SOUP

- ½ cup (125 mL) chopped onion
- 2 tablespoons (25 mL) minced garlic
- 1 to 3 teaspoons (5 to 15 mL) grated gingerroot
- ⅓ cup (75 mL) dry sherry
- 1 tablespoon (15 mL) olive oil
- 4 cups (1 L) peeled, seeded and cubed butternut squash
- 2 cups (500 mL) vegetable broth
- 1 tablespoon (15 mL) lemon juice
- ½ teaspoon (2 mL) ground coriander
- ½ teaspoon (2 mL) ground nutmeg
- ¼ teaspoon (1 mL) ground cumin
- ¼ teaspoon (1 mL) ground cinnamon
- 1 tablespoon (15 mL) grated lemon rind

4 to 6 servings

1 In 4-quart (4 L) stockpot, sauté onion, garlic and gingerroot in sherry and oil over medium-high heat for 6 minutes, stirring frequently.

2 Add squash and broth. Cover. Bring to a boil over medium-high heat. Reduce heat to low. Simmer for 25 min. Remove from heat and let cool for 10 minutes.

3 Place soup in food processor or blender. Process until smooth. Stir in lemon juice, coriander, nutmeg, cumin and cinnamon. Garnish with lemon rind.

Helpful Hint: *If vegetables stick while sautéing in step 1, add a small amount of broth to stockpot.*

▲ ROASTED GINGER SQUASH

- 1 butternut squash (2½ lbs./ 1.25 kg), peeled, halved, seeded and cut into 8 pieces
- 1 tablespoon (15 mL) grated orange peel
- 1 cup (250 mL) fresh orange juice
- 1 tablespoon (15 mL) grated gingerroot
- Freshly ground pepper (optional)
- Salt (optional)

8 servings

1 Heat oven to 400°F (200°C). Place squash pieces in 13 × 9-inch (3.5 L) baking pan. In small mixing bowl, combine peel, juice and gingerroot. Pour over squash. Cover with foil. Bake for 45 to 55 minutes, or until squash is tender.

2 Uncover. Baste squash with cooking liquid. Bake, uncovered, for additional 15 minutes. Sprinkle squash lightly with pepper and salt. Spoon cooking liquid over squash, if desired.

POTATOES & DRESSINGS

▲ TWICE-BAKED POTATOES

- 4 medium russet potatoes (8 to 10 oz./250 to 300 g each)
- ¼ cup (50 mL) milk
- ½ cup (125 mL) sour cream
- ½ cup (125 mL) shredded Cheddar cheese
- ¼ cup (50 mL) thinly sliced green onions
- 2 tablespoons (25 mL) snipped fresh parsley
- 1 tablespoon (15 mL) butter or margarine
- 2 teaspoons (10 mL) to 1 tablespoon (15 mL) prepared horseradish
- ½ teaspoon (2 mL) dried basil leaves
- ¼ teaspoon (1 mL) dried thyme leaves
- ¼ teaspoon (1 mL) salt
- ¼ teaspoon (1 mL) pepper
- Paprika

4 servings

1 Heat oven to 425°F (220°C). Pierce potatoes several times with fork. Place potatoes on rack in oven. Bake for 50 to 55 minutes, or until tender. Let stand for 10 minutes. Reduce oven temperature to 400°F (200°C).

2 Cut ¼-inch (5 mm) slice off top of each potato. Scoop out pulp, leaving ¼-inch (5 mm) shells. In medium mixing bowl, combine pulp and milk. Beat at medium speed of electric mixer until no lumps remain and mixture is light and fluffy. Add remaining ingredients, except paprika. Beat at low speed until well blended.

3 Pipe or spoon mixture evenly into potato shells. Sprinkle tops with paprika. Place stuffed shells on baking sheet. Bake for 20 to 25 minutes, or until potatoes are heated through and tops are golden brown.

Helpful Hint: *To save time, pierce potatoes several times with fork. Arrange on a paper towel in microwave oven. Microwave at High for 10 to 14 minutes, or until tender, rearranging once. Continue as directed.*

▲ GARLIC MASHED POTATOES

- 1½ lbs. (750 g) peeled red potatoes, cut into ½-inch (1.5 cm) cubes (4 cups/1 L), rinsed and drained
- ½ cup (125 mL) water
- 2 to 4 large cloves garlic, peeled and quartered
- ⅓ cup (75 mL) hot milk
- 1 tablespoon (15 mL) butter or margarine
- 1 tablespoon (15 mL) dried chives
- ½ teaspoon (2 mL) salt
- Paprika (optional)

6 servings

1 In 2-quart (2 L) saucepan, combine potatoes, water and garlic. Bring to a boil over high heat. Cover. Reduce heat to medium-low. Simmer for 10 to 14 minutes, or until potatoes are very tender, stirring occasionally. Drain.

2 In medium mixing bowl, combine potato mixture, milk, margarine, chives and salt. Beat at medium speed of electric mixer until smooth. Before serving, sprinkle with paprika.

POTATO ROSETTES ❄ FREEZE AHEAD

- 1½ teaspoons (7 mL) salt, divided
- ½ cup (125 mL) hot water
- 9 large baking potatoes, peeled and quartered
- ½ cup (125 mL) butter or margarine
- ½ cup (125 mL) dairy sour cream
- 2 tablespoons (25 mL) grated Parmesan cheese
- 2 cups (500 mL) milk
- 1 teaspoon (5 mL) dried chives
- Paprika

Makes 4½ to 5 dozen

1 Dissolve ½ teaspoon (2 mL) salt in water. In 3-quart (3 L) casserole, combine potatoes and salted water; cover. Microwave at High for 21 to 28 minutes, or until tender, stirring twice. Drain and mash.

2 In large mixing bowl, mix potatoes, butter, sour cream, cheese and 1 teaspoon (5 mL) salt. Add milk gradually, beating at high speed of electric mixer until smooth. Stir in chives.

3 Spoon potatoes into pastry bag using number 6 star tip. Squeeze into 2 to 2½-inch (5 to 6.5 cm) rosettes on wax-paper-lined baking sheets. Sprinkle with paprika. Freeze 3 hours or overnight.

4 Place rosettes in plastic bags. Freeze up to 1 week. To heat, place 15 rosettes on 12-inch (30 cm) plate; cover with wax paper. Microwave at 70% (Medium High) for 5 minutes. Rearrange rosettes with spatula so that those around outer edge are in center. Cover and microwave at 70% (Medium High) for 2 to 6 minutes, or until heated. Repeat with remaining rosettes.

WINTER FRUIT DRESSING

- 2 tablespoons (25 mL) butter or margarine
- 1 stalk celery, sliced (½ cup/ 125 mL)
- ¼ cup (50 mL) chopped onion
- 6 cups (1.5 L) cubed whole-grain bread (½-inch/1.5 cm cubes)
- 2 cups (500 mL) chopped mixed dried fruit (apples, apricots, cranberries, raisins)
- 1 to 1½ cups (250 to 375 mL) ready-to-serve chicken broth
- ½ cup (125 mL) pecan halves
- ½ teaspoon (2 mL) dried rubbed sage leaves
- ½ teaspoon (2 mL) dried rosemary leaves
- ¼ teaspoon (1 mL) dried thyme leaves
- Salt and pepper to taste

6 to 8 servings

1 Heat oven to 350°F (180°C). In medium skillet, melt butter over medium heat. Add celery and onion. Cook for 2 to 3 minutes, or until vegetables are tender-crisp.

2 In large mixing bowl, combine celery mixture, bread cubes and dried fruit. Stir in enough broth to just moisten mixture. Stir in remaining ingredients. Mix well.

3 Spray 2-quart (2 L) casserole with nonstick vegetable cooking spray. Spoon dressing into casserole. Cover and bake for 40 to 45 minutes, or until heated through.

Helpful Hint: *For a crisper top on dressing, uncover during last 15 minutes of baking.*

(See photo of this recipe with Roasted Goose, page 246)

SHERRIED SWEET POTATOES ▶

- 1 large sweet potato, peeled and cut into ½-inch (1.5 cm) cubes (3 cups/750 mL)
- ½ cup (125 mL) water

Sauce:

- ¼ cup (50 mL) packed brown sugar
- ¼ cup (50 mL) raisins
- ¼ cup (50 mL) apricot nectar
- 2 tablespoons (25 mL) dry sherry
- ¼ teaspoon (1 mL) ground nutmeg
- ¼ teaspoon (1 mL) ground ginger
- ¼ teaspoon (1 mL) salt

4 servings

1 Heat oven to 350°F (180°C). In 2-quart (2 L) saucepan, combine potato and water. Cover. Cook over high heat for 6 to 7 minutes, or until tender. Drain. Cover to keep warm.

2 Combine sauce ingredients in 1-quart (1 L) saucepan. Bring to a boil over high heat, stirring frequently. Boil for 1 minute. Remove from heat.

3 In 1½-quart (1.5 L) casserole, combine potato, sauce and pecans. Cover. Bake for 13 to 15 minutes, or until sauce bubbles.

Helpful Hint: *To microwave, place potato in 1½-quart (1.5 L) casserole (omit water). Cover. Microwave at High for 5½ to 7 minutes, or until tender. Drain.*

CRANBERRY CORN BREAD DRESSING

- 2 tablespoons (25 mL) butter or margarine
- ¾ cup (175 mL) chopped onion
- ¾ cup (175 mL) sliced celery
- 6 cups (1.5 L) dried corn bread stuffing mix
- 1½ cups (375 mL) water or chicken broth
- 1 cup (250 mL) dried cranberries
- ½ cup (125 mL) chopped walnuts
- 1¼ teaspoons (6 mL) poultry seasoning
- ½ teaspoon (2 mL) salt
- ¼ teaspoon (1 mL) freshly ground pepper

6 to 8 servings

1 Heat oven to 350°F (180°C). Spray 3-quart (3 L) casserole with nonstick vegetable cooking spray. Set aside. In 1-quart (3 L) saucepan, melt butter over medium heat. Add onion and celery. Cook for 3 to 5 minutes, or until vegetables are tender-crisp, stirring occasionally. Remove from heat.

2 In large mixing bowl, combine onion mixture, stuffing mix, water, cranberries and walnuts. Toss lightly to coat. Add poultry seasoning, salt and pepper. Toss to combine. Spoon mixture into prepared casserole. Cover and bake for 30 minutes. Uncover and bake for 10 to 15 minutes longer, or until top is golden brown.

(See photo of this recipe with Roasted Wild Turkey, page 236)

ACCOMPANIMENTS

PINEAPPLE CHUTNEY

- 2 cans (20 oz./560 g each) crushed pineapple, drained and ½ cup (125 mL) juice reserved

- 1½ cups (375 mL) raisins

- ¾ cup (175 mL) cider vinegar

- ⅔ cup (150 mL) packed brown sugar

- ⅓ cup (75 mL) chopped green pepper

- ¼ cup (50 mL) chopped onion

- 2 cloves garlic, minced

- 2 tablespoons (25 mL) finely chopped crystallized ginger

- ½ teaspoon (2 mL) salt

- ¼ teaspoon (1 mL) ground cinnamon

- ⅛ teaspoon (0.5 mL) ground cloves

- ⅛ teaspoon (0.5 mL) cayenne

About 6 cups (1.5 L) chutney

1 Place pineapple and reserved liquid in 3-quart (3 L) casserole. Combine with remaining ingredients. Cover and microwave at High for 10 minutes, stirring after 5 minutes.

2 Uncover. Microwave at High for 15 to 20 minutes, or until desired consistency, stirring every 5 minutes. Chill. Serve as a relish with meat.

Helpful Hint: *Mixture can be covered and stored in refrigerator or ladled into hot sterilized jars, sealed and processed.*

266

CRANBERRY-ORANGE RELISH

- 2 oranges
- 8 cups (2 L) fresh cranberries
- 1⅓ cups (325 mL) sugar
- ¼ cup (50 mL) chopped crystallized ginger
- ½ cup (125 mL) chopped pecans (optional)

12 to 14 servings

1 Wash oranges. Squeeze juice from oranges; refrigerate juice in covered container for other use. Remove and discard pulp from orange peels.

2 Cut peels in quarters; finely grind in food processor. Add half the cranberries and continue processing until finely ground. Repeat with remaining cranberries.

3 In large mixing bowl, combine ground cranberries, sugar and ginger; chill. Stir in pecans just before serving.

SPICED APPLE RELISH

- 6 cups (1.5 L) chopped peeled apples
- ⅓ cup (75 mL) chopped onion
- ¼ cup (50 mL) sugar
- ¼ cup (50 mL) chopped spiced peaches or raisins (optional)
- ¼ cup (50 mL) water
- ¼ teaspoon (1 mL) ground cloves
- Dash salt

About 3 cups (750 mL) relish

1 In 2-quart (2 L) casserole, combine all ingredients. Cover. Microwave at High for 10 to 15 minutes, or until apples are soft, stirring once or twice. Mash apples. Serve at room temperature with pork or poultry.

Helpful Hint: *Prepare relish the day before. Cover and refrigerate overnight. Serve at room temperature.*

▲ FRUITED WILD RICE

- ¾ cup (175 mL) wild rice, rinsed and drained
- ½ cup (125 mL) chopped carrots
- ¼ cup (50 mL) uncooked brown rice
- ¼ cup (50 mL) raisins
- ¼ cup (50 mL) sliced green onions
- 2 tablespoons (25 mL) butter or margarine
- ½ teaspoon (2 mL) salt
- ¼ teaspoon (1 mL) ground coriander
- 2¼ cups (550 mL) water
- ½ cup (125 mL) apple juice

4 to 6 servings

1 Combine all ingredients in oven cooking bag, except water and apple juice. Holding bag upright, add water and apple juice. Shake bag gently to mix. Secure bag loosely with nylon tie.

2 Place bag in 9-inch (2.5 L) square baking dish. Microwave at High for 5 minutes. Microwave at 50% (Medium) for 40 to 55 minutes longer, or until rice is tender and liquid is absorbed. Let bag stand for 5 to 8 minutes before serving.

DESSERTS

FRUIT DESSERTS

RUBY RED PEARS

- 1 cup (250 mL) red port wine
- ⅓ cup (75 mL) sugar
- 2 slices orange
- 1 stick cinnamon
- 4 whole cloves
- ½ teaspoon (2 mL) red food coloring
- 4 pears (about 8 oz./220 g each)
- 2 teaspoons (10 mL) cornstarch

4 servings

1 Combine wine, sugar, orange slices, cinnamon and cloves in 2-quart (2 L) casserole. Cover and microwave at High for 3 to 4 minutes, or until sugar dissolves, stirring once or twice. Add food coloring. Mix well. Set aside.

2 Peel pears. Core from bottom, being careful not to cut through stem end. Roll pears in wine mixture to coat. Cover. Microwave at High for 13 to 20 minutes, or until tender, turning pears over and basting with wine mixture 2 or 3 times.

3 Remove and discard cinnamon stick, cloves and orange slices. Refrigerate pears in wine mixture about 4 hours.

4 Drain wine mixture, reserving 1 cup (250 mL). Blend cornstarch into reserved mixture. Microwave wine mixture at High for 3½ to 4½ minutes, or until mixture is thickened and translucent, stirring once or twice.

5 Arrange pears on serving platter. Pour glaze evenly over pears. Garnish with sweetened whipped cream and mint leaves, if desired.

(See photo, page 269)

PHYLLO APPLE TURNOVERS ▶

Filling:

- 2 medium Granny Smith apples, peeled, cored and thinly sliced (3 cups/750 mL)
- ¼ cup (50 mL) dried currants
- ¼ cup (50 mL) sugar
- 1 tablespoon (15 mL) all-purpose flour
- ½ teaspoon (2 mL) ground cinnamon
- 2 tablespoons (25 mL) sugar
- ¼ teaspoon (1 mL) ground cinnamon
- 12 sheets frozen phyllo dough, defrosted
- 1 teaspoon (5 mL) butter or margarine, melted

6 servings

1 Heat oven to 375°F (190°C). In medium mixing bowl, combine filling ingredients. Set aside. In small mixing bowl, combine 2 tablespoons (25 mL) sugar and ¼ teaspoon (1 mL) cinnamon. Set aside.

2 Place 1 sheet of phyllo on flat work surface. (Keep remaining sheets covered with plastic wrap.) Spray sheet evenly with nonstick vegetable cooking spray. Lay second sheet of phyllo over first. Spray second sheet evenly with cooking spray. Cut layered sheets in half lengthwise. Lay one half of cut sheets on second half, forming 4 layers.

3 Place ½ cup (125 mL) filling at one end of layered sheets. Fold right bottom corner over filling, forming a triangle. Continue folding, keeping triangle shape. Place triangle seam-side-down on baking sheet. Repeat with remaining phyllo sheets and filling.

4 Brush tops of triangles with butter. Sprinkle evenly with sugar mixture. Bake for 15 to 18 minutes, or until turnovers are golden brown. Serve with praline or caramel ice cream, if desired.

SHERRY-MARMALADE ORANGES

- 2 large oranges, peeled, cut into ¼-inch (5 mm) slices
- ¼ cup (50 mL) orange marmalade
- 1 tablespoon (15 mL) dry sherry
- 2 tablespoons (30 mL) chopped pecans

4 servings

1 In 9-inch (22 cm) pie plate, arrange orange slices in overlapping circle.

2 In small bowl, combine marmalade and sherry. Spoon over oranges; top with pecans. Cover with wax paper. Microwave at High for 3 to 4 minutes, or until glazed and hot, rotating once.

BAKED APPLES

- 4 apples (3-inch/7 cm diameter)
- 4 tablespoons (60 mL) packed brown sugar
- 8 teaspoons (40 mL) butter or margarine

4 servings

1 Core apples. Pierce with fork. Place 1 tablespoon (15 mL) sugar and 2 teaspoons (10 mL) butter in each apple and arrange in baking dish with space between apples.

2 Cover with plastic wrap. Microwave for 8 to 11 minutes, or until tender, rotating dish once or twice. Let stand, covered, for 2 minutes.

APPLE CRISP

- 6 cups (1.5 L) cored, peeled and sliced cooking apples
- 1 tablespoon (15 mL) lemon juice
- ¼ cup (50 mL) plus 2 tablespoons (25 mL) butter or margarine, cut up
- ¾ cup (175 mL) packed brown sugar
- ¾ cup (175 mL) quick-cooking oats
- ½ cup (125 mL) all-purpose flour
- 1 teaspoon (2 mL) ground cinnamon

6 servings

1 Place apples in 9-inch (2.5 L) square baking dish. Sprinkle with lemon juice. In small mixing bowl, microwave butter at High for 1½ to 1¾ minutes, or until melted.

2 Stir in remaining ingredients until crumbly. Sprinkle evenly over apples; press down lightly. Microwave at High for 8 minutes. Rotate dish ½ turn.

3 Microwave at High for 6 to 10 minutes, or until apples are tender. Serve warm or cold. Top with whipped cream, if desired.

Cherry Crisp: *Follow recipe above, except substitute 1 can (21 oz./590 g) cherry pie filling for the apples and lemon juice. Microwave at High for 8 to 12 minutes, or until hot and bubbly in center.*

272

▲ CARAMEL FRUIT PLATTER

- 1 can (8 oz./220 g) pineapple chunks
- 1 medium apple, cut into chunks
- 1 banana, cut into chunks
- 1 pear, cut into chunks
- 1 dozen strawberries
- 1 pkg. (14 oz./396 g) caramels
- ¼ cup (50 mL) half-and-half

6 servings

1 Combine fruit in medium bowl. Toss to coat with pineapple juice. Drain. Set aside.

2 Arrange caramels in even layer in center of 12-inch (30 cm) round microwavable platter. Pour half-and-half over caramels. Microwave at High for 3½ to 5 minutes, or until caramels melt and mixture can be stirred smooth, stirring 3 or 4 times using a fork.

3 Arrange fruit around outside edges of platter. Serve fruit with wooden picks for dipping fruit in warm caramel.

HOT FRUIT COMPOTE

- 2 cups (500 mL) frozen peaches (about one-half of 16 oz./450 g bag)
- 1 can (16 oz./450 g) sliced pears, drained.
- 1 can (13½ oz./375 g) pineapple chunks, drained
- 1 cup (250 mL) seedless green grapes
- ½ cup (125 mL) coconut
- ¼ cup (50 mL) raisins
- 10 maraschino cherries
- 2 tablespoons (25 mL) packed brown sugar
- ⅛ teaspoon (0.5 mL) ground cinnamon
- 1 can (11 oz./305 g) mandarin orange segments, drained
- 1 cup (250 mL) miniature marshmallows

6 servings

1 Place frozen peaches in 2-quart (2 L) casserole. Microwave at High for 1½ to 2 minutes, or until partially defrosted, stirring after 1 minute.

2 Stir in remaining ingredients, except orange segments and marshmallows. Microwave at High for 5 to 6 minutes, or until thoroughly heated. Stir in orange segments and marshmallows. Serve warm.

▲ ORANGE-CARAMEL PEARS

- ½ cup (125 mL) caramel topping
- 1 tablespoon (15 mL) frozen orange juice concentrate
- ⅓ cup (75 mL) finely chopped pecans
- 2 medium fresh pears, cored and sliced

4 servings

1 In 4-cup (1 L) measure, combine caramel topping and orange juice concentrate. Microwave at High for 1 to 1½ minutes, or until hot, stirring once. Add pecans. Mix well.

2 Arrange pear slices on 4 individual dessert plates. Spoon warm caramel mixture over pears.

APPLE-PECAN CRUMBLE

- 5 pecan shortbread cookies (2 to 2¼-inch/5 to 6 cm)
- ¼ teaspoon (1 mL) ground cinnamon
- ⅛ teaspoon (0.5 mL) ground cloves
- 1 can (20 oz./560 g) apple pie filling
- ¼ cup (50 mL) raisins
- 2 tablespoons (25 mL) butter or margarine

4 servings

1 In food processor or blender, process cookies, cinnamon and cloves until crumbly. Set aside.

2 Divide apple pie filling evenly among four 10-ounce (280 g) custard cups. Add 1 tablespoon (15 mL) raisins to each custard cup. Stir to combine. Sprinkle each evenly with cookie crumb mixture.

3 In small bowl, microwave butter at High for 45 seconds to 1 minute, or until melted. Drizzle evenly over crumb mixture.

4 Arrange custard cups in microwave. Microwave at High for 6 to 8 minutes, or until mixture begins to bubble around edges, rearranging custard cups once. Cool 5 to 10 minutes. Serve warm. Top with ice cream, if desired.

BERRY FONDUE

- 1 pkg. (16 oz./450 g) frozen unsweetened whole strawberries
- ½ cup (125 mL) red raspberry spread

Dippers:

- Cantaloupe spears
- Whole fresh strawberries
- Fresh banana spears
- Pretzel twists or sticks
- Angel food cake, torn into bite-size pieces

18 servings,
2 tablespoons (25 mL) each

1 In 2-quart (2 L) casserole, combine frozen strawberries and raspberry spread. Cover. Microwave at High for 6 to 8 minutes, or until strawberries are defrosted and hot, stirring twice.

2 In food processor or blender, process mixture until smooth. Pour into serving dish. Cover with plastic wrap. Chill 4 hours, or until cold. Serve with desired dippers.

SUGARED PLUMS

- ¼ cup (50 mL) butter or margarine
- ½ cup (125 mL) sugar
- 1 teaspoon (5 mL) ground cinnamon
- 6 large ripe plums, cut in half and pitted

4 to 6 servings

1 In small dish, melt butter at High for 50 to 60 seconds. Combine sugar and cinnamon in bowl or on wax paper.

2 Dip plum halves in butter. Roll in cinnamon-sugar, coating generously. Place on serving plate. Cover with wax paper. Microwave at High for 2 to 3 minutes, or until tender, rotating dish and rearranging halves from center to outer edge after each minute. (Do not overcook.)

3 Let stand for 1 to 2 minutes. If desired, sprinkle with any remaining cinnamon-sugar before serving.

COLD ◀ CHERRY SOUP

- 2 cups (500 mL) frozen pitted dark sweet cherries
- ⅓ cup (75 mL) sugar
- ⅛ teaspoon (0.5 mL) ground cinnamon
- ¼ cup (50 mL) white wine
- 1 cup (250 mL) buttermilk
- 1 tablespoon (15 mL) sour cream

4 to 6 servings

1 Combine all ingredients, except buttermilk and sour cream, in 1½-quart (1.5 L) casserole. Mix well. Microwave at High for 7 to 10 minutes, or until mixture bubbles and sugar dissolves, stirring once.

2 Remove cherries with slotted spoon, reserving cooking liquid. In food processor or blender, process cherries until smooth. Blend in cooking liquid and buttermilk. Chill at least 1 hour.

3 Blend 1 teaspoon (5 mL) chilled soup and the sour cream in small bowl. Spoon soup into individual dishes. Top each serving with sour cream mixture. Using wooden pick, make a swirl design in each sour cream topping.

Peach Soup: *Follow recipe above, except substitute 2 cups (500 mL) frozen sliced peaches for cherries. Microwave at High for 10 to 15 minutes, or until peaches are tender, stirring once or twice.*

FROSTED CRANBERRY SOUP

- 1 pkg. (12 oz./330 g) fresh cranberries
- 1 cup (250 mL) orange juice
- ⅓ cup (75 mL) sugar
- ¼ teaspoon (1 mL) ground cloves
- ⅛ teaspoon (0.5 mL) ground nutmeg
- 2½ cups (625 mL) buttermilk

6 servings, ¾ cup (175 mL) each

1 In 2-quart (2 L) casserole, combine all ingredients except buttermilk. Cover and microwave at High for 9 to 12 minutes, or until very hot and cranberries are split, stirring twice. Chill mixture until completely cool.

2 In food processor or blender, process cranberry mixture until smooth. Pour into large mixing bowl. Add buttermilk. Mix well. Cover with plastic wrap and chill 4 hours, or until serving time. Serve cold.

PUDDINGS & CREAMS

RICE PUDDING WITH APRICOT SAUCE

- 2 cups (500 mL) hot cooked white rice
- 1½ cups (375 mL) skim milk
- 2 eggs, beaten
- ⅓ cup (75 mL) sugar
- ¼ teaspoon (1 mL) salt
- ⅓ cup (75 mL) chopped dried apricots
- ½ teaspoon (2 mL) vanilla
- ¼ teaspoon (1 mL) almond extract

Sauce:
- ¼ cup (50 mL) sugar
- 2 teaspoons (10 mL) cornstarch
- ⅔ cup (150 mL) apricot nectar
- 2 tablespoons (25 mL) toasted sliced almonds

6 servings

1 Combine rice, milk, eggs, ⅓ cup (75 mL) sugar and the salt in 2-quart (2 L) saucepan. Cook over medium-low heat for 17 to 22 minutes, or until pudding is slightly thickened, stirring frequently. (Do not boil.) Let cook for 15 minutes. (Pudding will thicken as it cools.) Stir in apricots, vanilla and almond extract.

2 To prepare sauce, combine ¼ cup (50 mL) sugar and the cornstarch in 1-quart (1 L) saucepan. Blend in nectar. Cook over medium heat for 3 to 7 minutes, or until sauce is thickened and translucent, stirring constantly. Remove from heat. Stir in almonds. Spoon sauce evenly over each serving of pudding.

BREAD PUDDING

- 2½ cups (625 mL) milk
- 2 cups (500 mL) dry bread cubes
- 2 tablespoons (25 mL) cornstarch
- ½ cup (125 mL) raisins
- ⅓ cup (75 mL) sugar
- ½ teaspoon (2 mL) ground cinnamon
- ½ teaspoon (2 mL) vanilla
- ¼ teaspoon (1 mL) salt
- 3 eggs, beaten
- Ground cinnamon

6 to 8 servings

1 In 4-cup (1 L) measure, microwave milk at High for 4 to 6 minutes, or until hot but not boiling. In 2-quart (2 L) casserole, toss bread cubes, cornstarch, raisins, sugar, cinnamon, vanilla and salt. Gradually stir in milk, then eggs. Microwave at High for 2 minutes; stir gently.

2 Reduce power to 50% (Medium). Microwave for 4 to 8 minutes, or until almost set in center, gently pushing outer edges toward center every 3 minutes. (Do not overcook.) Let stand directly on countertop for at least 30 minutes before serving. Serve warm or cold. Top with cream, if desired. Sprinkle with cinnamon before serving.

BAKED CUSTARD

- ⅓ cup (75 mL) sugar
- 1 teaspoon (5 mL) cornstarch
- 2½ cups (625 mL) milk
- 1 teaspoon (5 mL) vanilla
- ⅛ teaspoon (0.5 mL) salt
- 4 eggs, beaten
- Ground nutmeg

6 servings

1 In small bowl, combine sugar and cornstarch. Microwave milk in 1½-quart (1.5 L) casserole at High for 2 to 4 minutes, or until very hot but not boiling. Beat sugar mixture, vanilla and salt into eggs at low speed. Stir into milk. Sprinkle with nutmeg.

2 Place casserole in larger baking dish; add ½ inch (1.5 cm) hot water to baking dish. Microwave at 50% (Medium) for 7 to 12 minutes, or until slightly firm but still soft in center, rotating ¼ turn every 2 minutes. Let stand for at least 30 minutes before serving. Serve warm or chilled.

▲ WHITE CHOCOLATE-PEPPERMINT MOUSSE

- 1 pkg. (3⅛ oz./90 g) vanilla pudding and pie filling
- 2 cups (500 mL) milk
- ½ teaspoon (2 mL) peppermint extract
- 2 white baking bars (2 oz./60 g each)
- 1 container (12 oz./330 g) prepared whipped topping

6 servings

1 Place pudding mix in 8-cup (2 L) measure. Blend in milk and extract. Microwave at High for 6 to 9 minutes, or until mixture thickens and bubbles, stirring after first 3 minutes and then every minute. Place plastic wrap directly on surface of pudding. Chill about 4 hours, or until completely cool.

2 In small mixing bowl, microwave baking bars at 50% (Medium) for 3 to 4 minutes, or until bars are glossy and can be stirred smooth, stirring once. Add to chilled pudding. Mix well. Fold in whipped topping.

3 Spoon mousse into parfait glasses. Sprinkle with crushed peppermint candies, if desired.

BRANDY ALEXANDER CREAM

- 2 tablespoons (25 mL) sugar
- 2 teaspoons (10 mL) cornstarch
- 1 cup (250 mL) chilled whipping cream, divided
- ½ square (1 oz./30 g) semisweet chocolate
- 1 teaspoon (5 mL) dark crème de cacao liqueur
- 2 teaspoons (10 mL) brandy
- 1 tablespoon (15 mL) chopped hazelnuts (optional)

2 servings

1 In 1-quart (1 L) casserole, combine sugar and cornstarch. Blend in ½ cup (125 mL) whipping cream. Add chocolate and liqueur. Microwave at 50% (Medium) for 2 to 3 minutes, or until very thick, stirring every 30 seconds. Refrigerate 1 hour, or until chilled.

2 Beat brandy and remaining whipping cream in chilled bowl until soft peaks form. Fold into chilled chocolate mixture. Pour into two 6-ounce (175 g) serving bowls. Sprinkle with hazelnuts. Refrigerate before serving.

FUDGE-MINT DESSERT

Crust:

- ½ pkg. (1 lb., 4½ oz./575 g) low-fat fudge brownie mix (about 2 packed cups/500 mL)
- ⅓ cup (75 mL) hot water
- 2 egg whites, beaten
- 1 teaspoon (5 mL) vanilla

Filling:

- ¾ cup (175 mL) cold skim milk
- 1 pkg. (3.9 oz./125 g) instant chocolate pudding mix
- 2 tablespoons (25 mL) white crème de menthe
- 1 teaspoon (5 mL) vanilla
- 1½ cups (375 mL) frozen reduced-calorie nondairy whipped topping, defrosted

Topping:

- 1½ cups (375 mL) frozen reduced-calorie nondairy whipped topping, defrosted
- 2 teaspoons (10 mL) white crème de menthe
- 1 to 2 drops green food coloring (optional)
- 1 tablespoon (15 mL) miniature chocolate chips

9 servings

1 Heat oven to 325°F (160°C). Spray 9-inch (2.5 L) square baking pan with nonstick vegetable cooking spray. Set aside.

2 Combine crust ingredients in medium mixing bowl. Beat at low speed of electric mixer just until smooth, scraping sides of bowl frequently. Pour crust into prepared pan. Bake for 20 to 22 minutes, or until set. (Do not overbake.) Cool completely.

3 Combine milk, pudding mix, 2 tablespoons (25 mL) crème de menthe and the vanilla in medium mixing bowl. Beat at low speed of electric mixer for 1 minute, scraping sides of bowl frequently. Fold in 1½ cups (375 mL) whipped topping. Spread filling evenly over crust.

4 Place 1½ cups (375 mL) whipped topping in small mixing bowl. Fold in 2 teaspoons (10 mL) crème de menthe and the food coloring. Spread topping evenly over filling. Sprinkle chips evenly over top. Cover with plastic wrap. Chill. Cut into squares.

CAKES

GINGERBREAD WITH ORANGE SAUCE

Gingerbread:

- ¾ cup (175 mL) all-purpose flour
- ½ cup (125 mL) whole wheat flour
- ½ cup (125 mL) butter or margarine
- ⅓ cup (75 mL) packed brown sugar
- ⅓ cup (75 mL) dark molasses
- ¼ cup (50 mL) fresh orange juice

- 2 eggs
- 1 teaspoon (5 mL) grated orange peel
- ¾ teaspoon (4 mL) ground cinnamon
- ½ teaspoon (2 mL) baking soda
- ½ teaspoon (2 mL) ground ginger
- ¼ teaspoon (1 mL) ground cloves
- ¼ teaspoon (1 mL) salt

Orange Sauce:

- ½ cup (125 mL) fresh orange juice
- 1 tablespoon (15 mL) packed brown sugar
- 1 tablespoon (15 mL) butter or margarine
- ¾ teaspoon (4 mL) cornstarch
- ¼ teaspoon (1 mL) grated orange peel
- ⅛ teaspoon (0.5 mL) ground cinnamon

9 servings

1 In medium mixing bowl, combine all gingerbread ingredients. Beat at low speed of electric mixer until blended, scraping bowl constantly. Beat at medium speed for 2 minutes, scraping bowl occasionally. Pour batter into 9-inch (2.5 L) square baking dish. Shield corners of dish with foil.

2 Place dish on inverted saucer in microwave. Microwave at 50% (Medium) for 6 minutes, rotating dish ¼ turn after every 3 minutes. Remove foil. Increase power to High. Microwave for 3 to 9 minutes, or until center springs back when touched lightly and no uncooked batter remains on the bottom. Let stand on counter for 10 minutes.

3 In 1-cup (250 mL) measure, combine all Orange Sauce ingredients. Mix well. Microwave at High for 1½ to 2½ minutes, or until sauce thickens and bubbles, stirring once or twice. Spoon 1 tablespoon (15 mL) sauce over each serving of gingerbread.

PLUM CAKE

Topping:

- 3 tablespoons (50 mL) butter or margarine
- ½ cup (125 mL) packed brown sugar
- ½ cup (125 mL) chopped nuts
- 4 small ripe plums, pitted and diced (about 1 cup/ 250 mL)

Cake:

- 1 cup (250 mL) all-purpose flour
- ⅔ cup (150 mL) sugar
- 1 teaspoon (5 mL) baking powder
- ½ teaspoon (2 mL) salt
- ½ teaspoon (2 mL) vanilla
- ⅓ cup (75 mL) vegetable shortening
- 2 eggs
- ⅓ cup (75 mL) milk

One 9-inch (1.5 L) round cake

1 Line bottom of 9-inch (1.5 L) round baking dish with wax paper. Place butter in dish. Microwave at High for 45 to 60 seconds, or until melted. Spread butter evenly over bottom of dish. Sprinkle with brown sugar and nuts. Microwave at High for 2 minutes, rotating ½ turn after 1 minute. Top with diced plums. Set aside.

2 Place all cake ingredients in mixing bowl. Blend at low speed, then beat at medium speed for 2 minutes. Spoon cake batter evenly over fruit. Place dish on inverted saucer in microwave.

3 Reduce power to 50% (Medium). Microwave for 6 minutes, rotating ¼ turn every 1 to 2 minutes. Increase power to High. Microwave for 3 to 7½ minutes, or until top springs back and appears baked.

4 Cool directly on countertop for 5 minutes. Loosen edges well and turn out onto plate. Serve warm. Top with whipped cream, if desired.

◀ FESTIVE GELATIN CAKE

- 2 cups (500 mL) all-purpose flour
- 1¼ cups (300 mL) sugar
- 1 tablespoon (15 mL) baking powder
- 1 teaspoon (5 mL) salt
- 1 teaspoon (5 mL) vanilla
- ⅔ cup (150 mL) vegetable shortening
- ⅔ cup (150 mL) milk
- 2 eggs
- 4 egg whites
- 1 cup (250 mL) water
- 1 pkg. (3 oz./90 g) gelatin, any flavor
- Fluffy Frosting (below)

Two 8-inch (2 L) square cakes

1 Place all ingredients except water, gelatin and frosting in large bowl. Blend at low speed, scraping bowl constantly. Beat for 2 minutes at medium speed, scraping bowl occasionally. Divide batter between two 8-inch (2 L) square baking dishes.

2 Microwave one dish at a time at 50% (Medium) for 6 minutes, rotating twice. Increase power to High. Microwave for 1 to 5 minutes or until top springs back when touched lightly. Let stand for 10 minutes.

3 In 2-cup (500 mL) measure, microwave water at High for 1 to 3 minutes, or until boiling. Slowly add gelatin, stirring constantly. Pierce cakes at ¼-inch (5 mm) intervals with wooden pick. Pour half of gelatin mixture over each cake; cool. Frost with Fluffy Frosting (see below). Refrigerate.

FLUFFY FROSTING

- 1 cup (250 mL) sugar
- ⅓ cup (75 mL) water
- ¼ teaspoon (1 mL) cream of tartar
- ⅛ teaspoon (0.5 mL) salt
- 2 egg whites
- 1 teaspoon (5 mL) vanilla

Frosts two 8-inch (2 L) square cakes

1 In 2-quart (2 L) casserole, combine sugar, water, cream of tartar and salt. Cover and microwave at High for 2 minutes. Stir. Microwave at High, uncovered, for 1½ to 5 minutes, or until soft ball forms when small amount is dropped in cold water. (Do not undercook.)

2 Beat egg whites until stiff peaks form. Pour hot syrup slowly in thin stream into beaten egg whites, beating constantly, until stiff and glossy. Add vanilla during last minute of beating.

RASPBERRY ICE CREAM CAKE

- 1 frozen pound cake (16 oz./ 450 g)
- 1 pint (500 mL) raspberry sherbet
- 1 pint (500 mL) chocolate ice cream
- 1 square (1 oz./30 g) semisweet chocolate
- ½ teaspoon (2 mL) vegetable shortening
- ½ cup (125 mL) raspberry preserves
- 2 teaspoons (10 mL) light corn syrup
- Fresh raspberries (optional)

8 servings

1 Cut pound cake lengthwise into thirds. Place bottom cake layer on serving platter. Set aside. Remove lids from sherbet and ice cream. Microwave sherbet at 50% (Medium) for 30 seconds to 1 minute, or until softened. Repeat with ice cream.

2 Spread bottom cake layer with about 1 cup (250 mL) of the raspberry sherbet. Top with next cake layer. Spread second layer with about ½ cup (125 mL) of the chocolate ice cream. Place remaining cake layer on top.

3 Spread top with remaining raspberry sherbet. Spread sides with remaining chocolate ice cream. (If sherbet or ice cream becomes too soft, refreeze 10 to 15 minutes.) Freeze cake 15 to 30 minutes, or until very firm.

4 Combine chocolate and shortening in 1-cup (250 mL) measure. Microwave at 50% (Medium) for 1½ to 3 minutes, or until chocolate is glossy and can be stirred smooth, stirring once. Cool slightly. Drizzle chocolate over top of raspberry sherbet. Freeze uncovered until firm.

5 To serve, combine raspberry preserves and corn syrup in 1-cup (250 mL) measure. Microwave at 50% (Medium) for 1 minute, or until mixture is melted and can be stirred smooth. Drizzle raspberry sauce over servings of cake. Garnish each serving with fresh raspberries.

Helpful Hint: *Up to 1 week in advance, prepare cake Steps 1 through 4. When ready to serve, prepare raspberry sauce and continue with Step 5.*

CANDIES

PEANUT BRITTLE ❄️ FREEZE AHEAD

- 3 cups (750 mL) sugar
- 1½ cups (375 mL) light corn syrup
- ¼ teaspoon (1 mL) salt
- 4 cups (1 L) shelled salted roasted peanuts
- 3 tablespoons (50 mL) butter or margarine
- 2 teaspoons (10 mL) vanilla
- 1 tablespoon (15 mL) baking soda

3 lbs. (1.5 kg) brittle

1 Generously butter two large baking sheets. In 3-quart (3 L) bowl, mix sugar, syrup and salt. Microwave at High for 15 minutes, stirring 1 or 2 times. Stir in peanuts. Microwave at High for 10 to 15 minutes, or until syrup and peanuts are light brown, stirring after 2 and 4 minutes.

2 Stir in butter and vanilla until butter melts. Stir in baking soda until light and foamy. Pour half onto each baking sheet and spread quickly to ¼-inch (5 mm) thickness. Cool. Break into pieces. Freeze in single layer on trays until firm. Wrap, label and freeze no longer than 6 months.

3 To serve, unwrap and arrange in single layer on plate or tray. Let stand at room temperature for 15 to 20 minutes.

(See photo, page 285)

▲ CRANBERRY HAYSTACKS

- 1 pkg. (3 oz./85 g) cream cheese, softened
- 2 tablespoons (25 mL) milk
- 2 squares (1 oz./30 g each) white baking chocolate, melted and slightly cooled
- ½ teaspoon (2 mL) vanilla
- ¼ teaspoon (1 mL) salt
- 2 cups (500 mL) miniature marshmallows
- 1½ cups (375 mL) chow mein noodles
- ⅓ cup (75 mL) dried cranberries

1½ dozen cookies

1 Line baking sheets with wax paper. Set aside. In medium mixing bowl, combine cream cheese and milk. Beat at medium speed of electric mixer until smooth. Add melted chocolate, vanilla and salt. Beat at medium speed until smooth.

2 Stir in marshmallows, noodles and cranberries. Drop mixture by heaping teaspoons onto prepared baking sheets. Chill until set. Store in refrigerator.

TRUFFLES ❄ FREEZE AHEAD

- 3 bars (4 oz./125 g each) sweet cooking chocolate
- ¾ cup (175 mL) butter or margarine, cut into pieces
- 2 eggs, beaten
- 2 egg yolks, beaten
- 1¾ cups (425 mL) ground hazelnuts, divided
- ⅓ cup (75 mL) white crème de menthe
- 2 tablespoons (25 mL) cocoa

About 4 dozen truffles

1 Place chocolate in medium bowl. Microwave at 50% (Medium) for 2 to 5 minutes, or until melted, stirring 2 or 3 times. Stir in butter until melted. Blend in eggs and egg yolks.

2 Microwave at 50% (Medium) for 4½ to 5½ minutes, or until thickened, stirring with wire whip several times. Blend in 1 cup (250 mL) ground hazelnuts and crème de menthe. Refrigerate 3 hours, or until mixture is firm enough to shape into balls.

3 Shape into 1 to 1½-inch (2.5 to 3.5 cm) balls. Mix remaining ¾ cup (175 mL) hazelnuts and the cocoa. Roll balls in hazelnut mixture to coat. Freeze in single layer on tray until firm. Wrap, label and freeze no longer than 6 months.

4 To serve, unwrap 12 truffles and arrange in single layer on plate. Microwave at 30% (Medium Low) for 1 minute, rearranging once. Let stand for 10 minutes. Repeat, as desired.

287

◄ TURTLETTES *(Opposite, left)*

- 4 dozen large pecan halves, cut in half lengthwise
- 1 dozen large pecan halves, cut in half crosswise
- 2 dozen caramel candies
- 1 large recipe Chocolate Coating (right)

2 dozen candies

1 Arrange pecans on a sheet of wax paper, with 4 long pieces for legs and 1 short piece for head of each turtlette. Prepare 6 turtlettes at a time.

2 Grease a pie plate. Arrange 6 caramels evenly around edge. Microwave at High for 30 to 45 seconds, or until candies are soft but not melted on bottom, rotating plate once.

3 Press caramels down firmly over arranged nuts. Quickly form into turtle shape with fingers. If caramels become hard, microwave at High for 10 to 15 seconds. Repeat with remaining ingredients.

4 Frost with Chocolate Coating. Or dip each turtlette in Chocolate

Coating, using two forks. Place turtlettes on wax paper. Set aside and cool until set.

Chocolate Coating:

For large recipe, place 1 cup (250 mL) semisweet chocolate chips and 2 tablespoons (25 mL) vegetable shortening in a medium mixing bowl. For small recipe, use ½ cup (125 mL) chips and 1 tablespoon (15 mL) vegetable shortening.

Microwave at 50% (Medium) for 2½ to 5 minutes, or until chips can be stirred smooth. Stir well. Use to dip turtles or frost bars.

Helpful Hint: *With Chocolate Coating you can make a variety of quick and simple candies. Use it to dip large nuts, marshmallows, pretzels, animal crackers or other small cookies. If coating sets up while you are dipping, microwave at 50% (Medium) for 15 to 30 seconds to remelt. Refrigerate candies for faster setting.*

◄ PEANUT BUTTER HAYSTACKS *(Opposite, right)*

- 1 pkg. (6 oz./165 g) butterscotch chips
- ½ cup (125 mL) peanut butter
- ½ cup (125 mL) salted peanuts
- 2 cups (500 mL) chow mein noodles

About 2½ dozen candies

1 Combine chips and peanut butter in 2-quart (2 L) casserole or medium mixing bowl.

2 Microwave at 50% (Medium) for 3 to 5 minutes, or until chips can be stirred smooth.

3 Stir in salted peanuts and chow mein noodles. Drop mixture into mounds on wax paper. Cool at room temperature until set.

CREAM CHEESE MINTS ❄ FREEZE AHEAD

- 1 pkg. (8 oz./227 g) cream cheese
- 2 tablespoons (25 mL) butter or margarine
- ¾ teaspoon (4 mL) peppermint or wintergreen extract
- 6 to 7 cups (1.5 to 1.75 L) powdered sugar
- 3 drops food coloring (any color)

7 to 8 dozen mints

1 Place cream cheese in large bowl. Microwave at 50% (Medium) for 1 minute to soften. Add butter. Blend in extract. With electric mixer, beat in sugar until mixture is very stiff. Blend food coloring into candy.

2 With pastry bag and number 6 star tip, press mints, 1 to 1½ inches (2.5 to 3.5 cm) in diameter, onto wax-paper-lined baking sheet (if using different colors, wash pastry tube after each color). Let stand at room temperature for 24 hours. Freeze in single layer on baking sheet until firm. Wrap, label and freeze no longer than 1 month.

3 To serve, unwrap and arrange in single layer on plate. Let stand at room temperature for 5 to 10 minutes.

POPCORN BALLS

- 2⅔ cups (670 mL) sugar
- 1½ cups (375 mL) hot water
- ⅔ cup (150 mL) dark corn syrup
- 2 teaspoons (10 mL) vinegar
- 2 teaspoons (10 mL) vanilla
- 12 cups (3 L) popped popcorn

12 popcorn balls

1 Combine sugar, hot water, corn syrup and vinegar in 3-quart (3 L) casserole.

2 Microwave at High for 35 to 40 minutes, or until hard crack stage (300° to 310°F/150° to 155°C), when syrup separates into hard, brittle threads when small amount is dropped into cold water, stirring 3 or 4 times.

3 Stir in vanilla. Pour syrup over popcorn, stirring to coat. Quickly shape into balls, using buttered hands.

4 Place on wax paper; cool completely. Wrap each in plastic wrap.

▲ HAND-DIPPED CREAMS

Cream:
- 1 lb. (450 g) candy coating, any flavor
- ¼ cup (50 mL) vegetable shortening

Stir-Ins:

Stir one of the following into melted cream mixture.

- ¾ to 1 cup (175 to 250 mL) chopped nuts, peanuts, flaked coconut or raisins
- 1 teaspoon (5 mL) peppermint extract
- ½ cup (125 mL) peanut butter and 2 cups (500 mL) ready-to-eat cereal
- ½ cup (125 mL) peanut butter and 2 cups (500 mL) ready-to-eat cereal
- 1 teaspoon (5 mL) maple extract

Coating:
- ½ lb. (220 g) candy coating, any flavor
- 1 tablespoon (15 mL) vegetable shortening

1 Break candy coating into squares if it is in solid piece. Place 1 lb. (450 g) in single layer in 2-quart (2 L) casserole with ¼ cup (50 mL) shortening. Microwave at 50% (Medium) for 3 to 5 minutes, or until pieces are soft; stir after 3 minutes. Add stir-ins, if desired.

2 Spread in wax-paper-lined loaf dish. Let stand just until firm in center. Cut into 1-inch (2.5 cm) squares; let harden completely.

3 For coating, place ½ lb. (220 g) candy coating in small bowl with 1 tablespoon (15 mL) shortening. Microwave as directed for creams. Dip each square into candy coating to cover completely, using 1 or 2 forks. Let stand on wax paper until firm.

Helpful Hint: *For a more attractive appearance, use different flavor candy coatings for the cream and the dip. However, a white dip does not work as well with a darker candy.*

PEANUT BUTTER CUPS ❄ FREEZE AHEAD

- ¾ cup (175 mL) butter or margarine
- ¾ cup (175 mL) crunchy peanut butter
- 1½ cups (375 mL) graham cracker crumbs
- 1½ cups (375 mL) powdered sugar
- 1½ cups (375 mL) milk chocolate chips
- 3 tablespoons (50 mL) vegetable shortening
- 24 paper nut cups, 1¾ × 1¼-inch (4 × 3 cm)

2 dozen peanut butter cups

1 Combine butter and peanut butter in medium bowl. Microwave at 50% (Medium) for 2 to 4 minutes, or until butter melts, stirring 1 or 2 times. Stir in crumbs and sugar. Set aside.

2 Combine chocolate chips and shortening in small bowl. Microwave at 50% (Medium) for 1½ to 3 minutes, or until melted, stirring 1 or 2 times. Place bowl in container of hot water or microwave as necessary at 50% (Medium) for 30 seconds to 1½ minutes to keep chocolate from hardening.

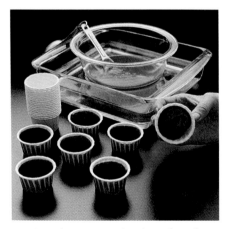

3 Coat bottom and sides of each paper cup with 1 to 1½ teaspoons (5 to 7 mL) chocolate. Let stand until chocolate hardens.

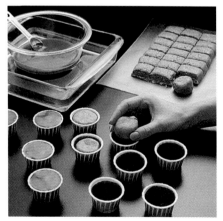

4 Press peanut butter mixture into each cup. Coat top with chocolate. Freeze in single layer on tray until firm. Wrap, label and freeze no longer than 6 months.

5 To serve, unwrap 12 and remove nut cups; place on plate in circle. Microwave at 30% (Medium Low) for 3 minutes, rearranging 2 times. Let stand for 10 minutes. Repeat, as desired.

◄ CARAMEL APPLES

- 12 medium red Delicious or McIntosh apples
- 12 wooden sticks
- 2 pkgs. (14 oz./396 g each) caramels
- ¼ cup (50 mL) half-and-half
- ½ cup (125 mL) chocolate-flavored or colored candy sprinkles

12 apples

1 Wash and dry apples. Insert sticks in stem ends. Place caramels and half-and-half in 2-quart (2 L) casserole. Microwave at High for 4 to 7 minutes, or until melted, stirring every minute.

2 Dip each apple in hot caramel until coated. Coat bottoms with candy sprinkles. Cool apples on wax paper.

PETITS FOURS

- 1 pkg. (2-layer size) white cake mix
- ½ teaspoon (2 mL) almond extract
- Petits Fours Icing (right)

50 petits fours

1 Prepare cake as directed on package, adding almond extract with the water. Divide batter between two 8-inch (2 L) square baking dishes. Microwave one at a time at 50% (Medium) for 6 minutes; rotate. Increase power to High. Microwave for 1 to 3 minutes, or until cake pulls away from side and wooden pick inserted in center comes out clean.

2 Let stand directly on counter for 5 minutes. Remove from pan; cool on wire rack. Trim edges from cooled cake. Cut each into 1½-inch (3.5 cm) squares or diamonds.

3 Place one-third of cake pieces, with space between sides, on wire rack over baking sheet. Spoon green icing evenly over top and sides until completely covered. If necessary, frost sides with metal spatula. Let icing dry. Spoon on second coat. Let dry. Repeat with white and pink icing, using one-third of the cake pieces for each color. Decorate with frosting flowers or whole almonds, if desired.

PETITS FOURS ICING

- 3 cups (750 mL) sugar
- ¼ teaspoon (1 mL) cream of tartar
- 1½ cups (375 mL) hot water
- 1 teaspoon (5 mL) vanilla or almond extract
- 1 cup (250 mL) powdered sugar
- 1 drop green food coloring
- 1 drop red food coloring

Frosts 50 petits fours

1 In 3-quart (3 L) mixing bowl, combine sugar, cream of tartar and water. Cover and microwave at High for 6 to 8 minutes, or until just boiling. Uncover. Microwave at High for 10 to 15 minutes, or until mixture reaches 226°F (110°C) on candy thermometer. Let stand on counter until cooled to 110°F (45°C).

2 Stir in vanilla and powdered sugar until icing is of pouring consistency and smooth. Divide among 3 bowls. Mix green food coloring into one, red food coloring into another and leave one white.

292

▲ BEST-EVER FUDGE

- 1 pkg. (6 oz./165 g) semisweet chocolate chips
- 6 oz./165 g) baking sweet chocolate, broken into squares
- 1 cup (250 mL) chopped nuts
- 1 cup (250 mL) marshmallow creme
- 2¼ cups (550 mL) sugar
- 1 can (5 oz./140 g) evaporated milk
- 1 tablespoon (15 mL) butter or margarine
- ⅛ teaspoon (0.5 mL) salt

2½ lbs. (1.12 kg) candy

1 Butter 9-inch (2.5 L) square baking dish. Set aside. In large mixing bowl, combine chocolate chips, sweet chocolate, nuts and marshmallow creme. Set aside.

2 In 2-quart (2 L) measure, combine sugar, evaporated milk, butter and salt. Mix well. Microwave at High for 2 minutes, stirring after every minute. Microwave at High for 1½ to 4 minutes, or until mixture comes to a full rolling boil.

3 Pour hot milk mixture over chocolate mixture. Mix until chocolate melts and marshmallow creme is blended. Spread mixture evenly into prepared dish. Chill until cool and set, about 3 hours. Cut into small squares.

PRALINE FUDGE ❄ FREEZE AHEAD

- 2 cups (500 mL) sugar
- 1 teaspoon (5 mL) baking soda
- 1 cup (250 mL) evaporated milk
- ¾ cup (175 mL) butter or margarine
- 1 teaspoon (5 mL) vanilla
- 2 cups (500 mL) chocolate chips
- 2 cups (500 mL) broken pecans

3 lbs (1.5 kg) fudge

1 Line 12 × 8-inch (3 L) baking dish with foil. In medium bowl, mix sugar, baking soda, evaporated milk and butter. Microwave at 70% (Medium High) for 22 to 27 minutes, or until syrup dropped into very cold water forms a soft ball that flattens on removal from water. Stir several times during cooking.

2 Add vanilla. Beat for 2 minutes at high speed of electric mixer, scraping bowl occasionally. Add chocolate chips. Beat with electric mixer until chips melt. Stir in pecans. Press into prepared baking dish. Refrigerate until set.

3 Remove from foil lining. Cut into serving pieces, but do not separate. Divide into three 1-lb. (450 g) sections. Wrap, label and freeze no longer than 6 months.

4 To serve, unwrap one package; separate pieces on plate. Microwave at 30% (Medium Low) for 2 minutes, rearranging every 30 seconds. Let stand for 5 to 10 minutes. Repeat, as desired.

▲ CARAMEL-NUT CANDY

- 1½ cups (375 mL) sugar
- ⅓ cup (75 mL) milk
- ¼ cup (50 mL) butter or margarine
- 1 bag (14 oz./396 g) caramels, unwrapped
- ¾ cup (175 mL) chopped nuts

2 lbs. (1 kg) candy

1 Butter 9-inch (2.5 L) square baking dish. Set aside. In 2-quart (2 L) measure, combine sugar, milk and butter.

2 Microwave at High for 2 minutes. Stir until butter melts. Microwave at High for 3 to 4½ minutes, or until syrup dropped into very cold water forms a soft ball that flattens on removal from water.

3 Carefully add caramels. Microwave at High for 1½ to 2½ minutes, or until caramels melt and can be stirred smooth. Stir in nuts. Spread mixture evenly into prepared dish. Chill until cool and set, about 3 hours. Cut into small squares.

BARS & COOKIES

◀ CANDY-TOPPED BROWNIES

Brownies:
- 1 cup (250 mL) sugar
- ½ cup (125 mL) butter or margarine, softened
- 1¼ cups (300 mL) chocolate-flavored syrup
- 3 eggs
- 2 teaspoons (10 mL) vanilla
- 1½ cups (375 mL) all-purpose flour
- ½ cup (125 mL) milk chocolate chips

Frosting:
- ⅓ cup (75 mL) butter or margarine
- ⅓ cup (75 mL) sugar
- ¼ cup (50 mL) milk
- 1 cup (250 mL) milk chocolate chips
- 1 cup (250 mL) candy-coated plain chocolate pieces

24 brownies

1 Heat oven to 350°F (180°C). Lightly grease 13 × 9-inch (3.5 L) baking pan. Set aside. In large mixing bowl, combine 1 cup (250 mL) sugar and ½ cup (125 mL) butter. Beat at medium speed of electric mixer until light and fluffy. Add syrup, eggs and vanilla. Beat at medium speed until well blended. Add flour. Beat at low speed until well blended. Stir in ½ cup (125 mL) chips. Spread mixture evenly in prepared pan.

2 Bake for 33 to 38 minutes, or until wooden pick inserted in center comes out clean. Cool completely.

3 In 1-quart (1 L) saucepan, combine ⅓ cup (75 mL) butter, ⅓ cup (75 mL) sugar and the milk. Bring to a boil over medium heat, stirring frequently. Boil for 1 minute. Remove from heat. Add 1 cup (250 mL) chips. Stir until smooth. Spread frosting evenly over brownies. Sprinkle frosting evenly with chocolate pieces.

RICH LAYERED BARS

- 6 tablespoons (75 mL) butter or margarine
- 1½ cups (375 mL) graham cracker crumbs
- 3 tablespoons (50 mL) sugar
- 2 cups (500 mL) flaked coconut
- 1 pkg. (6 oz./165 g) semisweet chocolate chips
- 1 pkg. (6 oz./165 g) butterscotch chips
- 1 cup (250 mL) chopped pecans
- 1 can (14 oz./396 g) sweetened condensed milk

3 dozen bars

1 Place butter in 9-inch (2.5 L) square baking dish. Microwave at High for 1½ to 1¾ minutes, or until butter melts. Stir in graham cracker crumbs and sugar. Mix well. Press mixture firmly against bottom of dish. Microwave at High for 2 minutes, rotating dish once.

2 Layer coconut, chocolate chips, butterscotch chips and pecans over crust. Pour sweetened condensed milk evenly over pecans. Reduce power to 50% (Medium). Microwave for 10 to 18 minutes, or just until bubbly around edges. Cool completely. Cut into squares.

(See photo of this recipe with Best-Ever Fudge and Caramel-Nut Candy, page 293)

▲ PEANUT-SCOTCH BARS

- ¼ cup (50 mL) plus 2 tablespoons (25 mL) butter or margarine
- 1 cup (250 mL) packed brown sugar
- ¼ cup (50 mL) peanut butter
- 1 cup (250 mL) all-purpose flour
- ½ cup (125 mL) Spanish peanuts
- 2 eggs
- 1 teaspoon (5 mL) vanilla
- ½ teaspoon (2 mL) baking powder
- ¼ teaspoon (1 mL) salt
- 1 small recipe Chocolate Coating (page 289)

1 Melt butter in 9-inch (2.5 L) square baking dish at High for 1½ to 1¾ minutes. Stir in sugar and peanut butter, then remaining ingredients, except Chocolate Coating. Spread evenly in dish. Place on inverted saucer in microwave.

2 Microwave at 70% (Medium High) for 9 to 12 minutes, or until top is no longer wet, rotating dish 2 or 3 times. Cool on counter. Prepare Chocolate Coating. Frost cooled bars.

12 to 16 bars

◀ MARSHMALLOW CRISPY BARS

- ¼ cup (50 mL) butter or margarine
- 1 pkg. (10 oz./283 g) marshmallows
- ¼ teaspoon (1 mL) vanilla
- 5 cups (1.25 L) crispy rice cereal

3 dozen bars

1 Microwave butter in 9-inch (2.5 L) square baking dish at High for 1¼ to 1½ minutes, or until melted. Stir in marshmallows and vanilla.

2 Microwave at High for 1½ to 3½ minutes, or until marshmallows are puffed, stirring after first minute. Stir until smooth.

3 Add cereal, one third at a time, stirring with fork until well coated. Press into dish. Cool. Cut into 36 bars.

Marshmallow-Peanut Crispies:

Follow recipe above, except stir in 1 cup (250 mL) salted peanuts after the cereal.

Peanut Butter-Marshmallow Crispies:

Follow recipe above, except add ¼ cup (50 mL) peanut butter with the marshmallows.

Chocolate-Peanut Crispies:

Follow recipe above, except add ¼ cup (50 mL) peanut butter and ½ cup (125 mL) chocolate chips with the marshmallows.

▲ ORANGE-SPICE SHORTBREAD

- 2¼ cups (550 mL) all-purpose flour
- ⅔ cup (150 mL) sugar
- 1 teaspoon (5 mL) grated orange peel
- ¼ to ½ teaspoon (1 to 2 mL) ground nutmeg
- Pinch of salt
- 1¼ cups (300 mL) cold butter, cut into small pieces

About 5 dozen cookies

1 Heat oven to 325°F (160°C). Lightly grease two 8-inch (2 L) square baking pans. Set aside. In large mixing bowl, combine flour, sugar, peel, nutmeg and salt. Using pastry blender, cut in butter until mixture resembles coarse crumbs. Form dough into ball.

2 Divide dough in half. Press halves evenly into prepared pans. Using fork, prick dough at 1-inch (2.5 cm) intervals. Bake for 30 to 35 minutes, or until light golden brown. Immediately cut shortbread into 2-inch (5 cm) squares, then cut each square diagonally to form triangles. Cool completely in pans before storing.

PEPPERMINT BONBONS

Cookies:

- 1 cup (250 mL) sugar
- ½ cup (125 mL) butter or margarine, softened
- ½ cup (125 mL) vegetable shortening
- ½ cup (125 mL) unsweetened cocoa
- ½ cup (125 mL) buttermilk
- 2 eggs
- ¼ teaspoon (1 mL) peppermint extract
- 3 cups (750 mL) all-purpose flour
- ½ teaspoon (2 mL) baking soda
- ¼ teaspoon (1 mL) salt

Frosting:

- 2 cups (500 mL) powdered sugar
- 2 to 4 tablespoons (25 to 50 mL) whipping cream
- 2 tablespoons (25 mL) butter or margarine, softened
- 1 or 2 drops green food coloring

5 dozen cookies

1 In large mixing bowl, combine sugar, ½ cup (125 mL) butter, the shortening, cocoa, buttermilk, eggs and peppermint extract. Beat at medium speed of electric mixer until well blended. Add flour, baking soda and salt. Beat at low speed until soft dough forms. Cover with plastic wrap. Chill 3 to 4 hours, or until firm.

2 Heat oven to 350°F (180°C). Shape dough into 1-inch (2.5 cm) balls. Place balls 2 inches (5 cm) apart on ungreased baking sheets. Bake for 10 to 14 minutes, or until set. Cool completely.

3 In medium mixing bowl, combine all frosting ingredients. Beat at low speed of electric mixer until smooth. Spread frosting evenly on cookies. Let dry completely before storing.

NUTMEG SQUARES

- ½ cup (125 mL) sugar
- ½ cup (125 mL) butter or margarine, softened
- 1 egg
- 1 tablespoon (15 mL) whipping cream
- 1 teaspoon (5 mL) vanilla
- 2 cups (500 mL) all-purpose flour
- 1 teaspoon (5 mL) baking powder
- ½ teaspoon (2 mL) baking soda
- ½ teaspoon (2 mL) ground nutmeg
- ½ cup (125 mL) semisweet chocolate chips
- 2 teaspoons (10 mL) vegetable shortening, divided
- ½ cup (125 mL) vanilla baking chips
- ½ cup (125 mL) coarsely chopped pistachios

About 3 dozen cookies

1 Heat oven to 350°F (180°C). In large mixing bowl, combine sugar, butter, egg, cream and vanilla. Beat at medium speed of electric mixer until well blended. Add flour, baking powder, baking soda and nutmeg. Beat at low speed until soft dough forms. Cover with plastic wrap. Chill 3 to 4 hours, or until firm.

2 On lightly floured surface, roll dough to ⅛ to ¼-inch (3 to 5 mm) thickness. Using 3-inch (8 cm) square cookie cutter, cut squares into dough. Place squares 2 inches (5 cm) apart on ungreased baking sheets. Bake for 8 to 10 minutes, or until edges are golden brown. Cool completely.

3 In 1-quart (1 L) saucepan, combine chocolate chips and 1 teaspoon (5 mL) shortening. Melt over low heat, stirring constantly. Set aside. Repeat with vanilla chips and remaining 1 teaspoon (5 mL) shortening. (If desired, transfer melted chips to custard cups.)

4 Dip one corner of each cookie into melted chocolate chips. Sprinkle pistachios evenly over dipped corners. Repeat with opposite corner in melted vanilla chips and remaining pistachios. Let dry completely before storing.

BROWN SUGAR COOKIES

Cookies:
- 1 cup (250 mL) butter or margarine, softened
- ½ cup (125 mL) packed brown sugar
- ¼ cup (50 mL) granulated sugar
- 1 teaspoon (5 mL) vanilla
- 2½ cups (550 mL) all-purpose flour
- ½ teaspoon (2 mL) salt

Frosting:
- ¾ cup (175 mL) packed brown sugar
- ¼ cup (50 mL) butter or margarine
- 1¼ cups (300 mL) powdered sugar
- 1 to 2 tablespoons (15 to 25 mL) half-and-half
- 1 teaspoon (5 mL) vanilla

About 6 dozen cookies

1 Heat oven to 300°F (150°C). In large mixing bowl, combine 1 cup (250 mL) butter, ½ cup (125 mL) brown sugar, the granulated sugar and 1 teaspoon (5 mL) vanilla. Beat at medium speed of electric mixer until light and fluffy. Add flour and salt. Beat at low speed until soft dough forms. Form dough into ball.

2 On well-floured surface, roll dough to ¼ to ½-inch (5 mm to 1 cm) thickness. Using 2-inch (5 cm) round cookie cutter, cut dough into circles. Place circles 2 inches (5 cm) apart on ungreased baking sheets. Bake for 20 to 25 minutes, or until golden brown. Cool completely.

3 In 1-quart (1 L) saucepan, combine ¾ cup (175 mL) brown sugar and ¼ cup (50 mL) butter. Cook over medium heat until butter is melted, stirring constantly. Remove from heat. Add remaining frosting ingredients. Stir until smooth. Spread frosting evenly on cookies. Let dry completely before storing.

▲ SPICY GUMDROP COOKIES

- ¾ cup (175 mL) packed brown sugar
- ½ cup (125 mL) granulated sugar
- ½ cup (125 mL) butter or margarine, softened
- ½ cup (125 mL) vegetable shortening
- 1 egg
- 1 teaspoon (5 mL) vanilla
- 2 cups (500 mL) all-purpose flour

- 2 cups (500 mL) uncooked quick-cooking oats
- ½ cup (125 mL) flaked coconut
- 1 teaspoon (5 mL) baking soda
- ½ teaspoon (2 mL) baking powder
- ¼ teaspoon (1 mL) salt
- 1 cup (250 mL) chopped spiced gumdrops

3½ dozen cookies

1 Heat oven to 375°F (190°C). Lightly grease baking sheets. Set aside. In large mixing bowl, combine sugars, butter, shortening, egg and vanilla. Beat at medium speed of electric mixer until light and fluffy. Add flour, oats, coconut, baking soda, baking powder and salt. Beat at low speed until soft dough forms. Stir in gumdrops.

2 Drop dough by heaping teaspoons 2 inches (5 cm) apart onto prepared baking sheets. Bake for 7 to 10 minutes, or until edges are golden brown. Let cool for 1 minute before removing from baking sheets. Cool completely before storing.

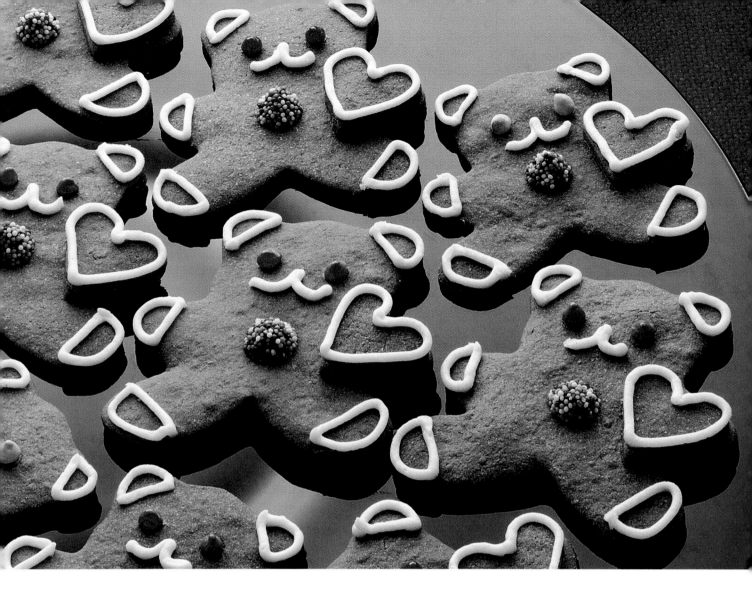

CHOCOLATE HEART PARTY BEARS

Cookies:

- 1 cup (250 mL) sugar
- 1 cup (250 mL) butter or margarine, softened
- 1 pkg. (3 oz./85 g) cream cheese, softened
- 1 egg
- 1 teaspoon (5 mL) vanilla
- ½ teaspoon (2 mL) chocolate extract
- 3 cups (750 mL) all-purpose flour
- ½ cup (125 mL) unsweetened cocoa
- Rainbow semisweet chocolate chips
- Miniature candy-coated semisweet chocolate chips

Frosting:

- 2 cups (500 mL) powdered sugar
- 2 to 3 tablespoons (25 to 50 mL) half-and-half
- 2 tablespoons (25 mL) butter or margarine, softened
- 1 or 2 drops red food coloring

5 dozen cookies

1 In large mixing bowl, combine sugar, 1 cup (250 mL) butter, the cream cheese, egg, vanilla and chocolate extract. Beat at medium speed of electric mixer until light and fluffy. Add flour and cocoa. Beat at low speed until soft dough forms. Divide dough in half. Cover with plastic wrap. Chill 1 to 2 hours, or until firm.

2 Heat oven to 350°F (180°C). On well-floured surface, roll half of dough to ¼-inch (5 mm) thickness. Using 3-inch (8 cm) teddy bear cookie cutter and 1-inch (2.5 cm) heart cookie cutter, cut shapes into dough. (Cut equal number of bears and hearts.)

3 Place bear shapes 2 inches (5 cm) apart on ungreased baking sheets. Place 1 heart on paw of each bear. Repeat with remaining dough. Decorate each bear with rainbow chip for belly button and miniature chips for eyes. Bake for 8 to 10 minutes, or until set. Cool completely.

4 In small mixing bowl, combine frosting ingredients. Using pastry bag with #2 writing tip, pipe outline on hearts, paws and ears. Pipe on mouth. Let dry completely before storing.

GINGERMAN SANDWICH COOKIES

- 12 oz. (375 g) white candy coating
- 1½ teaspoons (7 mL) vegetable shortening
- Red or green food color paste (optional)
- 3 pkgs. (5 oz./142 g each) gingerman cookies
- 30 pieces shoestring licorice (4-inch/10 cm lengths)
- Red cinnamon candies

2½ dozen cookies

1 Line baking sheets with wax paper. Set aside. In 1-quart (1 L) saucepan, combine candy coating and shortening. Melt over low heat, stirring constantly. Add food color paste. Mix well.

2 Spoon small amount of coating onto backs of half of cookies. Place cookies coated-sides-up on prepared baking sheets. Fold licorice pieces in half to form loops. Place 1 loop at head end of each cookie, with cut ends in coating on cookie.

3 Gently press backs of remaining half of cookies against filling to form sandwiches. Decorate one side, using wooden picks and remaining coating to attach cinnamon candies for eyes, nose and buttons. Let dry completely before storing.

Helpful Hint: *For a shortcut, microwave candy coating and shortening at 50% (Medium) for 2½ to 5½ minutes, stirring after every minute. Continue as directed.*

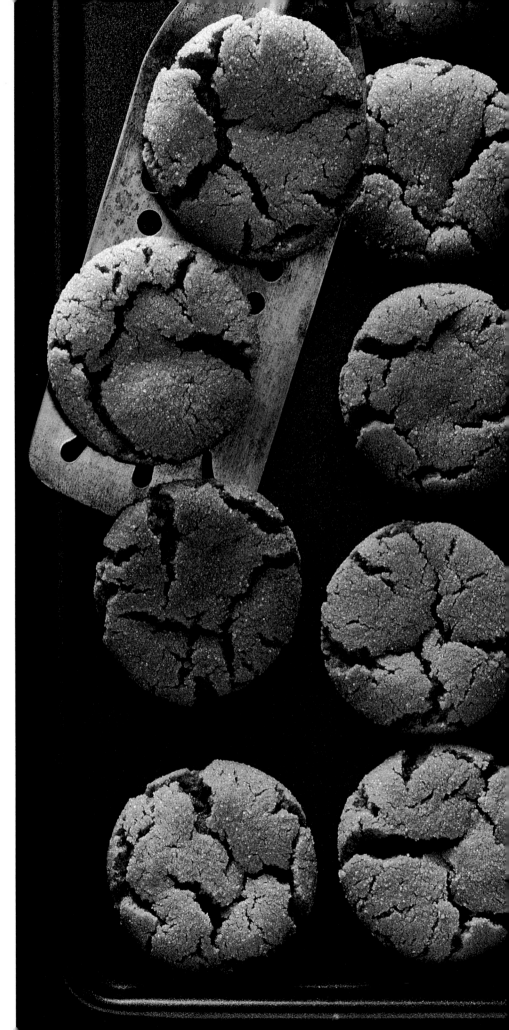

CRINKLED MOLASSES COOKIES

- 1 cup (250 mL) sugar
- ¾ cup (175 mL) vegetable shortening
- ¼ cup (50 mL) light molasses
- 1 egg
- 2 cups (500 mL) all-purpose flour
- 2½ teaspoons (12 mL) baking soda
- 1 teaspoon (5 mL) ground cinnamon
- 1 teaspoon (5 mL) ground ginger
- ½ teaspoon (2 mL) ground cloves
- ¼ teaspoon (1 mL) ground cardamom
- ¼ teaspoon (1 mL) salt
- Granulated sugar

6 dozen cookies

1 Heat oven to 350°F (180°C). In large mixing bowl, combine 1 cup (250 mL) sugar, the shortening, molasses and egg. Beat at medium speed of electric mixer until well blended. Add flour, baking soda, cinnamon, ginger, cloves, cardamom and salt. Beat at low speed until soft dough forms.

2 Shape dough into 1-inch (2.5 cm) balls. Roll balls in granulated sugar. Place balls 2 inches (5 cm) apart on ungreased baking sheets. Bake for 8 to 12 minutes, or until set. Cool completely before storing.

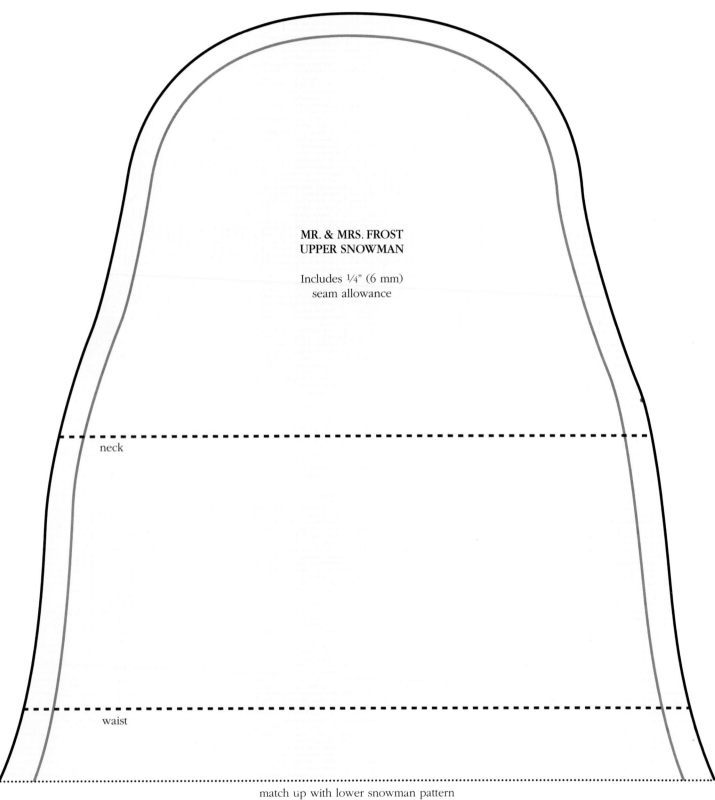

MR. & MRS. FROST
UPPER SNOWMAN

Includes ¼" (6 mm)
seam allowance

neck

waist

match up with lower snowman pattern

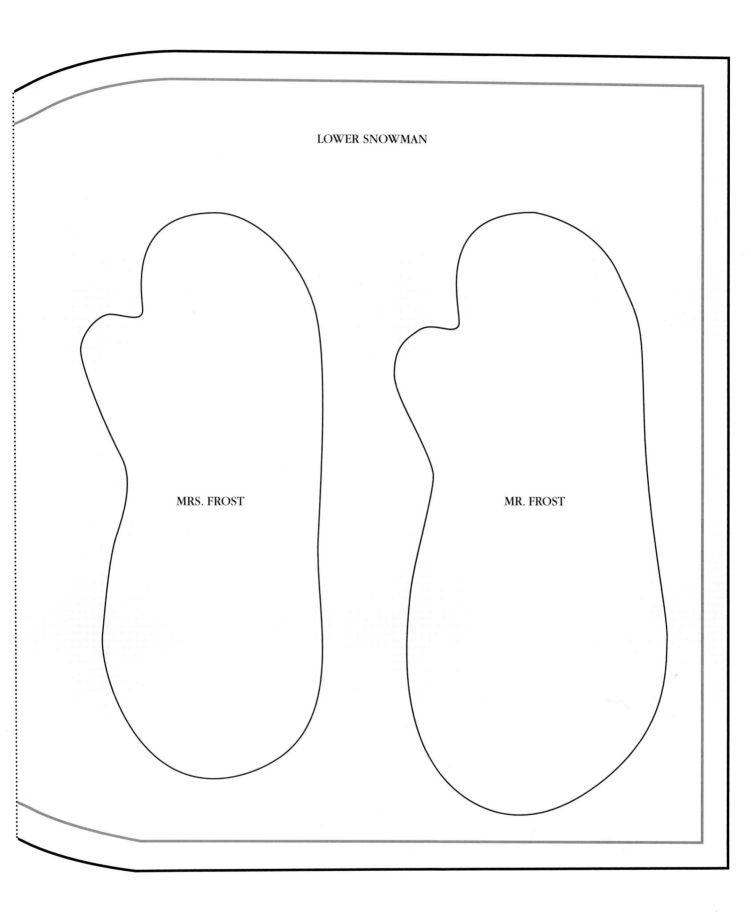

LOWER SNOWMAN

MRS. FROST

MR. FROST

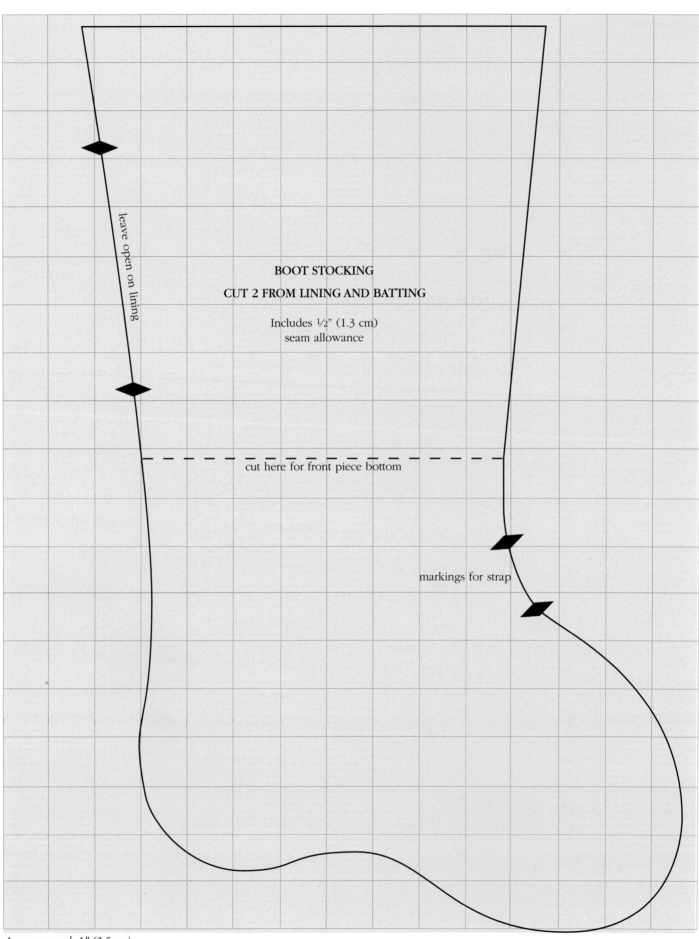

BOOT STOCKING

CUT 2 FROM LINING AND BATTING

Includes ½" (1.3 cm)
seam allowance

leave open on lining

cut here for front piece bottom

markings for strap

1 square equals 1" (2.5 cm)

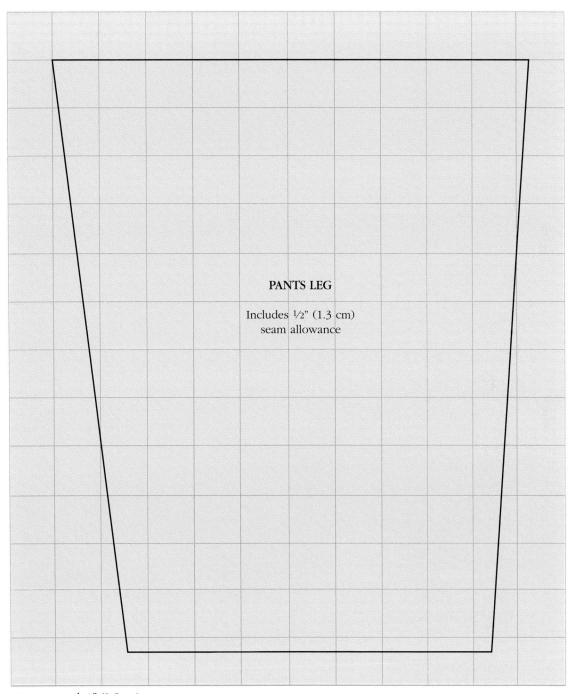

PANTS LEG

Includes ½" (1.3 cm)
seam allowance

1 square equals 1" (2.5 cm)

MITTEN GIFT BAG

Includes ¼" (6 mm)
seam allowance

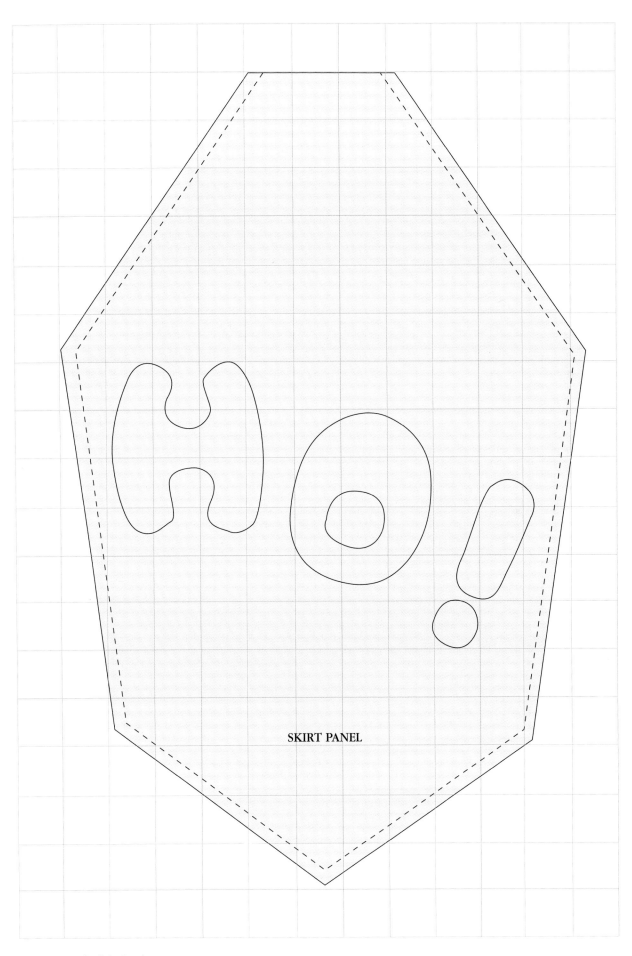

SKIRT PANEL

1 square equals 1" (2.5 cm)

309

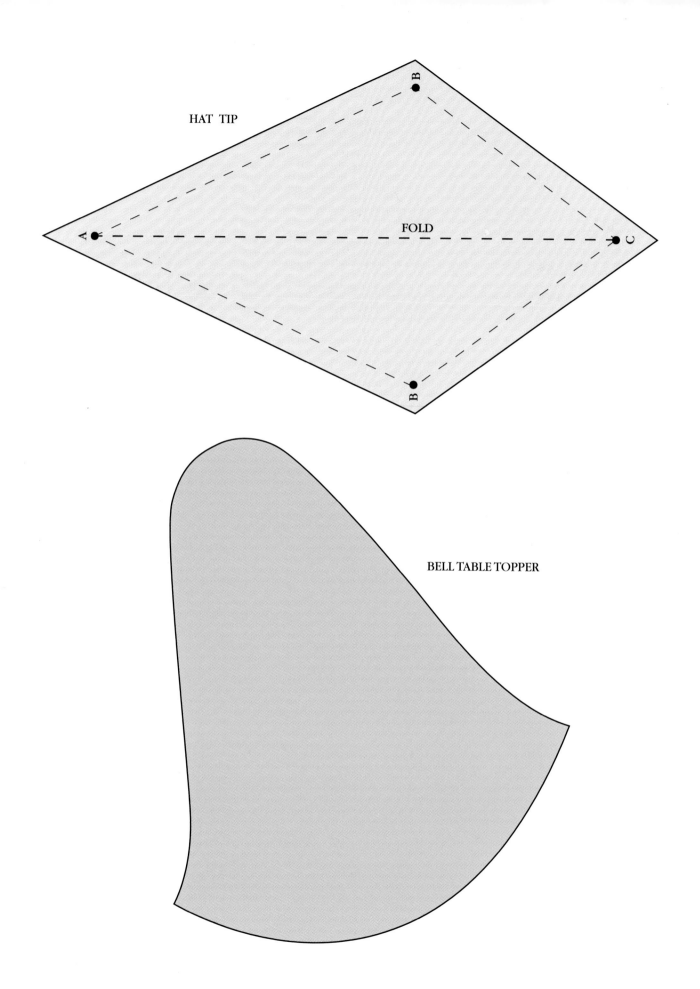

HAT TIP

B

FOLD

A

C

B

BELL TABLE TOPPER

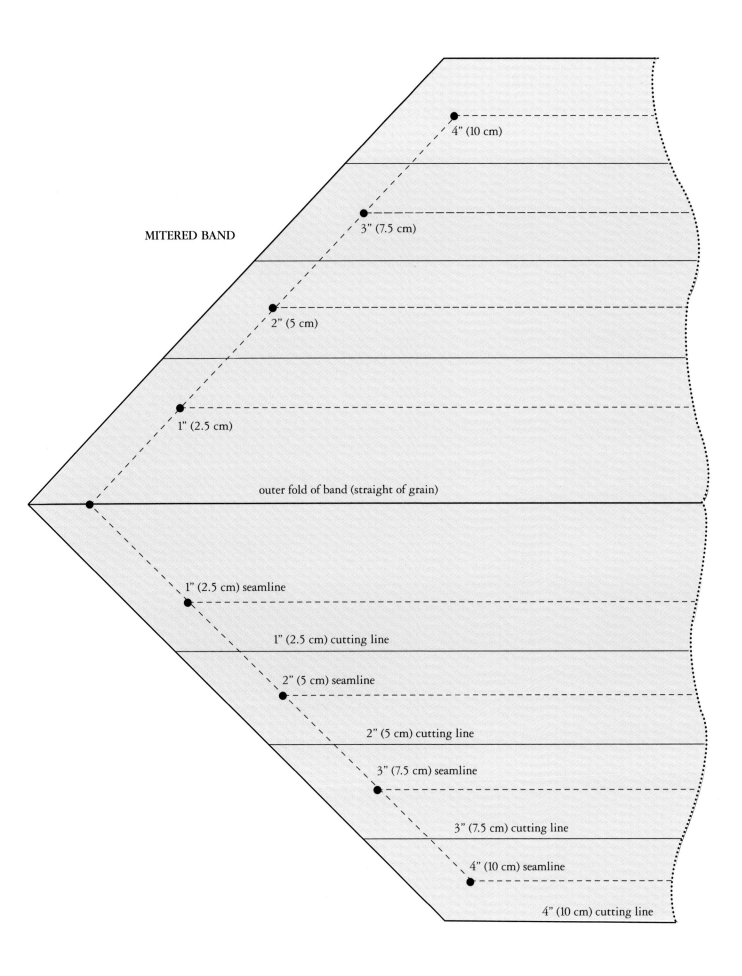

MITERED BAND

4" (10 cm)

3" (7.5 cm)

2" (5 cm)

1" (2.5 cm)

outer fold of band (straight of grain)

1" (2.5 cm) seamline

1" (2.5 cm) cutting line

2" (5 cm) seamline

2" (5 cm) cutting line

3" (7.5 cm) seamline

3" (7.5 cm) cutting line

4" (10 cm) seamline

4" (10 cm) cutting line

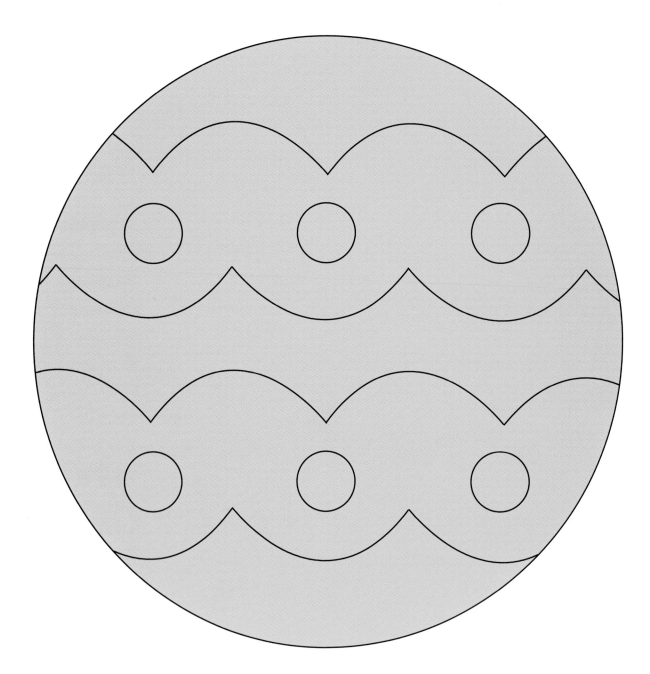

HOLIDAY ORNAMENT TRIVET

SANTA TRIVET

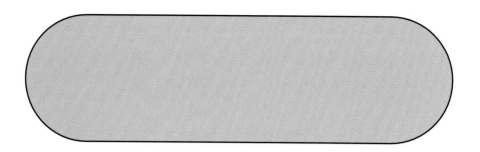

METAL NAPKIN RING

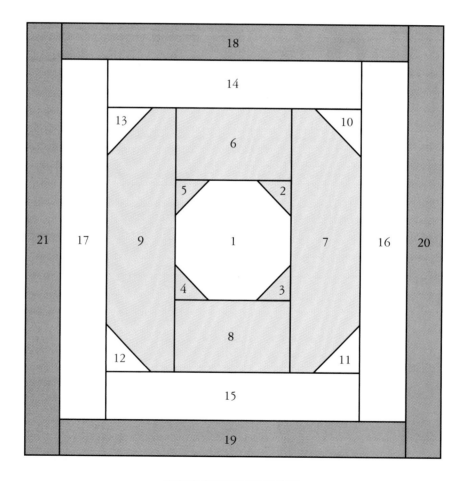

PAPER-PIECED WREATH

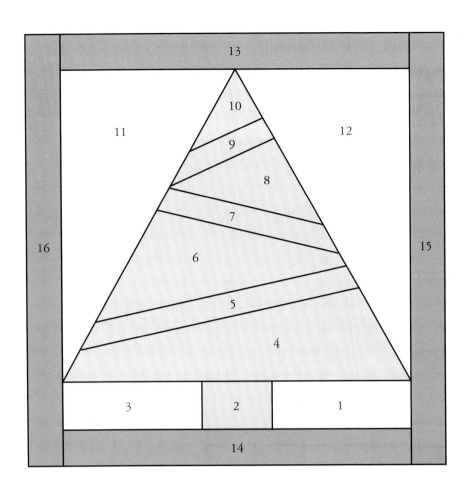

PAPER-PIECED TREE

PAPER-PIECED GIFT

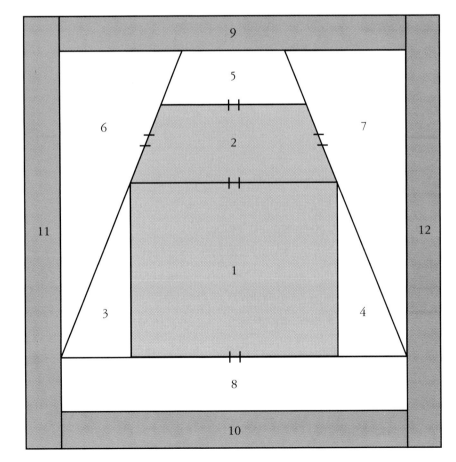

A

Accessories for entertaining,
  hooked rug trivet, 182-187, 312-313
  napkin rings, 192-197
  paper-pieced coasters, 203, 314-315
  scented coasters, 198-201
  tree trivet, 189-191
  woodburning designs, 176-181
Accompaniments,
  Cranberry-Orange Relish, 267
  Fruited Wild Rice, 267
  Pineapple Chutney, 266
  Spiced Apple Relish, 267
Advent decorations,
  calendar, 63-65
  wreath, 59-61, 157, 159
Angel ornament, seashell, 40-41
Appetizers, see: Cheese; Dips and
  spreads; Finger food
Apples,
  Apple Crisp, 272
  Apple-Pecan Crumble, 274
  Baked Apples, 272
  Brandied Apple Loaf, 213
  Caramel Apples, 292
  Phyllo Apple Turnovers, 270
  Sage Parsnips and Apples, 257
  Spiced Apple Relish, 267
Applesauce-Spice Loaf, 210
Appliqué linens, metallic, 118-121
Apricot Bread, 211
Arrangements, see: Centerpieces
Aspic, Tomato-Cucumber, 259

B

Bacon,
  Bacon and Horseradish Dip, 224
  Midwest Bacon and Cheese
    Company Canapés, 219
  Parmesan-Bacon Spread, 228
Bags, see: Gift bags
Baked Apples, 272
Baked Custard, 278
Baked French Toast, 207
Banana Bread, 211
Barbecued Meatballs, 218
Bars and cookies,
  Brown Sugar Cookies, 300
  Candy-Topped Brownies, 295
  Chocolate Heart Party Bears, 301
  Crinkled Molasses Cookies, 303
  Gingerman Sandwich Cookies, 302
  Marshmallow Crispy Bars, 297
  Nutmeg Squares, 299
  Orange-Spice Shortbread, 297
  Peanut-Scotch Bars, 296

Peppermint Bonbons, 298
  Rich Layered Bars, 295
  Spicy Gumdrop Cookies, 300
Beaded napkin rings, 192, 195-196
Beaded ornaments, 33-35
Beeswax decorations,
  molded candles, 163-165
  ornaments and garlands,
    166-167, 197
Beets with Sweet and Sour Apples, 256
Bell table topper, 133-135
  pattern, 310
Berry Fondue, 275
Best-Ever Fudge, 293
Beverages,
  Hot Bloody Mary, 215
  Hot Pineapple Punch, 215
  Mexican Hot Chocolate, 215
  Pink Zinger Punch, 214
Bias binding on a continuous curve,
  on table linens, 117
Bias strip, continuous, on table
  linens, 116
Birch-bark sconce, 17-18, 27
Bird feeders, 25-27
Bloody Mary, Hot, 215
Blue Cheese Log, 232
Boot stockings, 50-53
  patterns, 306-307
Bottles and jars, hostess gifts, 99-101
Box, Santa, 105-107
Brandied Apple Loaf, 213
Brandy Alexander Cream, 279
Bread Pudding, 278
Breads,
  Applesauce-Spice Loaf, 210
  Apricot Bread, 211
  Banana Bread, 211
  Brandied Apple Loaf, 213
  Cinnamon-Nut Loaf, 212
  Cran-Pineapple Bread, 209
  Date-Nut Bread, 210
  Pinwheel Bread Spread, 213
Breakfast recipes, see: Breads;
  Egg dishes
Brownies, Candy-Topped, 295
Brown Sugar Cookies, 300
Brunch recipes, see: Breads;
  Egg dishes
Brushed metal napkin rings, 192, 194
  pattern, 314

C

Cage ornament, 32, 34
Cakes,
  Festive Gelatin Cake, 282

Gingerbread with Orange Sauce, 281
  Plum Cake, 282
  Raspberry Ice Cream Cake, 283
Calendar, Advent, 63-65
Canapés, see: Finger food
Candleholders, painted glass, 171-173
Candles,
  embellishing, 168-169
  molded beeswax, 163-165
Candy,
  Best-Ever Fudge, 293
  Caramel-Nut Candy, 293
  Cranberry Haystacks, 286
  Cream Cheese Mints, 289
  Hand-Dipped Creams, 290
  Peanut Brittle, 286
  Peanut Butter Cups, 299
  Peanut Butter Haystacks, 289
  Praline Fudge, 293
  Truffles, 287
  Turtlettes, 289
Candy-Topped Brownies, 295
Caramel Apples, 292
Caramel Fruit Platter, 273
Caramel-Nut Candy, 293
Cards, paper art, 95-97
Carrots, Spicy Glazed, 255
Celery, Sautéed, with Toasted
  Almonds, 256
Centerpieces,
  cascading fruits and roses, 153-155
  fresh wreaths, 157-161
Changers, for pillows, 76-79
Charm ornament, Victorian, 37
Cheese,
  Blue Cheese Log, 232
  Cheese and Basil Pepper Spirals, 223
  Cheese Ball or Log, 233
  Cheesy Tomato Puffs, 220
  Chèvre and Sun-Dried Tomato
    Pâté, 226
  Crock Cheese, 233
  Party Cheese Ball, 230
  Port Wine Cheese Ball, 230
Cherried Ham Steak, 250
Cherry Soup, Cold, 276
Chèvre and Sun-Dried Tomato
  Pâté, 226
Chicken,
  Chicken and Broccoli Bites, 220
  Chicken-Pineapple Canapés, 222
  Hawaiian Chicken Company
    Canapés, 219
Chocolate Heart Party Bears, 301
Christmas tree,
  decorated in gold, 15
  shell-trimmed, 84-85

skirt for, patchwork Santa, 42-49,
   311-312
star topper, 30-31
topiary of lights, 23
also see: Ornaments
Chunky Salsa, 226
Chutney,
   Pineapple Chutney, 266
   Turkey Patties with Cranberry-Nut
      Chutney, 239
Cider-Sauced Turkey Breast, 240
Cinnamon-Nut Coffee Cake, 212
Cinnamon-Nut Loaf, 212
Classical gold wreath, 13-14
Coasters,
   paper-pieced, 203, 314-315
   scented, 198-201
   texturized, 141-143
Coffee Cake, Cinnamon-Nut, 212
Cold Cherry Soup, 276
Cold Peach Soup, 276
Company Canapés, 219
Cookies, see: Bars and cookies
Cornish hens,
   Cornish Hen and Vegetable
      Platter, 242
   Lime and Cumin Cornish Game
      Hens, 242
Crab, Seashore, Company
   Canapés, 219
Crackers, Hot Ham-n-Cheese, 229
Cranberries,
   Cranberry Corn Bread Dressing, 265
   Cranberry Haystacks, 286
   Cranberry-Orange Relish, 267
   Cranberry-Stuffed Turkey
      Tenderloins, 238
   Cran-Pineapple Bread, 209
   Frosted Cranberry Soup, 276
Cream Cheese Mints, 289
Creamed Pheasant and Biscuits, 247
Creams, see: Puddings and creams
Crinkled Molasses Cookies, 303
Crock Cheese, 233
Custard, Baked, 278

D

Date-Nut Bread, 210
Decorating trees, see: Christmas tree
Designs, woodburning, 176-181
Desserts, see: Cakes; Fruit desserts;
   Puddings and creams
Dips and spreads,
   Bacon and Horseradish Dip, 224
   Chèvre and Sun-Dried Tomato
      Pâté, 226
   Chunky Salsa, 226
   Herbed Garlic and Almond
      Spread, 228
   Hot Ham-n-Cheese Crackers, 229
   Indian Fruit Dip Platter, 228

Mexican Bean Dip, 227
Onion Dip, 225
Parmesan-Bacon Spread, 228
Pinwheel Bread Spread, 213
Dressings,
   Cranberry Corn Bread Dressing, 265
   Winter Fruit Dressing, 264
Duck,
   Traditional Roast, with Dressing, 247

E

Easy Velouté Sauce, 244
Egg dishes,
   Baked French Toast, 207
   Party Quiche, 207
   Puffy Omelet, 208
Embroidered linens, silk ribbon,
   127-131

F

Fabric-covered napkin rings, 192-194
Far-East Tuna Company Canapés, 219
Faux stained glass candleholders,
   171, 173
Feeders, bird, 25-27
Festive Gelatin Cake, 282
Feta and Pepper Appetizer Pizzas, 221
Figures, snowmen, Mr. and Mrs. Frost,
   87-91
   patterns, 304-305
Fillers, sconce, 18
Finger food,
   Barbecued Meatballs, 218
   Cheese and Basil Pepper Spirals, 223
   Cheesy Tomato Puffs, 220
   Chicken and Broccoli Bites, 220
   Chicken-Pineapple Canapés, 222
   Company Canapés, 219
   Feta and Pepper Appetizer
      Pizzas, 221
   Garlic-Chive Potato Crisps, 221
   Ham and Swiss Canapés, 222
   Stuffed Mushrooms, 218
Five-Spice Squash Soup, 261
Fluffy Frosting, 282
Fondue, Berry, 275
French Toast, Baked, 207
Fresh Fruit-Stuffed Turkey, 237
Fresh wreaths, 157-161
Fringed hem, how to sew on table
   linens, 113
Frosted Cranberry Soup, 276
Frosted glass candleholders, 171
Frosting,
   Fluffy Frosting, 282
   Petits Fours Icing, 292
Fruit desserts,
   Apple Crisp, 272
   Apple-Pecan Crumble, 274

Baked Apples, 272
Berry Fondue, 275
Caramel Fruit Platter, 273
Cold Cherry Soup, 276
Cold Peach Soup, 276
Frosted Cranberry Soup, 276
Hot Fruit Compote, 273
Orange-Caramel Pears, 274
Phyllo Apple Turnovers, 270
Ruby Red Pears, 270
Sherry-Marmalade Oranges, 270
Sugared Plums, 275
Fruited Pork Roast, 249
Fruited Wild Rice, 267
Fruit ornaments, beaded, 32, 35
Fruits and roses centerpiece, 153-155
Fruity Garlic-Roasted Pheasant, 243
Fudge,
   Best-Ever Fudge, 293
   Praline Fudge, 293
Fudge-Mint Dessert, 280

G

Garlands,
   beeswax, 166-167
   gold, 15
Garlic-Chive Potato Crisps, 221
Garlic Green Beans, 257
Garlic Mashed Potatoes, 263
Gift bags,
   mitten, 103, 308
   Santa, 105-107
Gifts, hostess, bottles and jars, 99-101
Gift-wrap pillow, 82
Gingerbread with Orange Sauce, 281
Gingerman Sandwich Cookies, 302
Glass candleholders, painted, 171-173
Glazed Ham and Sweet Potatoes, 250
Gold decorations, 13-15
Goose, Roast, 247
Grain stand bird feeder, 26
Green Beans, Garlic, 257

H

Ham,
   Cherried Ham Steak, 250
   Glazed Ham and Sweet Potatoes, 250
   Ham and Cheese Ring, 251
   Ham and Swiss Canapés, 222
   Ham Slices with Sweet Potatoes and
      Apples, 248
   Hot Ham-n-Cheese Crackers, 229
Hand-Dipped Creams, 290
Hawaiian Chicken Company
   Canapés, 219
Hems, sewing on table linens, 113-115
Herbed Garlic and Almond Spread, 228

Holiday bells table topper, 133-135
  pattern, 310
Hooked rug trivet, 182-187
  patterns, 312-313
Hostess gifts, bottles and jars, 97-101
Hot Bloody Mary, 215
Hot Chocolate, Mexican, 215
Hot Fruit Compote, 273
Hot Ham-n-Cheese Crackers, 229
Hot Pineapple Punch, 215

I

Icicle ornament, 33
Icing,
  Fluffy Frosting, 282
  Petits Fours Icing, 292
Indian Fruit Dip Platter, 228
Inserts on placemats, 137-139

J

Jars and bottles, hostess gifts, 99-101

L

Lights,
  indoor, candles, 163-165, 168-173
  outdoor, 19-23
Light sphere, 19-21
Lime and Cumin Cornish Game
  Hens, 242
Linens, table, see: Table linens

M

Mantel cloth, 54-58
Marshmallow Crispy Bars, 297
Mashed Potatoes, Garlic, 263
Meatballs, Barbecued, 218
Metallic appliqué linens, 118-121
Metal napkin rings, brushed, 192, 194
  pattern, 314
Mexican Bean Dip, 227
Mexican Hot Chocolate, 215
Midwest Bacon and Cheese Company
  Canapés, 219
Mitered band, how to sew on table
  linens, 112-113
  pattern, 311
Mitten gift bag, 103
  pattern, 308
Molded beeswax candles, 163-165
Mousse, White Chocolate-
  Peppermint, 279
Mushrooms,
  Stuffed Mushrooms, 218
  Wild Mushroom Sauce, 245

N

Napkin rings, 192-197
  pattern, 314
Nutmeg Squares, 299

O

Omelet, Puffy, 208
Onion Dip, 225
Orange-Caramel Pears, 274
Oranges, Sherry-Marmalade, 270
Orange-Spice Shortbread, 297
Ornaments,
  beaded, 32-35
  beeswax, 166-167, 197
  shell, 38-41
  Victorian, 36-37
Outdoor decorating,
  birch-bark sconce, 17-18, 27
  bird feeders, 25-27
  classical gold wreath, 13-14
  light sphere, 19-21
  snowflake wreath, 9-11
  topiary of lights, 23
Oval tablecloth, how to cut, 112
Overlay, sheer flanged, for pillows,
  76-79

P

Painted glass candleholders, 171-173
Painted placemats, 144-145
Painted Santa gift boxes and bags,
  105-107
Paper art cards, 95-97
Paper-pieced coasters, 203
  patterns, 314-315
Paper-pieced placemats, 123-125
Parmesan-Bacon Spread, 228
Parsnips, Sage, and Apples, 257
Party Cheese Ball, 230
Party Quiche, 207
Patchwork Santa tree skirt, 42-49
  patterns, 309-310
Patchwork Santa wall quilt, 66-69
Pâté, Chèvre and Sun-Dried
  Tomato, 226
Patterns, 304-315
Peach Soup, Cold, 276
Peanut Brittle, 286
Peanut Butter Cups, 291
Peanut Butter Haystacks, 289
Peanut-Scotch Bars, 296
Pears,
  Orange-Caramel Pears, 274
  Ruby Red Pears, 270
Peppermint Bonbons, 298
Peppers,
  Cheese and Basil Pepper Spirals, 223

Feta and Pepper Appetizer Pizzas, 221
Sautéed Peppers in Tarragon
  Vinaigrette, 258
Petits Fours, 292
Petits Fours Icing, 292
Pheasant,
  Creamed Pheasant and Biscuits, 247
  Fruity Garlic-Roasted Pheasant, 243
  Savory Pot Pie, 244
Phyllo Apple Turnovers, 270
Pillows,
  gift-wrap, 82
  Santa, 80-83
  shaped and tasseled, 71-73
  sheer flanged overlay, 76-79
  star, 71, 74-75
  toppers, 76-79
  tree, 71-73
Pineapple,
  Chicken-Pineapple Canapés, 222
  Cran-Pineapple Bread, 209
  Hot Pineapple Punch, 215
  Pineapple Chutney, 266
Pink Zinger Punch, 214
Pinwheel Bread Spread, 213
Pizzas, Feta and Pepper Appetizer, 221
Placemats,
  painted, 144-145
  paper-pieced, 123-125
  table runner, 147-149
  texturized, 141-143
  with sheer insert, 137-139
Plums,
  Plum Cake, 282
  Sugared Plums, 275
Popcorn Balls, 290
Pork,
  Fruited Pork Roast, 249
  Pork and Candied Yams, 251
  also see: Bacon; Ham
Port Wine Cheese Ball, 230
Potatoes,
  Garlic-Chive Potato Crisps, 221
  Garlic Mashed Potatoes, 263
  Potato Rosettes, 264
  Sherried Sweet Potatoes, 265
  Twice-Baked Potatoes, 263
Praline Fudge, 293
Puddings and creams,
  Baked Custard, 278
  Brandy Alexander Cream, 279
  Bread Pudding, 278
  Rice Pudding with Apricot Sauce, 277
  White Chocolate-Peppermint
    Mousse, 279
Puffy Omelet, 208
Pumpkin Soup, Spicy, 260
Punch recipes,
  Hot Pineapple Punch, 215
  Pink Zinger Punch, 214
Purchased candles, embellishing,
  168-169

Q

Quiche, Party, 207
Quilt, patchwork Santa wall, 66-69

R

Raspberry-Glazed Turkey Tenderloin
    Slices, 241
Raspberry Ice Cream Cake, 283
Relishes,
    Cranberry-Orange Relish, 267
    Spiced Apple Relish, 267
Ribbon ball ornament, Victorian, 37
Rice Pudding with Apricot Sauce, 277
Rich Layered Bars, 295
Rings, napkin, 192-197
    pattern, 314
Roasted Ginger Squash, 261
Roasted Wild Turkey, 237
Roast Goose, 247
Round tablecloth, how to cut, 112
Ruby Red Pears, 270

S

Sage Parsnips and Apples, 257
Salsa, Chunky, 226
Santa decorations,
    boot stocking, 50-53, 306-307
    gift box and bag, 105-107
    hooked rug trivet, 182-187, 313
    patchwork tree skirt, 42-49, 309-310
    patchwork wall quilt, 66-69
    pillows, 80-83
Sauces,
    Apricot Sauce, 277
    Easy Velouté Sauce, 244
    Orange Sauce, 281
    Wild Mushroom Sauce, 245
Sautéed Celery with Toasted
    Almonds, 256
Sautéed Peppers in Tarragon
    Vinaigrette, 258
Savory Pot Pie, 244
Scented coasters, 198-201
Sconce, birch-bark, 17-18, 27
Seashell ornaments, 38-41
Seashore Crab Company Canapés, 219
Sewing table linens, 111-117
Shaped and tasseled pillows, 71-73
Sheer flanged overlay for pillows,
    76-79
Shell ornaments, 38-41
Shell-trimmed Christmas tree, 84-85
Sherried Sweet Potatoes, 265
Sherry-Marmalade Oranges, 270
Shortbread, Orange-Spice, 297
Silk ribbon embroidered linens,
    127-131
Skirt, tree, patchwork Santa, 42-49

patterns, 309-310
Sliced Tomatoes with Goat Cheese
    Dressing Platter, 258
Snacks, see: Cheese; Dips and
    spreads; Finger food
Snowflake ornament, seashell, 38-39
Snowflake wreath, 9-11
Snowmen figures, Mr. and Mrs.
    Frost, 87-91
    patterns, 304-305
Soup,
    Cold Cherry Soup, 276
    Cold Peach Soup, 276
    Five-Spice Squash Soup, 261
    Frosted Cranberry Soup, 276
    Spicy Pumpkin Soup, 260
Spiced Apple Relish, 267
Spicy Glazed Carrots, 255
Spicy Gumdrop Cookies, 300
Spicy Pumpkin Soup, 260
Spreads, see: Dips and spreads
Squash,
    Five-Spice Squash Soup, 261
    Roasted Ginger Squash, 261
Stained glass candleholders, faux,
    171, 173
Star pillow, 71, 74-75
Star tree topper, 30-31
Steamed Vegetable Platter with
    Herbed Hollandaise, 255
Stockings, boot, 50-53
    patterns, 306-307
Stuffed Mushrooms, 218
Stuffed Vegetable Platter, 254
Suet house bird feeder, 26
Sugared Plums, 275
Sweet Potatoes, Sherried, 265

T

Table arrangements, see: Centerpieces
Tablecloths, how to cut, 112
Table linens,
    basics about, 111-117
    holiday bells table topper,
        133-135, 310
    metallic appliqué, 118-121
    painted placemats, 144-145
    paper-pieced placemats, 123-125
    placemats with sheer insert, 137-139
    placemat table runner, 147-149
    sewing, 111-117
    silk ribbon embroidered, 127-131
    tablecloths, how to cut, 112
    texturized, 141-143
Table runner, placemat, 147-149
Table topper, holiday bells, 133-135
    pattern, 310
Texturized table linens, 141-143
Tomato-Cucumber Aspic, 259
Tomatoes,

Cheesy Tomato Puffs, 220
Chèvre and Sun-Dried Tomato
    Pâté, 226
Sliced Tomatoes with Goat Cheese
    Dressing Platter, 258
Topiary of lights, 23
Toppers,
    pillow, 76-79
    table, 133-135, 310
    tree, 30-31
Traditional Roast Duck with
    Dressing, 247
Tree, decorating, see: Christmas tree
Tree pillow, 71-73
Tree skirt, patchwork Santa, 42-49
    patterns, 309-310
Tree trivet, 189-191
Trivets,
    hooked rug, 182-187, 312-313
    tree, 189-191
Truffles, 287
Tuna, Far-East, Company Canapés, 219
Turkey,
    Cider-Sauced Turkey Breast, 240
    Cranberry-Stuffed Turkey
        Tenderloins, 238
    Fresh Fruit-Stuffed Turkey, 237
    Raspberry-Glazed Turkey Tenderloin
        Slices, 241
    Roasted Wild Turkey, 237
    Savory Pot Pie, 244
    Turkey Patties with Cranberry-Nut
        Chutney, 239
Turnovers, Phyllo Apple, 270
Turtlettes, 289
Twice-Baked Potatoes, 263

V

Victorian ornaments, 36-37

W

Wall quilt, patchwork Santa, 66-69
White Chocolate-Peppermint
    Mousse, 279
Wild Mushroom Sauce, 245
Wild Rice, Fruited, 267
Winter Fruit Dressing, 264
Woodburning designs, 176-181
Wreath napkin ring, 192, 195
Wreaths,
    Advent, 59-61, 157-159
    classical gold, 13-14
    fresh, 157-161
    snowflake, 9-11

Copyright © 1999
Creative Publishing international, Inc.
5900 Green Oak Drive
Minnetonka, Minnesota 55343
1-800-328-3895
All rights reserved
Printed in U.S.A.

President: Iain Macfarlane
Director, Creative Development: Lisa Rosenthal
Executive Managing Editor: Elaine Perry

Created by: The Editors of Creative Publishing international, Inc.

Project Manager: Linnéa Christensen
Senior Art Director: Delores Swanson
Senior Editor: Linda Neubauer
Recipe Editors: Ellen Boeke, Carol Frieberg
Project Writer: Nancy Sundeen
Copy Editor: Janice Cauley
Design Intern: Michele Lehtis
Project Stylist: Joanne Wawra
Prop Stylist: Christine Jahns
Sample Production Manager: Elizabeth Reichow
Lead Samplemaker: Phyllis Galbraith
Sewing and Sample Production Staff: Karen Cermak, Arlene Dohrman,
   Sheila Duffy, Sharon Eklund, Bridget Haugh, Teresa Henn, Muriel Lynch,
   Dolores Minkema, Nancy Sundeen
Senior Technical Photo Stylist: Bridget Haugh
Technical Photo Stylists: Susan Jorgenson, Nancy Sundeen
Studio Services Manager: Marcia Chambers
Photo Services Coordinator: Carol Osterhus
Senior Photographer: Chuck Nields
Photographers: Tate Carlson, Jamey Mauk, Andrea Rugg
Photography Assistant: Greg Wallace
Publishing Production Manager: Kim Gerber
Mac Design Manager: Jon Simpson
Desktop Publishing Specialists: Laurie Kristensen, Brad Webster
Production Staff: Patrick Gibson, Laura Hokkanen, Kay Wethern
Contributors: American Efrid, Inc.; Clotilde, Inc.; Crafty Productions; Deco Art;
   Honey Wax; HTC-Handler Textile Corporation; Offray Ribbon; Plaid Enterprises,
   Inc.; Sulky of America; Thai Silks; Walnut Hollow; YLI Corporation

Printed on American paper by:
World Color
10 9 8 7 6 5 4 3 2 1

Creative Publishing international, Inc.
offers a variety of how-to books. For
information write:

> Creative Publishing international, Inc.
> Subscriber Books
> 5900 Green Oak Drive
> Minnetonka, MN 55343

Library of Congress Cataloging-in-Publication Data
Christmas Crafts and entertaining.
    p. cm.
   Includes index.
   ISBN 0-86573-178-0
   1. Christmas decorations. 2. Christmas cookery. I. Creative
  Publishing International.
  TT900.C4C447 1999
  745.594'2--dc21   99-24590